Philipp Josef Andelfinger

Identifying and Harnessing Concurrency for Parallel and Distributed Network Simulation

Identifying and Harnessing Concurrency for Parallel and Distributed Network Simulation

by

Philipp Josef Andelfinger

KIT Scientific Publishing

Dissertation, Karlsruher Institut für Technologie (KIT)
Fakultät für Informatik, 2016

Tag der mündlichen Prüfung: 10. Februar 2016
Referenten: Prof. Dr. rer. nat. Hannes Hartenstein, Dr. Kalyan Perumalla

Impressum

KIT Scientific Publishing

Karlsruher Institut für Technologie (KIT)
KIT Scientific Publishing
Straße am Forum 2
D-76131 Karlsruhe

KIT Scientific Publishing is a registered trademark of Karlsruhe Institute of Technology. Reprint using the book cover is not allowed.

www.ksp.kit.edu

Print on Demand 2016

ISBN 978-3-7315-0511-2
DOI 10.5445/KSP/1000054019

Zusammenfassung

Da Netzwerke von Computern inhärent parallele Systeme darstellen, können Simulationen von Computernetzen häufig durch parallele und verteilte Ausführung auf mehreren Prozessoren substantiell beschleunigt werden. Simulationsmodelle von Computernetzen können sich jedoch grundlegend in ihrer Eignung für eine Parallelisierung unterscheiden. Obwohl sich bereits eine Vielzahl von vorausgehenden Arbeiten mit der effizienten parallelen Ausführung von Netzwerkmodellen befasst hat, besteht ein Mangel an Verfahren, die Entscheidungen bezüglich der Parallelisierung von Netzwerkmodellen und die Wahl geeigneter Hardware-Plattformen, Simulatorarchitekturen und Synchronisationsansätze unterstützen. Zusätzlich hat die breite Verfügbarkeit kostengünstiger Manycore-Hardware das Spektrum möglicher Realisierungen von Simulatoren über die Möglichkeiten traditioneller CPU-basierter Ansätze hinaus erweitert.

Diese Dissertation betrachtet die effiziente Ausführung von Netzwerksimulationen aus zwei Perspektiven: zunächst werden Evaluationsmethoden vorgeschlagen, die eine Abschätzung des Parallelisierungspotentials von Netzwerkmodellen erlauben. Im Anschluss werden Ansätze vorgestellt, die das identifizierte Parallelisierungspotential mittels moderner Manycore-Hardware effizient ausnutzen.

Identifizierung von Nebenläufigkeit: wir stellen einen analytischen Ansatz vor, der die durchschnittliche Anzahl an Recheneinheiten abschätzt, die von einem idealisierten parallelen oder verteilten Simulationslauf eines gegebenen Netzwerkmodells ausgelastet werden können. Die Abschätzung erfolgt auf Basis von Modellwissen und einfachen Netzwerkstatistiken, die in sequentiellen Simulationsläufen gewonnen werden. Da das vorgestellte Verfahren nicht auf automatisierten Methoden wie der "Critical Path Analysis" beruht, erlauben die Schätzungen ein Verständnis von Zusammenhängen zwischen den Kommunikationsmustern im simulierten Netzwerk und der resultierenden Nebenläufigkeit des Netzwerkmodells. Ein Verständnis dieser Zusammenhänge kann Modelloptimierungen und die Auswahl geeigneter Simulatorarchitekturen unterstützen. Das Verfahren basiert auf einer näherungsweisen Bestimmung des Simulationsfortschritts unter dem Synchronisationsalgorithmus YAWNS. Wir legen den Zusammenhang zwischen Critical Path Analysis und YAWNS dar und beweisen die Gültigkeit unseres Ansatzes sowie existierender Arbeiten, die unsere Annahmen teilen. Eine Evaluation der Akkuratheit konkreter Schätzungen wird anhand einer Anwendung des Schätzverfahrens auf Implementierungen dreier Netzwerkmodelle in bekannten Netzwerksimulatoren durchgeführt.

Um zusätzlich zu den Eigenschaften des untersuchten Netzwerkmodells auch die zur Durchführung verwendete Hardware und den Synchronisationsansatz zu berücksichtigen, stellen wir ein Werkzeug vor, dass die Laufzeit paralleler und verteilter Simulationen auf Basis sequentieller Simulationen und Hardware-Messungen prädiziert. Das Werkzeug führt eine Simulation einer geplanten parallelen oder verteilten Simulation durch ("Simulation zweiter Ordnung"). Wir zeigen, dass im Falle von Netzwerkmodellen mit nicht-trivialen Berechnungen pro simulierter Nachricht eine angemessen akkurate Prädiktion erreicht wird.

Nutzung von Nebenläufigkeit: traditionelle Ansätze der parallelen und verteilten Simulation greifen zur Ausführung des Netzwerkmodells auf einen Verbund von CPUs zurück. In einigen existierenden Arbeiten ergaben sich für Modelle von Peer-to-Peer-Netzwerken durch Parallelisierung der Simulation nur geringe Laufzeitverbesserungen. Wir analysieren und vergleichen zwei Partitionierungsstrategien für Modelle von Netzwerken, die auf dem Protokoll Kademlia basieren. Ein Beispiel für ein solches Netzwerk ist die BitTorrent DHT, eines der größten öffentlichen Peer-to-Peer-Netzwerke. Mittels einer Partitionierung der Simulation basierend auf der logischen Topologie des Netzwerkes erreichen wir eine Beschleunigung der Simulation um einen Faktor von 6,0 im Vergleich mit einer sequentiellen Ausführung sowie eine nahezu lineare Reduktion des Speicherbedarfs pro Rechenknoten.

Da die mittels einer CPU-basierten parallelen und verteilten Ausführung erreichte Beschleunigung einer Simulation die hierzu erforderlichen Hardware-Ressourcen nicht in jedem Falle rechtfertigen kann, untersuchen wir die Ausführung von Netzwerksimulationen auf Grafikprozessoren (Graphics Processing Units, GPUs). Heutige GPUs sind in der Lage, allgemeine Berechnungen auf hunderten oder tausenden paralleler Recheneinheiten durchzuführen. Eine im Arbeitsplatzrechner eines Forschers vorhandene kostengünstige GPU kann dazu dienen, die Wartezeit zwischen Änderungen an einem Netzwerkmodell und dem Erhalten von Simulationsergebnissen zu verringern.

Zuächst vergleichen und evaluieren wir Architekturen zur GPU-Beschleunigung rechenaufwändiger Schritte einer CPU-basierten detaillierten Simulation drahtloser Netzwerke. Obwohl eine einzelne simulierte Nachrichtenübertragung bereits Möglichkeiten zur parallelen Verarbeitung bietet, zeigen unsere Messungen, dass eine signifikante Beschleunigung der Simulation es erforderlich macht, mehrere Nachrichtenübertragungen aggregiert zu betrachten. Um die Korrektheit der Simulation zu gewährleisten, muss hierbei die Möglichkeit von Interaktionen zwischen mehreren Sendevorgängen berücksichtigt werden. Unsere Ergebnisse demonstrieren daher, dass bereits im betrachteten Fall einer GPU-Beschleunigung einzelner Schritte einer durch eine CPU verwalteten Simulation Synchronisationsmechanismen aus dem Feld der parallelen und verteilten Simulationen erforderlich sind.

Schließlich stellen wir einen rein GPU-basierten Simulationsansatz vor, in welchem neben dem Netzwerkmodell auch die gesamte Simulationslogik auf einer GPU ausgeführt wird. Da auf eine Interaktion zwischen einer CPU des Host-Systems und der GPU weitestgehend verzichtet wird, eignet sich der rein GPU-basierte Ansatz auch im Falle von Netzwerkmodellen, deren Simulationsereignisse jeweils nur geringfügige Berechnungen erfordern. Im Gegensatz zu existierenden Arbeiten werden in unserem Ansatz die simulierten Knoten zu Gruppen zusammengefasst, welche jeweils gemeinsam betrachtet werden. Diese Aggregation erlaubt es, die Auslastung der Rechneneinheiten der GPU gegenüber dem Verwaltungsaufwand der Simulation abzuwägen, indem der Grad an Aggregation basierend auf Messungen der Simulationsleistung dynamisch zur Laufzeit angepasst wird. Eine Leistungsbewertung unserer Implementierung des Ansatzes anhand eines Modells Kademlia-basierter Netzwerke und des Benchmark-Modells PHOLD zeigt eine Beschleunigung der Simulationen um einen Faktor von bis zu 19,5 bzw. 27,5 im Vergleich mit einer sequentiellen CPU-basierten Ausführung, sowie eine Ereignisrate von bis zu $6{,}8 * 10^6$ bzw. $39{,}3 * 10^6$ Ereignissen pro Sekunde auf einer einzelnen GPU.

Abstract

Since computer networks are inherently parallel systems, simulations of computer networks can in many cases be accelerated substantially through parallel and distributed execution on a set of interconnected processors. Still, simulation models of computer networks vary significantly in their parallelization potentials. Although an enormous number of works consider the efficient parallel execution of specific network models, there is still a lack of guidelines that help in decisions on parallelization and in the selection of hardware platforms, simulator architectures and synchronization approaches that enable an efficient execution. Further, the advent of commodity many-core devices has broadened the range of possible simulator realizations beyond the possibilities of traditional CPU-based approaches.

This dissertation addresses the efficient execution of simulation models of computer networks from two perspectives: we propose evaluation methods to determine a model's parallelization potential and provide simulator realizations that efficiently exploit the identified potentials using modern many-core hardware.

Identifying Concurrency: we propose an analytical approach to estimate the concurrency of network models, i.e., the number of processors that can be occupied in an idealized parallel and distributed simulation run based only on model knowledge and simple network statistics from sequential simulation runs. By not relying on an automated "black-box" method such as critical path analysis, our estimation approach exposes the relationships between the communication patterns in a simulated network and the resulting concurrency of the simulation. Insights into these relationships may guide model optimizations and the selection of suitable simulator architectures. Our estimations approximate the progress of simulations performed using the well-known synchronization algorithm YAWNS. After clarifying the relationship between critical path analysis and YAWNS, we provide a proof that shows the validity of the general approach and that substantiates the results of previous works that share our assumptions. Empirical results on the example of three network models implemented in popular simulators demonstrate that the estimations are sufficiently accurate to evaluate the models' parallelization potential, while avoiding an automated "black-box" analysis of sequential simulation runs.

In order to take into account both the properties of the considered network model as well as the execution hardware and synchronization approach, we present a tool that predicts the runtime of parallel and distributed simulations on the basis of sequential simulation runs and hardware measurements. The tool performs a simulation of an envisioned parallel and distributed simulation ("second-order simulation"). We show that reasonably accurate runtime predictions are achieved for distributed simulation runs in the case of network models where simulated messages require non-trivial amounts of computation.

Harnessing Concurrency: traditionally, parallel and distributed simulations rely on interconnected CPUs for execution of the simulation model. In some previous works, models of peer-to-peer networks have been reported to benefit only to a small degree from parallelization in CPU-based execution environments. We analyze and compare two partitioning strategies for models of Kademlia-based networks such as the BitTorrent DHT, one of the largest public peer-to-peer networks. When applying a partitioning strategy based on the logical topology of the network, we achieve a simulation speedup of 6.0 compared to a sequential execution and a near-linear reduction of the memory requirements per execution node.

Since high-performance CPU-based parallel and distributed simulations can consume enormous amounts of hardware resources that may not be justified by the achieved runtime reductions, we consider the acceleration of network simulations using graphics processing units (GPUs). GPUs have evolved to support general-purpose computations on hundreds or thousands of parallel processing elements. An inexpensive GPU in a researcher's workstation can be used to shorten the feedback loop between changes to the network model and the retrieval of the corresponding simulation results.

We compare and evaluate architectures for a GPU-based coprocessing of detailed wireless network simulations. Although each simulated transmission already provides opportunities for parallel processing, we show that significant runtime reductions require an aggregated consideration of multiple transmissions in parallel. Since, in order to maintain correctness, the potential for interactions between multiple transmissions must be considered, the results show that even a simple GPU-based coprocessing requires synchronization mechanisms from the field of parallel and distributed simulation.

Subsequently, we propose a fully GPU-based simulation approach that executes all simulation logic as well as the network model on a GPU. Due to avoiding most interaction between a host CPU and the GPU, the fully GPU-based approach is applicable to network models where individual events require only small amounts of computation. Contrary to existing works, our approach aggregates sets of simulated nodes that are considered jointly. The aggregation enables the exploitation of a tradeoff between the utilization of the GPU's processing elements and simulation overheads by dynamically adapting the degree of aggregation according to performance measurements at simulation runtime. We conduct a performance evaluation of our implementation on the example of a model of Kademlia-based networks and the well-known PHOLD benchmark model. Using a single commodity GPU, we achieve a speedup of up to 19.5 and event rates up to 6.8×10^6 for the model of Kademlia-based networks. A speedup of up to 27.5 and event rates of up to 39.3×10^6 events per second of wall-clock time are achieved in the case of the PHOLD model.

Contents

List of Figures

List of Tables

1 Introduction

The recent decades have seen a vast increase in the scale and complexity of networked systems. The emergence of smart grids, the expected advent of smart cities and the Internet of Things will further accelerate the deployment of networked systems spanning cities or entire regions. The design of these large-scale systems is not possible without relying on *simulations* to evaluate different approaches, topologies and protocols. Frequently, networked systems are evaluated using *discrete-event* simulations, where changes in system state are represented by events occurring at discrete points in simulated time. However, the runtimes of discrete-event simulations can be prohibitively large: accurate simulation of highly dynamic systems at realistic scale entails processing vast numbers of events representing the complex interactions between, e.g., vehicles, mobile devices or systems in a smart grid. *Parallel and distributed simulation* is an approach to reduce simulation runtime by distributing the computational workload of an individual simulation run to a number of processors communicating using shared memory or a network. While parallel and distributed simulation is commonly applied when investigating systems whose state is subject to *continuous* changes, efficient parallel and distributed simulation of systems that are adequately described by *discrete-event* models is still regarded as a challenging problem, even after multiple decades of research. The main challenge in parallel and distributed discrete-event simulation is the synchronization between processors: to gain meaningful results, a synchronization mechanism must enforce an ordering of the simulation events so that the results of the parallel or distributed simulation are identical to those of a corresponding sequential run. In addition, an efficient parallelization depends on a sufficient amount of independence in the behavior of the components of the modeled system, i.e., sufficient numbers of events that can be processed independently, and on methods for efficient parallel execution of events during simulation runtime. We refer to the largest possible number of events that can be executed in parallel according to a network model's properties, averaged over a simulation run, as the *concurrency* of the simulation.

Due to the diminishing performance improvements of individual processor cores and the increasing prevalence of many-core devices with hundreds of cores, parallel and distributed simulation is becoming a key method to enable the evaluation of large-scale networked systems. However, since the runtime interactions between a network model and a simulator realization are difficult to predict, there is still a lack of guidance for decisions on whether a given model will benefit sufficiently from parallelization to justify the required development effort. The research question motivating this dissertation can therefore be stated as follows:

How can the parallelization potential of discrete-event models of computer networks be estimated and explained?

Since most existing approaches evaluate the parallelization potential of network models without a consideration of the causes for the respective results, novel evaluation approaches are needed to gain insights into the factors influencing a model's parallelization potential. Such insights may form guidelines for researchers to decide whether the parallelization of a model is worthwhile, and what simulator realization should be chosen.

While some network models exhibit enormous degrees of concurrency, achieving large performance gains through traditional parallel and distributed approaches can require significant hardware resources. Even if high simulation performance is achieved, the fine-grained computational tasks and the frequent need for communication between processors associated with the execution of many network models can render parallel and distributed simulations a comparatively inefficient use of large-scale computing resources.

In the past years, the massively parallel computing resources of graphics cards are increasingly applied to general computations in various scientific domains, enabling the high-performance execution of fine-grained parallel tasks. Since today, such many-core devices are readily available in commodity workstations, graphics cards can be utilized to accelerate network simulations without the need to allocate traditional high-performance computing resources. However, the heritage of graphics card architecture in computing three-dimensional graphics requires a reconsideration of simulator architecture in order to efficiently map the highly irregular tasks of discrete-event simulations to a graphics card's computing resources. Hence, our second research question can be stated as follows:

How can computationally intensive network simulations be executed efficiently on commodity graphics cards?

Whereas large-scale cluster resources in shared use can substantially reduce the overall time required for large parameter studies, an acceleration using commodity graphics cards is particularly applicable in exploratory phases of simulation studies, where a short feedback loop is the prime concern.

1.1 Contributions

The dissertation addresses the challenges of achieving high performance in parallel and distributed network simulation from two perspectives: we first consider the *identification of concurrency* in network simulation models by analytical and simulation-based methods. Subsequently, we focus on *harnessing concurrency* in network models by proposing high-performance simulator architectures and implementations running on CPU-based distributed systems as well as on GPU-based many-core devices.

Identifying Concurrency

After clarifying the key factors determining parallel simulation performance and the scope of existing evaluation approaches based on a categorization of the performance-critical factors such as synchronization costs and partitioning strategies, we expand the set of available performance evaluation approaches.

Analytical concurrency estimation approach: The most fundamental requirement for an efficient parallel execution of a network model is a sufficient degree of concurrency in the interactions between simulated nodes. However, the relationships between a simulated network's topology and communication patterns, and the resulting concurrency, are still not well understood. We present an analytical model to estimate the concurrency of network models that enables insights into the sources of concurrency based on an analysis of the communication patterns in the considered network model. Such insights are not easily obtained through an automated analysis of simulation traces in a "black-box" fashion, e.g., using critical path analysis. Our analytical estimations approximate the concurrency results obtainable using the well-known YAWNS synchronization algorithm that has been used for concurrency estimation of simulations in existing works. We provide a proof of the fundamental result that under common assumptions, the results of a concurrency analysis using the YAWNS algorithm shows only limited deviation from critical path analysis. Although a broader range of network models should still be considered in future work, we consider our results to be strong evidence towards the following statement:

The concurrency of network simulations can be estimated at reasonable accuracy without relying on an automated analysis of event traces.

We study models of three fundamentally different classes of networks: a peer-to-peer network, IP-based routing in a fixed topology, and a wireless network. The analysis exposes the relationships between the communication patterns among the simulated nodes of the considered network models, and the resulting concurrency.

Simulation-based performance estimation tool: To take into account both the properties of the network model as well as the simulator realization and execution environment, we present a tool that predicts the runtime of simulation runs. The prediction is performed by a simulation of the execution of an envisioned distributed network simulator ("second-order simulation") based on measurements of the costs of individual simulation events and of the communication between processors. The tool allows researchers to vary the configuration of the envisioned simulation system, e.g., the properties of the network model or the simulation scale, to evaluate performance potentials and limitations prior to parallelization.

Harnessing Concurrency

Subsequently, we propose and evaluate architectures and mechanisms for parallel and distributed network simulations for execution on different classes of network simulation studies and hardware environments.

Analysis of partitioning strategies for distributed simulations of Kademlia-based peer-to-peer networks: We consider the performance gains by distributed simulation of a model of the BitTorrent DHT, a widely deployed public peer-to-peer network based on the Kademlia protocol currently comprised of about 10 million nodes. Some previous works have reported models of peer-to-peer networks to benefit little from parallel and distributed simulation due to fine computational granularity and a need for frequent communication between processors. However, we show that for the considered network model, overheads can be reduced substantially using a partitioning approach that follows the logical topology of the network, whereas a spatial partitioning can moderately decrease the overheads required for inter-processor synchronization. Performance measurements in a high-performance cluster environment show a simulation speedup factor of up to 6.0 compared to a sequential run.

Evaluation of hybrid CPU-GPU-based simulator architectures: We evaluate the performance of different GPU-accelerated simulator architectures for acceleration of wireless network simulation. We show that GPUs can be applied to exploit the data parallelism in models where the low-level details of wireless transmissions are reflected by computationally expensive signal processing tasks. Since only the signal processing steps are executed on the GPU, whereas the remaining simulation tasks are handled by the CPU, substantial performance gains require a aggregated consideration of multiple packet receptions. Since the aggregation approach must maintain the correctness of the simulation, even a simple GPU-based coprocessing requires mechanisms from parallel and distributed simulation.

Adaptive fully GPU-based simulation: We propose a GPU-based simulation approach that performs all steps of discrete-event network simulations on a GPU and efficiently executes models that lack explicit data parallelism. Fully GPU-based network simulation entails a tradeoff between the utilization of the GPU's cores and the incurred simulation overheads. Contrary to previous works, we take this tradeoff into account by proposing an aggregated consideration of multiple simulated nodes. The proposed mechanism enables a runtime adaptation of the degree of aggregation to balance GPU utilization and simulation overhead according to the parametrization of the network model and the activity in the simulated network. Our results support the following statement:

A dynamically adaptable aggregation of simulated nodes substantially reduces the runtime of fully GPU-based network simulations.

In simulations of Kademlia-based peer-to-peer networks, a speedup factor of up to 19.5 in comparison with a sequential execution is achieved on a commodity graphics card. In simulations of the PHOLD benchmark model, we observed a speedup factor of up to 27.5. The simulator achieves event rates of up to 39.3×10^6 events per second of wall-clock time. In contrast to traditional distributed simulations in CPU-based supercomputing environments in shared use, the proposed simulation approach can be deployed on consumer GPUs in researchers' workstations and hence enables low turnaround times with respect to simulation results.

Parts of the contributions presented in this dissertation have been published in the following previous works:

- Philipp Andelfinger and Hannes Hartenstein. Model-Based Concurrency Analysis of Network Simulations. In *Proceedings of the ACM SIGSIM Conference on Principles of Advanced Discrete Simulation*, pages 223–234. ACM, 2015.
- Philipp Andelfinger and Hannes Hartenstein. Exploiting the Parallelism of Large-Scale Application-Layer Networks by Adaptive GPU-based Simulation. In *Proceedings of the Winter Simulation Conference*, pages 3471–3482. IEEE, 2014.

- Philipp Andelfinger, Konrad Jünemann, and Hannes Hartenstein. Parallelism Potentials in Distributed Simulations of Kademlia-based Peer-to-Peer Networks. In *Proceedings of the Conference on Simulation Tools and Techniques*, pages 41–50. ICST, 2014.
- Philipp Andelfinger and Hannes Hartenstein. Towards Performance Evaluation of Conservative Distributed Discrete-Event Network Simulations Using Second-Order Simulation. In *Proceedings of the ACM SIGSIM Conference on Principles of Advanced Discrete Simulation*, pages 221–230. ACM, 2013.
- Philipp Andelfinger, Jens Mittag, and Hannes Hartenstein. GPU-Based Architectures and Their Benefit for Accurate and Efficient Wireless Network Simulations. In *Proceedings of the International Symposium on Modeling, Analysis and Simulation of Computer and Telecommunication Systems*, pages 421–424. IEEE, 2011.

1.2 Thesis Outline

The dissertation is structured as follows: in Part I, we first give a brief overview of parallel and distributed discrete-event simulation. We propose a simple taxonomy for performance evaluation approaches in the context of parallel and distributed simulation and discuss related work. Since high simulation performance can require an adaptation of properties of the simulator to the considered network model, we discuss existing work on simulator adaptation. Part I concludes with a characterization and comparison of the specific network models that will serve as examples in the remainder of the dissertation.

In Part II, we propose methods to evaluate the parallelization potential of network models. We present an estimation approach that determines the number of processors that can be occupied by a parallel or distributed simulation of a given network model based only on model knowledge and basic network statistics obtained from sequential simulation runs. We provide a proof that shows the validity of the estimation approach. The estimation accuracy is evaluated empirically on the example of three network models. We detail the steps towards a refinement of the estimation approach and discuss the effects on the estimation results. Subsequently, we present a simulation-based tool that predicts the runtime of parallel or distributed simulations based on a simulation trace generated in a sequential simulation run and on measurements of the execution environment. The prediction accuracy is evaluated by a comparison with measurement results of simulations on physical hardware.

In Part III, we propose methods for efficient parallel and distributed execution of network simulations. First, we analyze and evaluate two partitioning strategies for distributed simulation of one of the largest existing peer-to-peer networks and show that the simulation runtime can be reduced substantially using a partitioning strategy that follows the logical topology of the peer-to-peer network. Subsequently, we study two approaches to accelerate network simulations using modern graphics processing units (GPUs): first, we propose architectures for accelerating a traditional sequential simulator using GPU-based execution of computationally expensive simulation tasks. Finally, we propose an approach for fully GPU-based execution of network simulations without the need for a CPU-based management of simulation tasks. The approach is evaluated using a comparison of its time complexity with existing works and measurements of simulation performance.

Chapter 12 provides conclusions from our results and sketches directions for future work.

Part I
Fundamentals

2 Parallel and Distributed Network Simulation

A frequent goal of researchers and engineers is to gain an understanding of properties of a real-world or envisioned system. If the system in question is a computer network, the relevant properties may for instance be the maximum throughput in a given network topology, the time required to route a packet between two nodes, or the scalability of a novel network protocol. To determine the desired properties, a number of evaluation methods present themselves [Law14]: if the network under study already exists or can be constructed with tolerable effort, it is possible to perform experiments on it directly by triggering the relevant behavior and conducting measurements of the desired properties. If the topology of the network under study and the behavior leading to the desired property are sufficiently simple, it can be possible to construct an analytical model that enables a mathematical derivation of the desired properties. In many cases, however, the network under study does not yet exist, is expensive to construct and, due to its complexity, defies analytical modeling. Such networks under study are typically evaluated using *simulation*. Averill Law defines the term simulation as follows: "In a simulation we use a computer to evaluate a model numerically, and data are gathered in order to estimate the desired true characteristic of the model." [Law14] The behavior of computer networks is usually described adequately by simulation models that involve a notion of time, that contain probabilistic components, and that change their state at discrete points in simulated time. These properties characterize the class of *discrete-event* models. An *event* is an "instantaneous occurrence that may change the state of the system" [Law14].

An event is represented by two elements: a timestamp specifying the event's point of occurrence in simulated time, and a code segment referred to as an *event handler* that performs the required changes in system state. For instance, an event may increment a counter representing the number of messages received by a node in a simulated network. In addition, an event may schedule new events to be executed at a later point in simulated time.

A discrete-event *simulator* performs the task of executing the events in a simulation in chronological order of their occurrence. In the simulator, the events to be executed are held in a data structure called the *future event list* (FEL). The task of executing events in timestamp order is performed by iteratively removing the earliest event from the FEL and executing the event by calling its event handler.

A discrete-event simulation model of a computer network (*network model*) typically includes the following elements:

- A description of a static or dynamic **network topology**, i.e., of the links between the nodes in the network. Depending on the modeling detail, the maximum throughput of each link is specified, while the latency of each link or each message passing over a link is given as a constant value or drawn from a probability distribution.
- An implementation of one or more **network protocols** that govern the behavior of the nodes. The protocols are implemented in the form of event handlers that are scheduled to be called on the arrival of a message at a node or after a certain period of simulated time has passed. For reasons of development cost or simulation performance, the protocol implementations may abstract from details of the protocol specification or of a reference implementation.
- An implementation of the behavior of one or more **applications**. The applications rely on the functionality specified in the implemented protocols.

An initial set of events is inserted into the FEL during initialization of the simulation. All further behavior of the network model is induced by the initial events and new events scheduled during simulation.

The complexity and scale of a realistic network model translates to immense computational demands and huge memory requirements to execute the simulation, rendering some simulation studies prohibitively expensive due to the large simulation runtimes, and others infeasible due to memory constraints.

Frequently, to study the sensitivity of a network model's behavior to a range of parameters, simulation studies involve multiple executions of the simulation model under various parameter combinations. Since most simulations include probabilistic components, additional repetitions are required to achieve an acceptable degree of confidence in the results. Hence, a simple way to reduce the overall time required for a simulation study is to distribute the required executions of the model to a number of processors ("Multiple Replications in Parallel", MRIP [EMP97]). Since the separate executions can be processed independently, an interaction between processors is required solely to aggregate the results of all executions. However, MRIP does not reduce the runtime and memory requirements of individual model executions.

Individual discrete-event model executions can offer substantial potential for parallelization as well. In fact, Le Boudec considers concurrency to be an inherent property of simulations: "A first task of a simulation program is to simulate parallelism: several parallel actions can take place in the real system, and in the program, they are serialized." [LB10].

Parallel and distributed simulation (PADS) describes mechanisms to distribute the computational workload of individual model executions to a set of processors interconnected using shared memory or a network [Fuj01]. Hence, PADS can be seen to reverse the serialization of the parallel actions of the modeled system. PADS can reduce both the runtime and memory consumption of individual model executions. Similarly to parallel and distributed computing in other domains, one of the challenges of PADS is to maximize the computational throughput by finding a partitioning of the network model that balances the computational workload evenly between the available processors. Contrary to the use of the term in mathematics, in the PADS literature, the term *partition* refers to only one individual segment of a partitioned network model. We additionally use the term *logical process* (LP) to refer to a partition of a network model together with the simulator instance managing its execution. The interactions between nodes simulated in separate LPs are reflected by the exchange of events in the form of messages between LPs transferred via shared memory or a network. We subsume these two communication mechanisms under the term *interconnect*.

In PADS, determining a suitable partitioning can be particularly difficult due to the potentially highly dynamic behavior of the simulated entities, which may require dynamic adaptations of the partitioning strategy. An additional challenge is given by the requirement for maintaining a consistent behavior of the simulated entities with respect to simulated time. In other words, it must be ensured that the results of a parallel or distributed simulation correspond to those of a sequential execution on a single processor. For instance, the observed behavior of a simulated node may differ substantially depending on the ordering of incoming messages. The need for a correspondence between the results of a sequential simulation run and a parallel or distributed run is equivalent with the requirement for an execution of all events pertaining to an individual simulated node *in non-decreasing timestamp order*. In the literature, this requirement is referred to as the *local causality constraint* [Fuj01].

2.1 Synchronization of Simulated Time

There are two fundamental classes of synchronization algorithms that ensure the correctness of PADS results. *Conservative* algorithms guarantee a non-decreasing timestamp order previous to each event execution, whereas *optimistic* algorithms detect violations of timestamp order and subsequently perform rollbacks to a previous correct simulation state.

A survey of the literature on synchronization algorithms, on which the following overview is based, is given by Fujimoto [Fuj01].

2.1.1 Conservative Algorithms

Conservative synchronization algorithms adhere to the local causality constraint by ensuring *a priori*, i.e., prior to the execution of each event, that the execution of the event does not create the possibility of a violation of timestamp order. Events for which violations can be ruled out are called *safe* events. Identifying safe events efficiently is the main challenge in the design of conservative synchronization algorithms.

The earliest well-known first synchronization algorithm was described in publications by Bryant [Bry77], and Chandy and Misra [CM79] and is commonly referred to as the *Chandy-Misra-Bryant* (CMB) algorithm. In CMB, each LP owns queues that each hold the events that arrive from one of the remote LPs in "first-in first-out" (FIFO) order. Events both created locally and to be executed locally are also inserted into a FIFO queue. Since events are assumed to be sent in timestamp order and since this order is assumed to be maintained by the interconnect, the events in all FIFO queues are in non-decreasing timestamp order. Hence, the timestamp of the last received event in each FIFO queue serves as a lower bound for the timestamps of any event received from the LP associated with the queue. Now, each LP can calculate the minimum of the last received timestamps in all of its FIFO queues to determine a lower bound on the timestamp of any further event received by another LP (*earliest input time*, EIT [BT00]). All events in the local queues with timestamps lower than the EIT are safe and can therefore be processed in timestamp order without the risk of a violation of the local causality constraint. If the EIT does not render any events safe, the LP blocks until more events are received. Without further mechanisms, CMB will frequently create deadlocks: if there is a cycle of empty FIFOs and the timestamps of the last received events in the FIFOs are too small to allow any LP to execute further events, the simulation cannot proceed. Deadlocks can be avoided by exchanging *null messages* containing the earliest possible timestamp of an event created by one LP to be executed in another LP. The timestamp in a null message is the sum of the earliest possible timestamp of an event received by an LP and the minimum timestamp delta between an event and its creation. This minimum timestamp delta is called the *lookahead* τ and must be determined based on knowledge of the network model. CMB with the addition of null messages is frequently called the *Null Message Algorithm* (NMA). Both CMB and NMA are *asynchronous* algorithms in the sense that the LPs independently alternate between waiting for events to become safe and the processing of events.

Under *synchronous* algorithms, the LPs alternate in lockstep between EIT calculation and the processing of events. A well-known synchronous algorithm is YAWNS [NMI89, Nic93] (cf. Figure 2.1): before events are processed, the global minimum timestamp $t_{\min}$ of all events in the simulation is determined. The sum $t_{\max} = t_{\min} + \tau$ of the global minimum and the lookahead is the earliest possible timestamp of a new event created by any event in the simulation. Hence, all events in the *lookahead window* $\{t_{\min}, t_{\min}+1, \ldots, t_{\max}\}$ are safe to be processed. Now, each LP executes all events in the lookahead window in timestamp order before the next lookahead window is calculated.

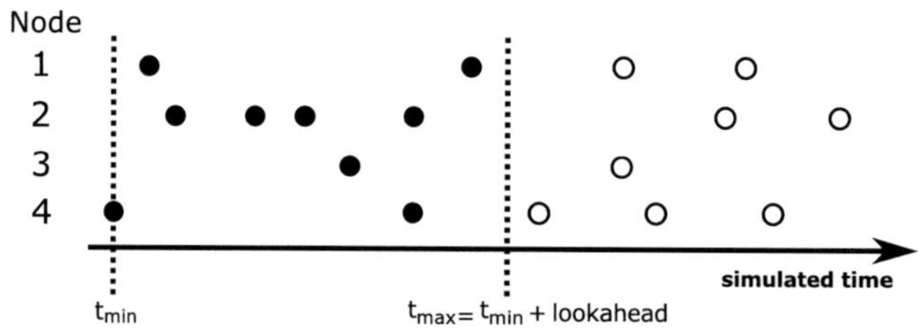

Figure 2.1: A simulation round using YAWNS: events in $\{t_{\min}, t_{\min}+1, \ldots, t_{\max}\}$ create no events with timestamps below $t_{\max}$ and are thus safe to be executed in parallel.

2.1.2 Optimistic Algorithms

Since the remainder of the thesis focuses on conservative synchronization, we give only a brief sketch of optimistic synchronization algorithms. The main idea of optimistic synchronization is to allow for violations of the local causality constraint, but to perform rollbacks of the simulation to restore correctness after a violation. A well-known optimistic algorithm is Time Warp [Jef85]:

each LP creates periodic checkpoints of the simulation state. If an LP receives an event with a lower timestamp than a non-empty set of previously executed events, the LP restores its state to a point before the execution of the set of erroneously executed events. Since the erroneously executed events may have created new events for remove LPs, so-called anti-messages are sent to these LPs to delete the erroneously created events. To limit the amount of memory required for checkpoints, the lower bound of the timestamp of a rollback is calculated periodically. All checkpoints created earlier than this lower bound can be discarded.

Optimistic synchronization can perform better than conservative synchronization in cases where violations of the causality constraint can be ruled out for only small ranges in simulated time, but where actual violations occur only infrequently. In these cases, small lookahead values lead to slow progress using conservative synchronization. On the other hand, optimistic synchronization requires the simulator engine to store sufficient data so that a previous model state can be recovered. Hence, optimistic synchronization can incur substantial memory requirements. Substantial reductions in the memory requirements of optimistic synchronization and further performance increases are possible using reversible computing [CPF99, Per13].

2.2 Performance Evaluation

The benefits of PADS vary immensely depending on the network model and the simulator realization. Due to the complex interactions between the behavior of the network model during simulation runtime and the mechanisms used for communication and synchronization between the processors executing the simulation, estimating the performance of parallel and distributed simulations is a difficult task that has been the focus of a substantial body of research.

A particular challenge is given by the fact that simulation is typically applied in cases where the behavior of a system cannot be easily predicted analytically. Hence, since the runtime behavior of the model can strongly affect the simulation performance, predicting the simulation performance becomes difficult as well.

2.2.1 Taxonomy

A multitude of performance estimation and evaluation approaches have been proposed, each focusing on a subset of the factors determining the observed performance of a real-world execution of a simulation model. In the following, we will give an introduction to the key performance-critical factors, categorizing previous works in the field of performance evaluation according to the considered subset of factors.

We motivate our focus on sets of performance-critical factors with the observation that real-world networked systems are highly parallel and work in real-time. Hence, in theory it should be possible to simulate these systems in real-time by imitating the parallelism that is inherent in the real-world systems. However, the reported benefits of PADS vary immensely. In some cases, a large speedup compared to a sequential execution was achieved [PFP04], while in other cases there were only modest performance gains or runtime even increased after parallelization [QRT12]. These results raise the question: *if the modeled system itself contains high amounts of parallelism, why is the parallelism not exploited by PADS?*

To approach this question, we first distinguish between three key metrics that describe different aspects of PADS performance and which we will return to repeatedly throughout the remainder of the thesis:

- *Speedup* is the ratio between the execution time of a sequential simulation run and a parallel or distributed simulation run. It is influenced by the network model, the synchronization algorithm, the simulator implementation, and the execution hardware.
- *Parallelism* is the measured average number of events executed in parallel in a parallel or distributed simulation run.
- *Concurrency* is the average number of events in a simulation run that *can* be executed in parallel, assuming an unlimited number of processors and no costs for synchronization and communication between logical processes. The concurrency is a property of the network model and scenario configuration and forms an upper bound for the parallelism in a simulation run.

The distinction between parallelism and concurrency is made in analogy to the use of the terms in the literature on software engineering. For instance, Briot et al. describe concurrency as "referring to the non-sequential semantics of a program", and parallelism as "referring to the actual implementation of a concurrent system" [BGL98]. Note that in contrast to the software engineering domain, where the terms are used in a more qualitative sense to refer to aspects of software systems and their execution, we define both concurrency and parallelism as specific measurable quantities.

To enable a more fine-grained categorization of performance evaluation approaches, we propose a taxonomy of the main factors that determine PADS performance (cf. Figure 2.2), tracing the properties of the network model itself (the root node of the tree) to the measured or estimated performance of a full simulation run (the leaf node on the deepest level of the tree).

The literature has focused on the performance-critical factors depicted in Figure 2.2:

1. **Lookahead:** Under a conservative synchronization algorithm, in order to adhere to the local causality constraint, only *safe* events are executed. Depending on properties of the network model, it may be sufficient to determine a global and constant minimum timestamp delta between an event and its creation and choose this value as a fixed lookahead. In other cases, the lookahead must be determined dynamically for efficient simulation. Limited lookahead can restrict the portion of the concurrency of a network model that can be exploited in a simulation run.

2. **Partitioning:** Given a limited number of processors to perform the simulation on, sets of nodes in the network must be assigned to logical processes (LPs), each handling a segment of the simulated network. Partitioning the network to n LPs introduces two limitations with respect to the network model's concurrency. First, since only a maximum of n LPs can execute events in parallel, the maximum number of parallel events is n. Second, as events in each LP are executed in timestamp-order, previously independent events are given a sequential order to be followed in the simulation. We can model the changes in the number of parallel events by additional edges in an event precedence graph (cf. Figure 2.3) that describes the order between events that must be maintained during execution to guarantee the correctness of the simulation. The impact of the partitioning on the precedence graph and the resulting

number of parallel events can be influenced by the number of LPs chosen and the strategy by which nodes are assigned to LPs. Event precedence graphs are considered in more detail in Chapter 5.

3. **Communication:** Simulated messages crossing LP boundaries require physical communication between LPs. In parallel simulations using shared memory, physical communication takes the form of synchronized accesses to memory. The amount of inter-LP communication is dependent on the chosen partitioning strategy. Hence, all vertices containing the factor C in Figure 2.2 also contain the factor P.

4. **Synchronization:** Synchronization is required to maintain the causal relationships between nodes simulated in different LPs. There is a dependence of the costs of the synchronization algorithm on the partitioning strategy and on the number of LPs.

The remainder of this section provides an overview of existing work on performance evaluation of PADS, categorizing the approaches by the considered performance-critical factors.

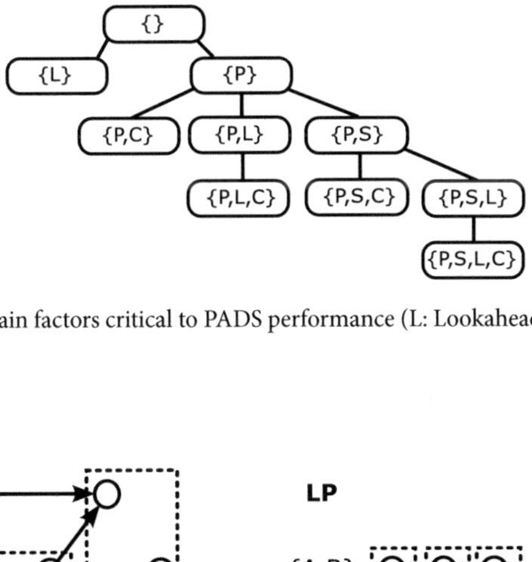

Figure 2.2: Taxonomy of the main factors critical to PADS performance (L: Lookahead, P: Partitioning, C: Communication, S: Synchronization).

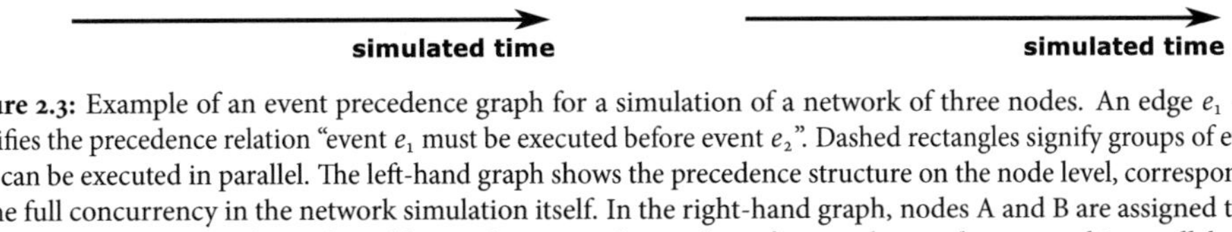

Figure 2.3: Example of an event precedence graph for a simulation of a network of three nodes. An edge $e_1 \rightarrow e_2$ signifies the precedence relation "event e_1 must be executed before event e_2". Dashed rectangles signify groups of events that can be executed in parallel. The left-hand graph shows the precedence structure on the node level, corresponding to the full concurrency in the network simulation itself. In the right-hand graph, nodes A and B are assigned to the same logical process, which is reflected by a reduction in the number of events that can be executed in parallel.

2.2.2 Strategies

Measurements

A wide variety of works study the performance of PADS by benchmarking simulation runs on physical hardware. Measuring the runtime of a simulation run considers the effects of the model partitioning, the costs of communication and synchronization, as well as the available lookahead ($\{P, L, C, S\}$). Many works in this category focus on the impact of the choice of synchronization algorithm (e.g., [RJD89, KY91, BRA95]). While benchmarking results can accurately represent the simulation performance on a given hardware platform, the measured runtime is affected by all of the performance-critical factors. Hence, it can be difficult to generalize measurement results.

To isolate the impacts of the costs for synchronization, the Ideal Simulation Protocol (ISP) [JB96, BT00] enables performance measurements while excluding synchronization costs. ISP requires two simulation runs: in the first run, a trace is generated that contains the timestamp ordering of all events. In the second run, the information of the trace can be used to execute all events in non-decreasing timestamp order without resorting to a traditional conservative or optimistic synchronization algorithm. Blocking of LPs is required only when the earliest next event is yet to be created or is still being transferred over the interconnect. Hence, the second simulation run is performed with only minimal costs for synchronization. When comparing the simulation performance under a traditional synchronization algorithm with ISP, the costs for synchronization can be studied in isolation. Simulation studies using ISP compare simulation runs under the performance-critical factors $\{P, L, C\}$ with runs under the factors $\{P, L, C, S\}$. De Munck et al. [DMVB13] applied ISP to study the costs of conservative synchronization algorithms in the context of modern hardware environments. By studying two different simulation models and various traditional and novel variants of the null message algorithm, their results show the large dependence of PADS performance on the interaction between the simulation model and the synchronization algorithm, in particular with respect to the null message sending strategy.

Analytical Modeling

While a detailed analytical description of the performance of a full simulation run on physical hardware is usually unattainable, analytical modeling can still provide insights into the impact of isolated performance-critical factors or give coarse indications of the expected performance.

Critical Path Analysis is a method that processes an event precedence graph to determine the path containing the events that must be executed in order, i.e., that cannot be executed concurrently. If no weights are assigned to the vertices of the graph representing events, the sum weight of the vertices represents the minimal number of event execution iterations that must be performed to complete the simulation. If this number is divided by the total number of events in the simulation, we arrive at the concurrency of the network model in isolation, i.e., $\{\}$ in Figure 2.2. Traditional critical path analysis assumes can be considered to assume sufficient lookahead to enable optimal synchronization between logical processes. In Chapter 5 we give an algorithmic description of critical path analysis and propose a variant that assumes a configurable fixed lookahead value.

Liu et al. [LNPP99] performed micro-benchmarks on physical hardware and performed back-of-the-envelope calculations of the expected performance of parallel simulations under synchronous conservative synchronization. Their estimations consider the performance-critical aspects $\{P, S, L, C\}$ and in an experiment are able to approximate the runtime of a parallel simulator implementation with an error below 10%. In Chapter 5, we present an analytical estimation method that predicts the raw concurrency of a network model. While Liu et al. assume an even distribution of events to LPs, our approach focuses on the imbalances in event counts between the simulated nodes, enabling concurrency estimations for models of comparatively large complexity.

Park et al. [PFP04] constructed an analytical estimation model for the number of null messages generated in large-scale network simulations. Hence, they consider an aspect of the synchronization costs ($\{S\}$) in a simulation. Their estimations enable predictions of the synchronization overhead in PADS using the null message algorithm.

Pienta et al. [PF13] modeled the concurrency in simulations of networks with node degrees following a power law (scale-free networks). Under an assumed communication pattern between nodes, a recursive term is derived for the number of events executed in each iteration of a simulation under synchronous conservative simulation. Again, calculated concurrency values reflect the concurrency of the network model itself, without considering further performance-critical factors, i.e., $\{\}$. The analytical approach presented in Chapter 5 provides more direct insights into a network model's concurrency by not requiring an iterative model. Like Pienta et al., we base our estimations on the YAWNS algorithm (cf. Section 2.1.1). We provide a proof of the soundness of this approach by determining an upper bound for the deviation between the results obtained using YAWNS and critical path analysis under commonly applied assumptions. Additionally, our experiments focus on concrete network models implemented in popular network simulators.

Second-Order Simulation

PADS is frequently applied for the evaluation of networked systems. However, the PADS system comprised of a set of interconnected processors, a synchronization algorithm, and a network model can be considered a networked system in itself and can consequently be evaluated using simulations. Based on this observation, a number of previous works have created simulation models of PADS systems similar to simulation models for performance evaluation of general sequential, parallel, and distributed applications [BM02, ZKK04, BKR07, HMS+09, RHB+11, BRM12]. We refer to the simulation of a simulation as *second-order simulation.*

Using second-order simulation approaches, it is possible to consider all performance-critical aspects ($\{P, S, L, C\}$), while individual aspects can still be suppressed to determine their impact on performance in isolation.

Swope et al. [SF87] simulate the execution of distributed simulations using assumed costs for execution of the first-order model code, and for system calls and communication between processors in the first-order simulator. Similarly to the Ideal Simulation Protocol (cf. Section 2.2.2), knowledge of the sequence of future events enables optimal synchronization. Hence, their approach enables an evaluation of the expected simulation performance under the performance-critical factors $\{P, L, C\}$.

The following works consider the full set of performance-critical factors $\{P, S, L, C\}$.

Wong et al. [WHL95] simulate a conservatively synchronized parallel execution of a simulation during a sequential run of an instrumented simulator implementation.

Juhasz et al. [JTKG01] propose a second-order simulation tool to estimate the expected benefit of parallelization of a simulation model. A trace of the events executed in a sequential run of the first-order simulator is used to guide the execution of the second-order simulation under a number of synchronization algorithms.

Perumalla et al. [PFT+05] propose a trace-based second-order simulation approach with a focus on selecting a suitable synchronization algorithm for a given type of first-order model.

Ewald et al. [EHU+06] present a second-order simulation approach implemented in the simulation system JAMES II. Their approach extends the execution of an unmodified first-order simulation model by a second-order simulation model predicting the time required for the interactions between LPs.

Gianni et al. [GID10] combine network model knowledge with benchmarking results on physical hardware to generate a queuing network model of distributed simulations. The PADS runtime is determined by simulating the queuing network in the simulation framework OMNet++.

A key challenge in performance prediction of PADS is the estimation accuracy given events associated with low computational costs. In such cases, two issues pose difficulties: first, it is difficult to accurately measure and predict the costs of fine-grained computations. Second, low per-event computation times tend to increase the impact of network overheads on the resulting simulation performance. However, without a detailed model of the interconnect between LPs, the costs of individual communication operations between LPs will be limited.

Previous works have not focused on estimation accuracy with respect to models with fine-grained computations. In Chapter 6, we present a second-order simulation tool that we use to predict the estimated runtime of simulation of multiple network models with fine-grained computations. We evaluate the prediction accuracy by comparing the predictions to the runtime of PADS runs on physical hardware.

2.3 Simulator Adaptation

A variety of previous works has studied the adaptation of the simulator configuration to the given network model. Although some simulations may perform well under a suitable *static* configuration determined prior to the simulation run, network models with highly dynamic or unpredictable behavior may require adaptations of the simulator configuration *at runtime* to achieve high simulation performance. In this section, we give an overview of existing approaches to static and runtime adaptation of the simulator configuration. The overview is structured according to the considered performance-critical factors. Since the impact of the performance-critical factor *communication* is largely determined by the interconnect and the chosen network model *partitioning*, approaches to reduce communication in PADS are discussed as part of the works on partitioning.

2.3.1 Lookahead

The lookahead is central to the performance of PADS under conservative synchronization, since the lookahead determines the length of periods in simulated time that LPs can process without blocking to wait for events or null messages from other LPs. The maximum lookahead that is possible in a simulation is a property of the network model. Typically, the maximum lookahead in a network model is not fully exploited, since in general, the answer to the associated question *"What is the earliest possible timestamp of an event that the current LP will create for another LP"* is not trivially answered. A common approach in the field of network simulations is the use of a fixed lookahead value according to a lower bound on the delta in simulated time between an activity in an LP and a resulting activity in a remote LP [Nic96], e.g., the smallest possible link latency between network nodes simulated in separate LPs. To extract further lookahead, it is possible to supply model-specific knowledge to the simulator [MB98, LN02, CK06, PVM09, WDYR13]. A more general solution is given by modeling the state and control flow of the model and analyzing the resulting graph statically or dynamically to determine the shortest possible timestamp of an event created in the current LP for another LP [CS89, MB99, ZP01].

Based on the observation that the generation of pseudo-random numbers is conducted in a deterministic fashion, the pseudo-random numbers determining future event creations can be calculated in advance, so that LPs can determine the timestamp of future events at an earlier point in simulated time [LL90, BT00, LF00].

The evaluation of approaches to extend the lookahead can be performed based on the achieved reduction in simulation runtime and of synchronization overhead, e.g., by measurements of the number of null messages required for conservative synchronization.

Since the Ideal Simulation Protocol (ISP) enables an evaluation of synchronization overhead in isolation, some authors applied ISP to study the achieved synchronization efficiency under their lookahead extension approaches [MB99, PVM09].

A further object of evaluation is the quantity of simulated time between events created by an LP in measurements of a simulation run, i.e., the maximum lookahead available in the model, in relation to the lookahead actually extracted by a given synchronization algorithm. The lookahead ratio [Fuj88] and the null message inverse lookahead ratio [PL90] enable an empirical assessment of the fraction of the maximum lookahead that is extracted in a given simulation run.

2.3.2 Partitioning

When distributing the computational load of the simulation to a number of processors, intuitively, the largest benefit is achieved under an even distribution over the available processors. In the case of network simulations, the corresponding partitioning problem can be formulated based on an activity graph of the network. Vertices represent the nodes in the network and are weighted by the number of events pertaining to the node. Edges reflect direct links between nodes and are weighted by the number of events, i.e., messages, travelling over the link. A naïve partitioning strategy that considers only the workload balance between LPs could for instance aim to minimize the largest sum weight of the vertices assigned to a single LP. However, if the activity in the network shifts between nodes over simulated time, it is not sufficient to consider such a fixed representation of the network activity. Achieving an optimal partitioning would potentially require an update on each change in activity in the network. Since calculating a partitioning and redistributing the simulation workload is associated with a cost, in practice, dynamic partitioning approaches redistribute the simulated nodes periodically after a certain interval in simulated time or wall-clock time.

The partitioning problem is further complicated by the fact that the simulated communication between nodes may require physical communication via shared memory or a network in case the simulated communication crosses LP boundaries. To minimize physical communication, the minimum edge cut could be determined for a desired number of logical processes. However, in general, the maximum workload balance and the minimum edge cut will be achieved for different partitionings. In addition, the effect of a given partitioning strategy on synchronization costs depends on the synchronization algorithm and may be non-obvious.

Finally, a full description of the optimization problem sketched above is not available in the general case. Whenever the simulation approach implies that the steps leading to a certain behavior, i.e., the sending and reception of messages, must actually be performed to observe the behavior we are interested in, the vertex and edge weights cannot be estimated with full accuracy prior to simulation. Instead, dynamic partitioning strategies in practice perform the partitioning based on weights gathered from observing the simulated network activity of the immediate past with respect to simulated time, under the assumption that past behavior serves as a reasonable estimate of the immediate future. Additionally, since acquiring a global knowledge of the vertex and edge weights of the nodes handled by all LPs can be costly, the partitioning is typically conducted without global knowledge of the model state using a distributed partitioning algorithm.

In 1993, Nandy et al. [NL93] discussed the challenges of the PADS synchronization problem and proposed a distributed partitioning algorithm. They showed that when considering a closed queuing network, PADS performance under conservative synchronization using the null message algorithm depends linearly both on the imbalance in vertex weights, i.e., of the computational workload of individual simulated nodes, and on the weight of the total edge cut, i.e., the number of messages passed between nodes simulated in separate LPs.

A multitude of works have proposed static and dynamic partitioning strategies in the context of simulations of various domains (e.g., [NS88, KHW95, KY95, BF00, FGF00, Bou01]).

2.3.3 Synchronization

While it is clear that different synchronization algorithms perform best for different types of network models, only few guidelines exist for deciding upon an algorithm for a given simulation study: for instance, optimistic synchronization seems to perform better than conservative synchronization if only a small amount of lookahead is available in the network model [Fuj01]. Further degrees of freedom are given by the exact realization of the algorithm, e.g., the frequency of sending null messages in a conservative algorithm [PFP04].

Depending on the requirements of the simulation study, it is possible to relax the local causality constraint to achieve higher simulation performance. Lin et al. [LPGZ05] proposed the use of a relaxation window larger than the lookahead window. Whether the relaxation window can be applied and to what size it can be set depends on the research questions to be answered in the simulation study. Any question whose answer requires an exact timestamp ordering of events, e.g., the search for deadlock situations in a distributed algorithm, will not be able to apply the proposed optimization. In the example given by Lin et al., it is assumed that any delay in the processing of messages that does not lead to a timeout in the simulated peer-to-peer network can be tolerated.

In 2000, Fujimoto [Fuj00] proposed partial orderings of simulation events that exploit the temporal uncertainty given when modeling many real-world systems. Instead of fixed timestamps, events are assigned intervals in simulated time within which they must be processed. Now, events that would not be considered safe to be processed in parallel under a traditional conservative synchronization algorithm can be considered concurrent and can hence be executed simultaneously.

Of course, the applicability of the relaxation of the temporal ordering depends on the requirements of the given simulation study. While the proposed synchronization scheme enables comparatively high-performance PADS of models with low amounts of lookahead, the effects on the validity of simulation results are difficult to quantify.

Since the performance of optimistic synchronization algorithms depends strongly on the frequency of violations of the local causality constraint and the subsequent rollbacks, optimizations have focused on limiting the optimism so that the rollback frequency is reduced [Fuj01]. While early approaches were based on a user-configured parameter to restrict the optimism, later approaches monitor the rollback frequency during simulation runtime and adapt the optimism parameter appropriately [Fuj01]. In [KSGW12], the interactions between events are monitored during simulation to estimate the likelihood of future causality violations caused by optimistic event execution.

3
Considered Network Models

In the subsequent parts of this dissertation, we investigate the parallelization potential of several network models. The statements that can be made based on analyzing a network model or measuring the performance of a simulator implementation depend strongly on the selected type of network model: studying a network model that accurately reflects aspects of a real-world network enables insights of immediate relevance to simulationists in the respective domain. However, generalizing the results poses the challenge of uncovering the causal relationships between the model characteristics and the observed results. In contrast, simulation models created specifically for benchmarking allow researchers to vary key model characteristics such as the network topology and the communication patterns in the network. Hence, the relationship between model parameters and parallelization results can be studied more directly. However, the chosen parameters may deviate strongly from the properties of models of any real-world network, calling into question the direct applicability of the results.

Therefore, we investigate both models of real-world networks and benchmark models. Two of the selected network models – a model of large-scale peer-to-peer networks and a model of wireless networks – are intended as close representations of their real-world counterparts. The models differ strongly in their computational intensity and in the communication patterns among the simulated nodes. Additionally, we consider two models traditionally used as benchmarks for parallel and distributed simulators: a model of a simple wired network topology, and a purely synthetic benchmark model. The characterization of the network models is based on descriptions presented in our previous publications [AMH11, AJH14, AH15].

The models are applied in multiple ways in this thesis: in Part II, the models are used for evaluation of the proposed evaluation methods and are investigated with respect to their parallelization potential. In Part III, the models serve as examples to demonstrate the performance gains through efficient parallel and distributed simulator architectures.

3.1 Peer-to-Peer Overlay Network

The first considered network model represents a distributed hash table (DHT) established for use by the BitTorrent file sharing application[1]. A DHT is the realization of a hash table using a peer-to-peer network. Today, the BitTorrent DHT is also used in the contexts of video streaming[2], file synchronization[3] and instant messaging[4]. While the models considered here focus on the BitTorrent DHT, which is a separate network used to identify peers of the main BitTorrent network that store a desired piece of information, the main BitTorrent network used to perform data transfers was previously modeled by LaFortune et al. [LCSH07].

The BitTorrent DHT is based on the Kademlia [MM02] protocol. In the peer-to-peer network that represents the DHT, peers as well as contents are identified by identifiers (IDs) numbers taken from a 160-bit space. The logical distance between IDs is defined by the XOR metric $d(x, y) = x \oplus y$. All interactions between peers are performed using remote procedure calls (RPCs), each of which is comprised of a request and a subsequent response. RPCs form the basis for *lookups*. In this description, we focus on *FIND_NODE* lookups, which serve to identify the closest nodes to a desired target ID. A *FIND_NODE* lookup is initiated by sending requests to a number of peers, each message requesting the closest peers to a target ID. Additional requests are sent to the peers received in the incoming responses to iteratively retrieve closer peers. The peer that initiated the lookup maintains a sorted list of the peers closest to the desired key. Once the first k peers in the list have responded to RPCs and have not returned any closer peers, the lookup terminates. In addition to *FIND_NODE*, further lookup types are used for the actual storage and retrieval of data. These lookup types extend *FIND_NODE* by a fixed number of RPCs to retrieve the located value or to store the value on the identified nodes. Since the principle mechanisms of all lookup types are identical, we do not discuss the remaining lookup types in further detail.

Each peer in the DHT maintains a routing table containing other peers in the network. The topology of the overlay network established by the DHT is comprised of the entries in the peers' routing tables. The routing table is a binary tree of *k-buckets*, each holding at maximum k, usually 8, peers. Each k-bucket holds peers in a subsegment of the 160-bit ID space so that the set of all k-buckets in a peer's routing table covers the full ID space without overlap. When a peer A becomes aware of another peer B in the network, an attempt is made to insert B in the k-bucket covering the ID range corresponding with B's ID. If the k-bucket holds less than k peers, B is added to the k-bucket. If the k-bucket is full of alive peers, one of two possible steps is performed:

1. If the k-bucket covers the ID of peer A itself, the corresponding k-bucket is split in two, each new k-bucket handling half of the original k-bucket's ID range. Peer B is added to the new bucket corresponding to its ID.
2. If the k-bucket does *not* cover the ID of peer A itself, peer B is discarded.

Due to the splitting mechanism, a peer's routing table tends to contain more peers close to its own ID than peers with large XOR-distance.

The sources for traffic induced by the protocol are as follows.

[1] http://www.bittorrent.com/
[2] http://www.tribler.org/
[3] https://www.getsync.com/
[4] http://www.bleep.pm/

- **Bootstrapping**: when entering the DHT, each peer is bootstrapped by executing a lookup targeting its own ID to populate its routing table.
- **Routing table maintenance**: if a peer attempts to add a new peer to a k-bucket that is full, requests are sent to peers in the k-bucket that have not sent a message in the past 15 minutes. If one of the probed peers does not respond within a timeout interval, it is replaced by the new peer. Additionally, if the contents of a k-bucket do not change within 15 minutes, the k-bucket is refreshed by performing a lookup for a random ID in the k-bucket's range.
- **User-initiated lookups**: when a user requests the value associated with a given key, a lookup is triggered.

As each peer's routing table is biased towards peers with IDs close to its own, bootstrapping and routing table maintenance induce traffic concentrated in XOR-proximity of the peer. The traffic resulting from user-initiated lookups converges against the lookup's target ID, which in the simulation is drawn from a uniform distribution on the ID space.

In the remainder of the dissertation, we consider three variants of the Kademlia model, each representing the network on a different level of abstraction. The different model variants were created to limit the development effort incurred by targeting fundamentally different simulator architectures. Of course, direct comparisons between two simulator architectures can be made only in the cases where a given model variant exists for both simulator architectures. Limitations in the statements that are possible given the available set of network model implementations will be discussed in the performance evaluation of the simulator architectures presented in Part III. We consider the following model variants:

1. **Kademlia$_A$** models the behavior and state of the peers accurately according to the BitTorrent DHT specification [LN08]. Routing table maintenance traffic as well as user-initiated lookups are part of the model. The amount of user-initiated traffic can be configured. The transport layer and lower layers are not modeled explicitly. Instead, the latency of each message between simulated peers is drawn from a uniform distribution. Given an initial number of peers in the simulated network, the topology is created by providing each peer entering the network with a fixed number of remote peers drawn uniformly from the existing network. Subsequently, as specified by the protocol, the new peer performs a lookup targeting its own ID to learn about further peers. Peers join and leave the network at a configurable rate. The model was originally implemented by Jünemann, who later presented a refined model parametrization according to measurements in the BitTorrent DHT [Jün15].

2. **Kademlia$_B$** is simplified in multiple regards. First, the network topology is generated at the start of the simulation and is not changed during simulation. Hence, after the initialization phase, the set of peers in the network as well as their routing tables contents remain constant. In consequence, the model omits the routing table maintenance traffic of the peers.

3. **Kademlia$_C$** is a slight simplification of Kademlia$_B$. Each peer executes at most one lookup concurrently. Still, as in the other model variants, multiple RPCs can be performed concurrently by each individual lookup.

3.2 TCP/IP in a Fixed Topology

The second considered network model was created as part of the DARPA "Network Modeling and Simulation" (NMS) program[5]. The model is distributed with the popular network simulator NS-3[6] and is frequently used as a benchmark for parallel and distributed simulators [LLH09, PR11, SIR14]. This section is based on [AH15].

The simulated network topology is created from so-called campus networks interconnected in a ring topology. Given n campus networks, the campus network i communicates with its neighboring network $(i + 1)\ MOD\ n$.

Each campus network is composed of three subnetworks (cf. Figure 3.1). The nodes in Network 0 and Network 1, and between Network 0, 1 and 3 are connected by a 1 Gbps link with 5ms latency. The local area networks in network 2 and 3 contain a configurable number of user workstations connected to a switch using 100 Mbps links with 1 ms of latency. The campus networks are interconnected using links with a latency of 200 ms. For each of the LAN nodes, a TCP stream with a constant data rate of 500 kbps is transmitted by one of the nodes 1:2, 1:3, 1:4 or 1:5 of the neighboring campus network.

NS-3 accurately models TCP and IP. In the local area networks, media access control is handled by a simple CSMA mechanism. All other interconnections are point-to-point links.

In the remainder of the dissertation, we will refer to this network model as **NMS**.

3.3 Wireless Ad-Hoc Communication

We consider two models of wireless communication according to IEEE 802.11 a, g, and p. The following description of these models is based on [AMH11] and [AH15]. The considered scenarios reflect a setup commonly used when studying wireless ad-hoc communication of vehicles: a configurable number of nodes is placed spatially on one or more straight lines, representing highway segments. The nodes periodically emit beacon messages containing, e.g., their current location and speed, to establish a mutual awareness that can be leveraged by applications to increase traffic safety and efficiency. To determine whether a transmitted message can be successfully received by each of the receivers, the effects of the wireless channel, e.g., by path loss and fading, must be modeled. Typically, abstract analytical models are used to model the channel effects and to determine a probability of successful reception depending on the distance between the sender and the receiver and the transmission power. These analytical models incur only little computational costs, but model each reception on the level of individual packets as the smallest unit of consideration. Hence, for instance, changes in signal strength within individual packets cannot be represented by these models. Mittag et al. presented *PhySim*, an extension to NS-3 that enables a more detailed modeling of wireless network transmissions [MPHS11]. Using PhySim, instead of considering packet as the smallest unit of consideration, each wireless transmission is represented by the electromagnetic signals transmitted and received by the wireless transceivers. Channel effects are modeled by degrading the transmitted signal according to one of a number of detailed channel

[5] `http://www.cs.dartmouth.edu/~nicol/NMS/baseline/`
[6] `http://www.nsnam.org/`

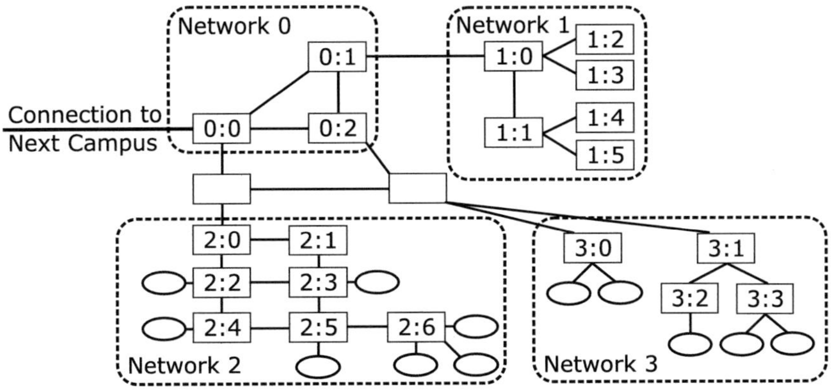

Figure 3.1: A single campus network of the topology defined in the context of the NMS program (Figure adapted from [PR11]).

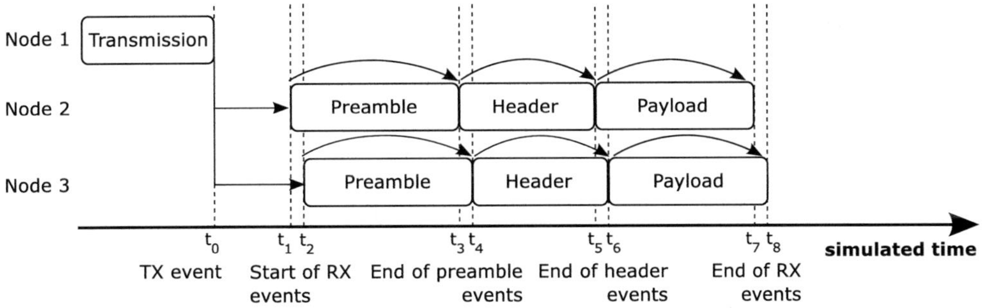

Figure 3.2: Sequence of events during a transmission in the wireless network model.

models. Simulation on the signal level enables an accurate modeling of the physical layer and the wireless channel. However, PhySim requires the execution of the computationally expensive signal processing steps of a wireless transceiver. Performing these signal processing steps in software incurs an increase in the runtime of the simulation of more than three orders of magnitude [Mit12].

In the signal-level model, the transmission and reception process has to be divided into several events to represent the temporal extent of the signal representing each transmitted packet. As illustrated in Figure 3.2, a packet transmission leads to several events at each potential receiver: first, an event that indicates the arrival of the first time sample is scheduled, followed by events that reflect the points in time at which the three parts of the packet, i.e., the preamble, the packet header, and the payload, have been received. At each of these events, a decision is made whether the reception process of the packet is continued depending on the successful handling of the previous part of the packet.

In the subsequent parts of the dissertation, we will refer to the packet-level model as **Wireless$_A$** and to the signal-level model as **Wireless$_B$**.

3.4 PHOLD Benchmark Model

In addition to simulation models of specific network protocols and scenarios, we consider the PHOLD model [Fuj87], a synthetic benchmark model frequently used in the literature to evaluate the performance of simulator implementations and to compare synchronization strategies. PHOLD adopts the basic mechanisms of the classical hold benchmark model [VD75, MS81] for sequential discrete-event simulators and extends the model for parallel and distributed simulation. The hold model is used to determine the raw event rate, i.e., the number of events processed per second wall-clock time, of a sequential simulator. In the hold model, an initial population of events is created at the start of the simulation. Now, events are executed in timestamp order. During the execution of each event, exactly one new event is created. The time delta between each event and its creation time is drawn from a configured probability distribution. Since the execution of each event entails no computational costs apart from the generation of a new event, the model mainly exercises the core event management procedures of the simulator. In particular, the hold model is well-suited to evaluate the performance of different implementations of the future event list [RA97].

The PHOLD model extends the hold model by assigning each event to a specific logical process. Hence, newly created events may need to be physically transferred between logical processes via shared memory or a network. The model can be parametrized with respect to the following aspects: a configured topology connecting the logical processes is used to decide randomly which logical processes a new event can be assigned to. Additionally, a configured probability distribution determines which of the neighboring logical processes a new event is forwarded to. Finally, to imitate the computations associated with events of a network model, a configured distribution determines the amount of time spent on dummy computations during each event execution.

In the remainder of the dissertation, we will refer to this network model as **PHOLD**.

3.5 Comparison

We illustrate the core differences in the properties of the described network models by comparing the core characteristics that affect to parallel and distributed performance (cf. Table 3.1).

- *Computational granularity:* In general, a more abstract network model that confines itself to a probabilistic representation of low-level details of each network transmission requires less computation time per event than a network model that accurately represents all details of each transmission. Hence, the lowest OSI layer that is represented accurately in the model provides a rough indication of the costs of each event, i.e., the *computational granularity* of the simulation. All else being equal, larger computational granularity tends to increase the benefit of parallelization, since the relative impact of overheads incurred by communication and synchronization between processors decreases. We measured the event processing times of the considered networks models in sequential simulation runs on an Intel Xeon E5-2670 processor running at 2.6 GHz, using the accurate cycle counter available in recent Intel processors [Pao10]. While each event of the packet-level models **Kademlia**$_{\mathbf{A,B,C}}$, **NMS**, **Wireless**$_{\mathbf{A}}$ and the synthetic model **PHOLD** can typically be processed within a few microseconds of wall-clock time, events of the signal-level model **Wireless$_B$** require multiple milliseconds of processing time.

- *Topology and communication patterns:* The topology of the modeled network restricts the possible communication patterns between simulated nodes, which in turn strongly affect the concurrency of the network model and the requirement for physical communication between logical processes with respect to a selected partitioning strategy. In the **Kademlia$_{A,B,C}$** models, the topology is generated by notifying newly created peers about a set of existing peers selected uniformly at random. Existing peers to insert into the new peer's routing table are selected according to the routing table management procedure described in the BitTorrent DHT specification [LN08]. The protocol aims to maintain the *small-world* property, i.e., a low average hop count between arbitrary peers. The **NMS** model uses the fixed topology described in Section 3.2. Each campus network transmits a TCP flow with a constant rate to the neighboring campus network. The network models **Wireless$_{A,B}$** reflect a broadcast medium where a packet transmitted by a sender is received by all other nodes, analogously to a fully meshed wired network. In the **PHOLD** network, an arbitrary topology can be configured. In our experiments, we configure the network to be fully meshed. Messages are passed between nodes uniformly at random. A delta in simulated time is drawn from an exponential distribution and added to a fixed configured lookahead value.
- *Maximum number of nodes*: Finally, the number of nodes in the simulated networks can affect both the required physical communication between logical processes and the memory requirements of the simulation. Additionally, since the local causality constraints mandates a non-decreasing timestamp order in the execution of events per node, only event per node can be executed at the same time. Hence, the total number of nodes is a trivial upper bound for the concurrency of a network model. The numbers of nodes listed in Table 3.1 are intended as rough estimates of the upper limits used in typical studies of the respective domain.

In Part II of the dissertation, we investigate how the differences in the core characteristics of the network models translate to differences in their concurrency and expected parallel and distributed simulation performance. In Part III, we present simulator architectures suitable to exploit the parallelization potentials given by the different network models' characteristics.

	Kademlia$_{A,B,C}$	**NMS**	**Wireless$_{A,B}$**	**PHOLD**
Lowest OSI Layer	5	2	A: 2, B: 1	N/A
Computational Granularity	$\leq 5\mu s$	$\leq 10\mu s$	A: $\leq 10\mu s$, B: $\approx 5ms$	$\approx 0.7\mu s$
Topology	probabilistic small-world network	static sub-networks	broadcast medium (fully meshed)	fully meshed
Communication Patterns	lookups to routing table and random IDs	constant-rate TCP flows	periodic single-packet broadcasts	uniform receivers, exponential delays
Max. Number of Nodes	10 000 000	arbitrary	100	arbitrary

Table 3.1: Comparison of the considered network models.

Part II
Identifying Concurrency

4
Identifying Concurrency – Introduction

The benefits of parallel and distributed simulation of network models reported in the literature vary immensely. In some cases, substantial performance increases are achieved in comparison to a sequential execution, while in other cases gains are modest to non-existent. Since the runtime performance of a parallel and distributed simulation is subject to the complex interaction of the properties of the network model and the simulator realization, performance estimation and evaluation is non-trivial. In particular, it is difficult to determine whether low performance is due to fundamental limitations given by the network model at hand, or due to the specific choice of synchronization algorithm, hardware platform or simulator implementation. Hence, there is a need to study these aspects both in isolation and in interaction.

In the past forty years, a multitude of evaluation approaches have been proposed to determine upper bounds and realistic estimations for parallel and distributed simulation performance. Depending on the level of abstraction chosen by the approaches, different types of questions about simulation performance are addressed.

In this chapter, we introduce methods to trace the performance of conservative parallel and distributed simulations from the most fundamental upper bounds given by properties of the network model to predictions of the real-world simulation performance on physical hardware. The approaches enable an assessment of a network model's parallelization potentials on different levels of detail:

First, we propose an analytical approach to estimate the available concurrency in network simulations based on scenario parameters and the communication patterns defined by the network model. In contrast to existing methods, the approach enables insights into the *causes* for the given amounts of concurrency, allowing simulationists to analytically estimate the effects of varying scenario parameters and model properties without requiring a repeated automated analysis of event traces gathered from simulation runs. The approach is applied to three models implemented in well-known network simulators, exposing fundamental upper bounds on the model's potential for parallelization.

Second, to demonstrate the more accurate performance prediction that is enabled when considering the overheads for inter-processor communication and synchronization, we present a simulation-based performance estimation tool. The tool performs a simulation of an envisioned parallel or distributed simulation (a *second-order simulation*) based on measurements gathered from a sequential simulation run and benchmarking results of the execution network. The resulting performance predictions enable users to evaluate the benefits of a parallel or distributed variant of a network model prior to parallelization. At the cost of larger modeling and measurement effort, the simulation-based approach allows for a detailed modeling of the simulator realization and the execution platform.

5 Analytical Concurrency Estimation Approach

In Section 2.2, we presented a categorization of the factors that determine the performance of parallel and distributed simulations. When abstracting from the concrete realization of a simulation, i.e., from the costs induced by partitioning, communication and synchronization, we consider only the properties of the network model itself. These properties define an upper bound for the speedup by parallelization of the model, independently of the simulator and hardware in use.

The largest possible speedup through parallelization of a discrete-event network simulation is achieved in case every event in the simulation is executed as early as possible given the *local causality constraint*, i.e., non-decreasing timestamp ordering of events per simulated node. By the precedence relationships between events, the minimum simulation time can be calculated. From the minimum runtime, it is possible to deduce the average number of events that can be executed in parallel. This number, which we refer to as the simulation's *concurrency*, can be interpreted as the average number of processors that can be occupied by a parallel simulation run of the model when assigning one simulated node to each processor and disregarding the overheads of inter-processor communication.

In a real-world setting, a simulator will usually not fully exploit the concurrency in a network model, since communication overheads tend to increase with larger numbers of active processors. However, in the context of modern many-core hardware architectures, large numbers of processor cores can be employed with comparatively low overhead [Per06, KSGW12, AH14]. Hence, the concurrency of a network model is meaningful from two perspectives: first, it indicates the parallelization potential of the model. Therefore, the results may help understand the original system or guide model optimizations. Second, the results may suggest a suitable simulator architecture to be used for the network model. For instance, given a network model with very low concurrency, it is obvious that the simulation will not fully exploit the hardware resources of a many-core device.

Critical path analysis (cf. Section 2.2.2) is a well-known approach to determine the minimum simulation time from a precedence graph gathered from a sequential simulation run. However, since critical path analysis determines a simulation's concurrency without revealing the underlying model properties, insights into the key model properties that determine the concurrency may require a sensitivity analysis based on large numbers of simulation runs and subsequent critical path analysis.

In this chapter, we make the following contributions:

- **Analytical estimation model**: we propose a model to estimate the concurrency of network models based on model knowledge and statistics describing the communication in the modeled network. The approach exposes the relationships between model properties and concurrency.
- **Proof of validity**: our estimations are performed by approximating the progress of the well-known synchronization algorithm YAWNS. We prove the limited deviation of the results of YAWNS using critical path analysis: when assuming fixed event processing times and fixed lookahead, the concurrency determined using YAWNS is at least 1/3 of the concurrency determined using critical path analysis.
- **Network model analysis**: we perform a concurrency analysis of three network models implemented in popular network simulators. The estimations serve as examples of the application of the proposed estimation approach and are used for empirical validation of the estimation accuracy.
- **Estimation refinement**: we describe the steps required to consider variable event processing times and discuss the impact on estimations and their interpretation.

This chapter is based on [AH16]. Here, we substantiate our previous results [AH15] by analyzing the algorithmic relationships between critical path analysis and the YAWNS algorithm. We provide a proof of a fundamental upper bound on the deviation between the results of the two methods under common assumptions. Further, we present a refined estimation model that eliminates the assumption of fixed event processing times and study the effects on the estimation results.

The proposed approach and estimation results apply to parallel simulation using *conservative* synchronization, where events are executed only in case future violations of the local causality constraint can be ruled out. *Optimistic* synchronization approaches may in some cases be able to exceed the presented concurrency results.

The remainder of the chapter is structured as follows: in Section 5.1, we discuss existing trace-based concurrency evaluation approaches that are fundamental to our analytical estimation approach. In Section 5.2, we show the close relationship between YAWNS-based synchronization and critical path analysis before introducing the proposed analytical concurrency estimation model. We prove the limited deviation between the analysis results of YAWNS and critical path analysis the two approaches under the stated assumptions. In Section 5.3, we analyze three concrete network models to derive concurrency estimations. In Section 5.4, we first study the sensitivity of the considered network models to scenario parameters. Subsequently, we validate our estimation results by comparison with the results of a critical path analysis. In Section 5.5, we investigate the steps necessary to extend the proposed estimation model to consider measured event processing time distributions and discuss the effects on concurrency estimations. In Section 5.6, we discuss the applicability and limitations of our approach. Section 5.7 summarizes our results.

5.1 Fundamental Algorithms

In this section, we give a brief summary of trace-based concurrency estimation approaches, which determine the concurrency in a network model by an automated analysis of event traces generated during sequential simulation runs. These approaches determine the concurrency in the model accurately, but are performed in a black-box fashion that limits insights into the sources of the identified concurrency. The assumptions and terminology of the trace-based approaches will be used when we propose an analytical estimation model in Section 5.2.3.

In discrete-event network models, communication activities are modeled as timestamped *events* representing instantaneous state changes of the simulated nodes. The communication patterns in a given network model define a precedence relation governing the event execution order. For instance, subsequent message arrivals at a single node must be simulated in timestamp order to maintain the correctness of the node state. An event can safely be executed as soon as no remaining precedence relationships demand the prior execution of other events.

Critical path analysis [BJ85, Liv85] is a classical method to determine a lower bound on the runtime of a simulation model by traversing a graph reflecting the precedence relationships between the events of a previous sequential simulation run of the considered model. A precedence graph is a directed acyclic graph $G = (V, E)$ where vertices represent simulation events, and edges represent precedence relationships. In the example depicted in Figure 5.1, events are represented by circles. An arrow between events e_1 and e_2 reflects the precedence relationship "e_1 before e_2". There are two causes of precedence relationships: first, events cannot be processed prior to their creation in the course of the simulation. Hence, there are edges reflecting the precedence of an event e over any new events created by e. Second, to enforce timestamp ordering of events in each node, there is an edge between an event e and the latest event that occurs before e and pertains to the same node. In the general case, vertices are weighted with their associated processing times. The path with the largest sum of vertex weights in the precedence graph is the critical path. The sum of the vertex weights on the critical path is a lower bound on the runtime of the simulation. The pseudo code in Algorithm 1 (from [YM89], modified to represent events as vertices), determines for each event $u \in V$ the maximum processing time sum of any path ending in u. Given an event u, $P(u)$ is the *number* of predecessor events of u. $S(u)$ is the *set* of successor events of u. $W(u)$ is the processing time of u. In subsequent sections, we will further characterize an event u by its timestamp $T(u)$ and its assignment to a simulated node $N(u)$. Q is a double-ended queue that holds the events

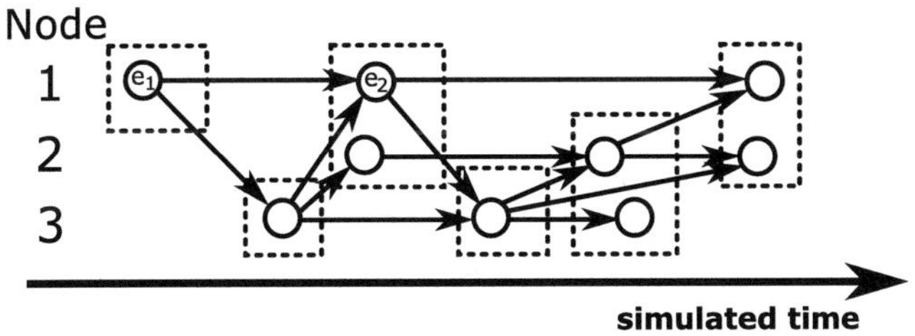

Figure 5.1: Critical path analysis of a precedence graph with fixed event processing times.

to be traversed next and is initialized with the set $V_{\text{initial}} \subseteq V$ of events that exist at the start of the simulation. The algorithm returns the largest path weight in the precedence graph G.

Contrary to Algorithm 1, in the case considered in the following, we assume identical processing times for all events. This assumption corresponds to a simulation where in each iteration independent events are executed in parallel, each processor acting on at most one event. A new iteration begins once all processors have finished executing the current event. We refer to each iteration of such a simulation as an *execution*. As an example, some discrete-event simulators running on graphics cards [PF10, AH14] are instances of the above execution scheme. We are interested in the average number of events that can be processed in an execution, which we refer to as the *concurrency* of the simulation. The concurrency can be interpreted as the average number of events that can be executed in parallel assuming an unlimited number of processors and no overheads for inter-processor communication. With a processing time of 1 unit of wall-clock time for all events, the sum vertex weight on the critical path is identical to the maximum number of vertices on any path in the precedence graph (cf. Algorithm 2). In contrast to Algorithm 1, a specific ordering of the events in Q is not required. The maximum number of vertices on any single path is the minimum number of executions required to process all events in the graph. From the minimum number of executions and the total number of events in the simulation, we can determine the concurrency of the simulation. In Figure 5.1, dashed rectangles indicate groups of events that can be processed in parallel. Nine events are processed in a total of six executions. Hence, the concurrency is $9/6 = 1.5$.

YAWNS [Nic93] (cf. Section 2.1) is a well-known synchronization algorithm for parallel and distributed simulation. Synchronization using YAWNS is illustrated in Figure 5.2. A pseudo code description of the algorithm will be given in Section 5.2. First, the timestamp t_{min} of the earliest event is determined. A fixed *lookahead* value τ determined according to model properties gives a lower bound on the timestamp delta between an event e and any new event created by e. Given $t_{\text{min}} \in \mathbb{N}$ and $\tau \in \mathbb{N}$, all events in the *lookahead window* $\{t_{\text{min}}, t_{\text{min}} + 1, \ldots, t_{\text{min}} + \tau\}$ are guaranteed to create no events with timestamps below $t_{\text{min}} + \tau$. Events in the current lookahead window are referred to as *safe* events. Safe events pertaining to separate nodes can be processed concurrently without allowing for violations of timestamp order per node. Still, safe events pertaining to a single node must be processed one after the other in non-decreasing timestamp order. Hence, the number of executions required to process a lookahead window is the largest number of events pertaining to a single node. This observation can also be understood in terms of Amdahl's law [Amd67]: the largest number of events assigned to a single node is the inherently sequential portion of the considered partial simulation. Another interpretation is given by considering the largest sequence of events assigned to a single node as the critical path within the considered lookahead window. In the example, nine events in the lookahead window can be processed in four executions. Hence, the concurrency within the shown lookahead window is $9/4 = 2.25$. YAWNS has already been used as a basis for analytical concurrency estimation in previous works [Nic93, PF13]. Here, we employ YAWNS in two ways: we analytically estimate the expected YAWNS concurrency based on key properties of network models. Further, we show analytically and empirically that the results between a concurrency analysis using critical path analysis and YAWNS are sufficiently close to use these approaches interchangeably to roughly estimate the potential of network models for parallelization.

Algorithm 1: Critical path analysis.

```
INPUT: G = (V, E); V_initial
OUTPUT: Critical path weight of G
for each u ∈ V do
    D(u) ← 0
for each u ∈ V_initial do
    D(u) ← W(u)
Q ← V_initial
while Q ≠ ∅ do
    u ← head of Q
    remove u from Q
    for each v ∈ S(u) do
        P(v) ← P(v) − 1
        if D(v) < D(u) + W(v) then
            D(v) ← D(u) + W(v)
        if P(v) = 0 then
            insert v at tail of Q
return max({D(u) : u ∈ V})
```

Algorithm 2: Critical path analysis assuming identical processing times for all events.

```
INPUT: G = (V, E); V_initial
OUTPUT: Critical path weight of G

Q ← V_initial
X ← 0

while Q ≠ ∅ do
    X ← X + 1
    Q_new ← ∅
    for each u ∈ Q do
        for each v ∈ S(u) do
            P(v) ← P(v) − 1
            if P(v) = 0 then
                insert v into Q_new
        remove u from Q
    Q ← Q_new
return X
```

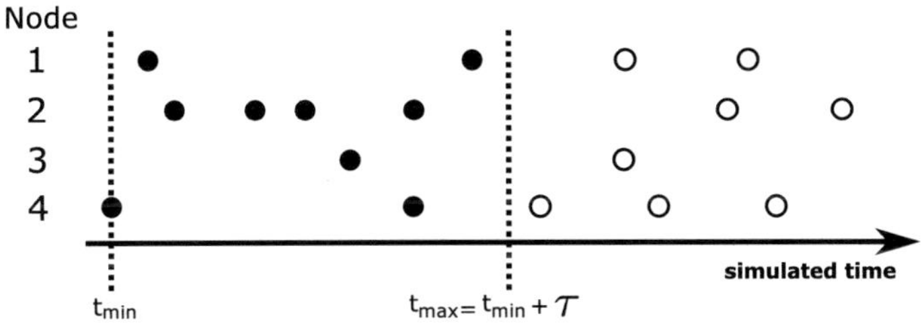

Figure 5.2: Synchronization using YAWNS. Events with timestamps $\leq t_{\text{max}}$ can be processed safely.

5.2 Methodology

In this section, we first describe the building blocks and assumptions of our concurrency estimation methodology. We then propose an analytical concurrency model as a basis for the analysis of specific network models. Finally, we provide a proof of the soundness of the estimation approach.

5.2.1 Consideration of Fixed Lookahead

Critical path analysis can be used to perform a trace-based calculation of the concurrency in a simulation under the assumption of full knowledge of all events that will be received by each processor, i.e., assuming optimal synchronization. However, since parallel network simulation is typically performed under a fixed lookahead value, at each point during simulation, only events within a limited window in simulated time can be considered for parallel execution. Thus, the results given by critical path analysis provide only loose upper bounds on a model's concurrency.

To gather more realistic estimates, we adapt critical path analysis by applying fixed lookahead at each point where events are considered for execution. The adapted critical path analysis (ACPA) determines an upper bound on the average number of events that can be executed in parallel given an unlimited number of processors and assuming no overhead for communication between processors, but under a fixed lookahead. A pseudo code description of ACPA is given in Algorithm 3.

Algorithm 3: Adapted critical path analysis (ACPA) assumes fixed event processing times and fixed lookahead.

```
INPUT: G = (V, E); V_initial; τ   OUTPUT: Number of executions required to process G
Q ← V_initial; X ← 0
while Q ≠ ∅ do
   t_min ← min({T(u) : u ∈ Q})
   Q_safe = {u ∈ Q : T(u) ≤ t_min + τ}
   while Q_safe ≠ ∅ do
      X ← X + 1
      for each u ∈ Q_safe do
         for each v ∈ S(u) do
            P(v) ← P(v) − 1
            if P(v) = 0 then
               insert v into Q
         remove u from Q and Q_safe
      t_min ← min({T(u) : u ∈ Q})   [remark: with YAWNS, t_min is not updated at this point.]
      Q_safe = {u ∈ Q : T(u) ≤ t_min + τ}
return X
```

Symbol	Description
G	Precedence graph
V	Events in G
V_{initial}	Initial events
E	Precedence relation on V
e_{global}	#Events in the simulation
$N(u)$	Node assignment of event u
$P(u)$	#Predecessors of event u
$S(u)$	Set of successors of event u
$T(u)$	Timestamp of event u
$W(u)$	Weight of event u
τ	Lookahead
t_{min}	Min. timestamp of remaining events
Q	Events to consider for processing
Q_{safe}	Events within lookahead window
$D(u)$	Largest path weight of event u
X_{ACPA}	ACPA: #Executions required to process G
X_{YAWNS}	YAWNS: #Executions required to process G
C_{ACPA}	ACPA concurrency of the simulation
C_{YAWNS}	YAWNS concurrency of the simumlation

Table 5.1: Symbols used in algorithms.

The set Q holds events with no remaining predecessors. We now determine the earliest timestamp $t_{\min}$ of all events in Q. An event u in Q can be executed, i.e., eliminated from our consideration, if two conditions both hold: the event is safe, i.e., the timestamp $T(u)$ of u is in the lookahead window $\{t_{\min}, t_{\min} + 1, \ldots, t_{\min} + \tau\}$, and u has no remaining predecessors. The set $Q_{\text{safe}} \subseteq Q$ holds the events that are safe to be executed. The number X of executions required until Q is empty is a lower bound on the number of executions required to complete the simulation. After termination of the algorithm, the concurrency C, i.e., the average number of events that can be executed in parallel, can be determined based on the number e_{global} of events: $C_{\text{ACPA}} = e_{\text{global}}/X$.

5.2.2 Relationship between Critical Path Analysis and Synchronization Algorithms

ACPA assumes fixed event processing times and a fixed lookahead. The resulting analysis method closely resembles synchronous conservative synchronization algorithms: comparing ACPA with a YAWNS-based analysis of a precedence graph (cf. the remark in Algorithm 3), the only difference is that with YAWNS, the lookahead window remains constant as long as any events remain in the current lookahead window, whereas with ACPA, a new lookahead window is calculated after each execution. If there is a large imbalance in the numbers of events assigned to different processors, many processors may remain idle with YAWNS, whereas with ACPA, the newly calculated lookahead window may contain new events to consider for execution. Hence, the concurrency determined using ACPA is equal or larger than the concurrency determined using a YAWNS-based analysis.

Our goal is to estimate the concurrency of network simulations without relying on the processing of precedence graphs. To this end, ideally, we would derive an analytical model to estimate ACPA results directly. However, since ACPA allows for overlapping lookahead windows, the sets of events contained in consecutive lookahead windows cannot be considered independently, rendering a mathematical analysis cumbersome.

In contrast, when analyzing YAWNS, each lookahead window can be considered separately. Therefore, our proposed analytical model (cf. Section 5.2.3) estimates concurrency according to YAWNS. Figure 5.3 illustrates the relationships between the concurrency results of ACPA, YAWNS and our analytical estimation approach: for the analytical results to be meaningful, it is important that the estimations are close to the reference results of ACPA. To show that this is the case, in Section 5.2.4, we prove that the concurrency analysis results using YAWNS are never larger than 3 of the results using YAWNS. Further, we show that with larger event densities or larger lookahead, the upper bound tends towards 2. In Section 5.4, we study the accuracy of our analytical estimations and show empirically that for the considered concrete network models, almost all concurrency estimations are above a factor 1/2 of the ACPA results.

ACPA Concurrency ≥ **YAWNS Concurrency** ≈ **Estimated Concurrency**

YAWNS — Proof: at least 1/3 of ACPA

Estimated — Empirically: at least 1/2 of ACPA

Figure 5.3: Relationships between concurrency results of ACPA, YAWNS and our estimation approach.

5.2.3 Analytical Concurrency Estimation Model

In this section, we propose an approach to derive a concurrency estimation of network models based only on model knowledge and basic network statistics gathered from sequential simulation runs. The estimation workflow can be sketched as follows:

1. Given a network model specification or implementation, we manually determine the event patterns resulting from the communication patterns in the modeled network.
2. Based on the event patterns, categories of nodes with approximately identical numbers of event per unit of simulated time are identified.
3. The expected number of events within each lookahead window in each node category and in total is determined based on the desired scenario parameters.
4. From the expected number of events within a lookahead window in each node category and in total, the estimated concurrency of the network model is calculated.

In the following, we detail the calculation of the concurrency in step 4 given the results of the previous steps. Examples of the analysis of the event patterns of concrete network models are given in Section 5.3.

In Section 5.1, we have seen that the concurrency within a single lookahead window of a YAWNS-based simulation is the total number of events e_{total} in the lookahead window, divided by the largest number m of events pertaining to a single processor. Since our goal is to estimate the number of processors that can be occupied when fully exploiting the independence of events, we assume an assignment of a single node to each processor. Hence, given estimates of m and e_{total}, the estimated concurrency of the network model is:

$$C_{\text{est}} := \frac{e_{\text{total}}}{m}$$

While e_{total} can easily be estimated based on the communication activity in a network model, we need to derive m from an estimate of the distribution of events to simulated nodes, i.e., we need to answer the question "what is the expected largest number m of events within a lookahead window that are assigned to single node?" Our estimation of m is based on the hypothesis that is it possible to identify categories of simulated nodes so that within each category, events are distributed approximately uniformly among the nodes. The number of nodes in each category and the number of events assigned to each category are the inputs from which our analytical model derives m. In Section 5.3, we will show how these inputs can be determined for concrete network models.

More formally, we divide the nodes of the simulated network into c categories so that all n_i nodes in category i share the same estimated number of events e_i per lookahead window. Within each category, we consider the assignment of events to nodes as a sequence of Bernoulli trials with probability $p_i = 1/n_i$ each. The probability that a *single* node of category i is assigned $\leq k$ events follows the binomial distribution:

$$F_i(k) = \sum_{j=0}^{k} \binom{e_i}{j} {p_i}^j (1 - p_i)^{e_i - j}$$

The probability that *all* nodes of category i are assigned $\leq k$ events is:

$$G_i(k) = F_i(k)^{n_i}$$

By considering all node categories, we arrive at the probability that all nodes *of all categories* are assigned $\leq k$ events:

$$G(k) = \prod_{i=1}^{c} G_i(k)$$

We are interested in the expectation of G, i.e., the expected largest number of events any single node is assigned in a lookahead window [ABN92]. Using the probability density function g of the cumulative distribution function G, the expectation is:

$$m = \sum_{k=1}^{\infty} k g(k)$$

In a YAWNS-based analysis limited to a single lookahead window, m is identical with X, the expected number of parallel event executions required to process the lookahead window. Now, the estimated concurrency of the simulation is: $C_{\text{est}} := e_{\text{total}}/m$.

5.2.4 Limited Deviation between ACPA- and YAWNS-Based Concurrency

The proposed concurrency estimation approach approximates the results of a YAWNS-based analysis, even though ACPA may expose larger concurrency. In this section, we show that considering YAWNS in place of ACPA introduces only a limited error. To this end, we prove the following statement:

Theorem 1 *The concurrency determined using YAWNS is at least 1/3 of the concurrency determined using ACPA.*

Before providing the full proof, we first sketch the individual proof steps: let G be an arbitrary precedence graph containing $e_{\text{global}}(G)$ events. Let $X_{\text{YAWNS}}(G)$, $X_{\text{ACPA}}(G)$ be the number of executions required to process G using YAWNS and ACPA, respectively. Since $C_{\text{YAWNS}}(G) = e_{\text{global}}(G)/X_{\text{YAWNS}}(G)$, $C_{\text{ACPA}}(G) = e_{\text{global}}(G)/X_{\text{ACPA}}(G)$, and $e_{\text{global}}(G)$ is constant, it suffices to prove $X_{\text{YAWNS}}(G) \leq 3X_{\text{ACPA}}(G)$:

1. We show how a reduced precedence graph G' can be constructed from G so that YAWNS still requires the same number of executions, i.e., $X_{\text{YAWNS}}(G') = X_{\text{YAWNS}}(G)$.
2. Since the events in G' are a subset of the events in G: $X_{\text{ACPA}}(G') \leq X_{\text{ACPA}}(G)$.
3. By exhaustively analyzing all cases of event executions with respect to G', we show: $X_{\text{YAWNS}}(G') \leq 3X_{\text{ACPA}}(G')$.
4. Applying 1. to 3. shows: $X_{\text{YAWNS}}(G) \leq 3X_{\text{ACPA}}(G')$.
5. With 2.: $X_{\text{YAWNS}}(G) \leq 3X_{\text{ACPA}}(G') \leq 3X_{\text{ACPA}}(G)$.

For the full proof, we begin with the observation that when considering a fixed precedence graph G, YAWNS and ACPA both process the same number of events $e_{\text{global}}(G)$. Both with YAWNS and ACPA, the concurrency is the mean number of events processed in each execution, i.e., the total number of events divided by the number of executions $X_{\text{YAWNS}}(G)$ or $X_{\text{ACPA}}(G)$, respectively. For instance, $C_{\text{YAWNS}}(G) = e_{\text{global}}(G)/X_{\text{YAWNS}}(G)$. The number of events $e_{\text{global}}(G)$ is independent of the analysis method used. Hence, to prove the above statement, only the ratio $X_{\text{YAWNS}}(G)/X_{\text{ACPA}}(G)$ is of interest.

1. We now consider the analysis of a precedence graph using YAWNS in more detail. We make two observations: First, in YAWNS, the placement of each lookahead window in simulated time is determined by the earliest event that exists in the simulation at the time a new lookahead window is calculated. Second, the number of executions required to process the events in a single lookahead window using YAWNS is equal to the largest number of events in the lookahead window that pertain to a single node.

Given an arbitrary precedence graph, we can utilize the two observations to construct a *reduced* precedence graph that contains only the earliest event $z_{\text{earliest},i}$ of the i-th lookahead window and the set $Z_{\text{largest},i}$ of events pertaining to the node with the largest number of events in the i-th lookahead window. If there is a non-empty subset of $Z_{\text{largest},i}$ of events that have the lowest timestamp in the i-th lookahead window, let $z_{\text{earliest,i}}$ be an arbitrary element of this subset instead of an event $\notin Z_{\text{largest},i}$, if any.

The reduced precedence graph has the property that a YAWNS-based analysis requires exactly the same number of executions for processing the reduced precedence graph as for processing the original full precedence graph. Figures 5.4 and 5.5 depict an example of a full precedence graph and its reduced counterpart. Let τ be the fixed lookahead value of the considered network model. Each lookahead window covers an interval $L_{\text{YAWNS},i} = \{t_{\text{min},i}, t_{\text{min},i} + 1, \ldots, t_{\text{min},i} + \tau\}$, which is identical for the full and reduced precedence graph. Since further, YAWNS processes at least one event in each execution, the following holds true: $X_{\text{YAWNS}}(G') = X_{\text{YAWNS}}(G) \leq e_{\text{global}}(G') \leq e_{\text{global}}(G)$.

2. Since all events in the reduced precedence graph are also contained in the full precedence graph, ACPA, just as YAWNS, must process at least the events of the reduced precedence graph. Hence, the number of executions required to process G' using ACPA is a lower bound on the number of executions required to process G.

3. We now consider all cases of event executions that are possible when analyzing a reduced precedence graph using ACPA to show $X_{\text{ACPA}}(G') \geq e_{\text{global}}(G')/3$ by proving the invariant *"at most 3 events can ever be processed in a single execution"*.

ACPA iteratively selects the timestamp $T(z_{\text{current}})$ of the earliest remaining event z_{current} in the precedence graph and processes all events without remaining predecessors in the lookahead window $L_{\text{ACPA,current}} = \{T(z_{\text{current}}), T(z_{\text{current}} + 1, \ldots, T(z_{\text{current}}) + \tau\}$ in a single execution. Let $V_{\text{remaining}}$ be the set of events in G' that have not been processed previously and let Q_{ready} be the set of events ready to be processed. $N(u)$ is the node an event $u \in V_{\text{remaining}}$ pertains to. If all events in a set U pertain to the same node, $N(U)$ is the node the events pertain to. An event $r \in Q_{\text{ready}}$ has three properties: r is in the lookahead window, no other event in Q_{ready} pertains to the same node as r, and r has the earliest timestamp of any event pertaining to $N(r)$, i.e., $(T(r) \leq T(z_{\text{current}}) + \tau) \wedge (\forall u \in Q_{\text{ready}} : N(u) \neq N(r) \vee u = r) \wedge (\forall u \in V_{\text{remaining}} : T(r) \leq T(u) \vee N(r) \neq N(u))$.

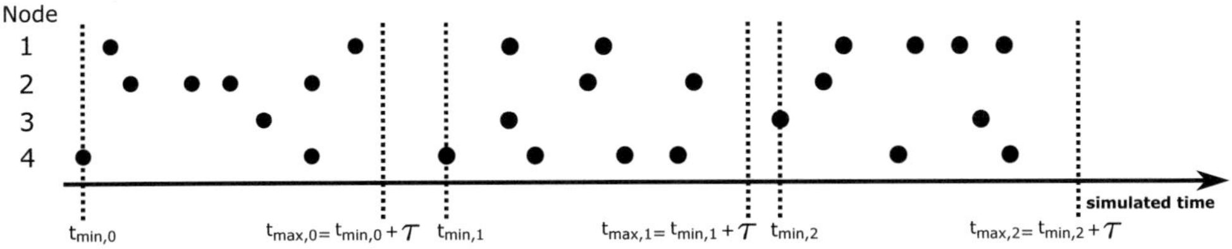

Figure 5.4: Full precedence graph.

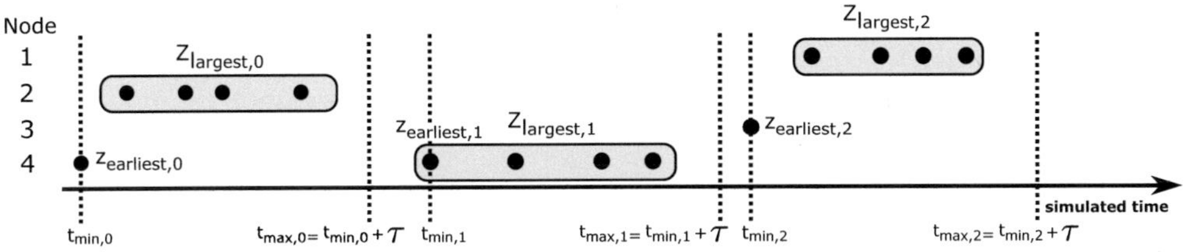

Figure 5.5: Reduced precedence graph.

We now consider an arbitrary execution of ACPA on a reduced precedence graph. The current lookahead window begins at $T(z_{\text{current}})$. If there are multiple events that share the timestamp $T(z_{\text{current}})$, the event z_{current} can be chosen arbitrarily from these events without affecting any statements made in the following.

We investigate the event z_{current} by comparison with a YAWNS-based analysis. Any event apart from z_{current} may have already been processed previously. The timestamp $T(z_{\text{current}})$ of z_{current} is in a YAWNS-based lookahead window $L_{\text{YAWNS},i} = \{t_{\min,i}, t_{\min,i} + 1, \ldots, t_{\min,i} + \tau\}$ for a fixed $i \in \mathbb{N}$. Figure 5.6 illustrates the different cases. We first differentiate by the position of $T(z_{\text{current}})$ in $L_{\text{YAWNS},i}$. There are two possibilities:

1. $T(z_{\text{current}}) = T(z_{\text{earliest},i})$: then, $L_{\text{YAWNS},i} = L_{\text{ACPA,current}} = \{T(z_{\text{current}}), T(z_{\text{current}}) + 1, \ldots, T(z_{\text{current}}) + \tau\}$. In this case, the current ACPA lookahead window coincides with one of the YAWNS-based lookahead windows. Due to the construction of the reduced precedence graph, the events in a single YAWNS-based lookahead window pertain to at most two separate nodes: the node of the event at $T(z_{\text{current}})$ that defines the lower bound $t_{\min,i}$ of the i-th YAWNS-based lookahead window, and a possibly empty set of events $Z_{\text{largest},i}$ that all pertain to a single, but arbitrary node. $L_{\text{ACPA,current}}$ fully covers the timestamps of any events in $Z_{\text{largest},i}$.

   Due to the construction of the reduced precedence graph, all events in the set $Z_{\text{largest,i}}$ pertain to the same node. Now, there are three possibilities:

   - $Z_{\text{largest},i} \setminus \{z_{\text{current}}\} = \emptyset$, i.e., z_{current} is the only event in $L_{\text{YAWNS},i}$. Then, only z_{current}, i.e., a single event, is processed in the current execution.
   - $Z_{\text{largest},i} \setminus \{z_{\text{current}}\} \neq \emptyset \wedge N(Z_{\text{largest},i}) = N(z_{\text{current}})$. Then, only z_{current}, i.e., a single event, can be processed in the current execution.

- $Z_{\text{largest},i} \setminus \{z_{\text{current}}\} \neq \emptyset \wedge N(Z_{\text{largest},i}) \neq N(z_{\text{current}})$. Then, z_{current} and the earliest event in $Z_{\text{largest,i}}$, i.e., two events, can be processed in the current execution.

2. $T(z_{\text{current}}) > T(z_{\text{earliest},i})$: again, $T(z_{\text{current}})$ is in $\{t_{\text{min},i}, t_{\text{min},i} + 1, \ldots, t_{\text{min},i} + \tau\}$ for a fixed $i \in \mathbb{N}$ and the current lookahead window is $L_{\text{ACPA,current}} = \{T(z_{\text{current}}), T(z_{\text{current}}) + 1, \ldots, T(z_{\text{current}}) + \tau\}$. We consider two disjoint segments of this interval separately: due to the construction of the precedence graph, all events in $\{T(z_{\text{current}}), T(z_{\text{current}}) + 1, \ldots, t_{\text{min},i} + \tau\}$ pertain to the same node. Hence, only a single event from this interval can be processed. The remainder of the lookahead window is $\{t_{\text{min},i} + \tau + 1, t_{\text{min},i} + \tau + 2, \ldots, T(z_{\text{current}}) + \tau\}$. For any event z_{next} of the set of events Z_{next} in this interval, we must differentiate two cases:

   - z_{next} is the earliest event in the next YAWNS lookahead window $L_{\text{YAWNS},i+1}$, i.e., $z_{\text{next}} = z_{\text{earliest},i+1}$ and $T(z_{\text{next}}) = t_{\text{min},i+1}$. Then z_{next} can pertain to an arbitrary node. Since the $i+2$nd lookahead window begins at a timestamp of $t_{\text{min},i+1} + \tau + 1$ or larger, there can be at most one event of this kind in $\{t_{\text{min},i} + \tau + 1, t_{\text{min},i} + \tau + 2, \ldots, T(z_{\text{current}}) + \tau\}$. If such an event exists, we refer to the event as z_a.
   - $z_{\text{next}} \in Z_{\text{largest},i+1} \setminus \{z_{\text{earliest},i+1}\}$. All events in $Z_{\text{largest},i+1}$ pertain to the same node. Hence, only an event with the lowest timestamp in the set can be processed in the current execution. If such an event exists, we refer to the event as z_b.

   Considering the set of candidate events for concurrent processing $\{z_{\text{current}}\} \cup Z_{\text{next}}$, the maximum number of events that can be processed in the current execution is 3. This is the case when $N(z_{\text{current}}) \neq N(z_a) \neq N(z_b)$. Since z_a is the earliest event of a YAWNS-based lookahead window, this situation arises at most once per lookahead window of the YAWNS-based analysis. Since the width of each lookahead window is $\tau + 1$, in a precedence graph that covers t units of simulated time, three events can therefore be processed in a single execution at most $t/(\tau + 1)$ times. In all other cases, at most two events can be processed in a single execution.

We have now considered all possible cases of processing events in ACPA. Since the largest number of events that can be processed in a single execution is three, ACPA requires at least $e_{\text{global}}(G')/3$ executions to process the reduced precedence graph G'.

4. Since YAWNS requires at most $e_{\text{global}}(G)$ executions to process both the reduced and the full precedence graph, so far we have shown $X_{\text{YAWNS}}(G) \leq 3X_{\text{ACPA}}(G')$.

5. Since $G' \subseteq G$: $X_{\text{YAWNS}}(G) \leq 3X_{\text{ACPA}}(G') \leq 3X_{\text{ACPA}}(G)$.

The concurrency is given by $C_{\text{YAWNS}}(G) = e_{\text{global}}(G)/X_{\text{YAWNS}}(G)$ and $C_{\text{ACPA}}(G) = e_{\text{global}}(G)/X_{\text{ACPA}}(G)$, respectively. Since $e_{\text{global}}(G)$ is independent of the analysis method used, the factor between the calculated concurrency is $C_{\text{ACPA}}(G)/C_{\text{YAWNS}}(G) = X_{\text{YAWNS}}(G)/X_{\text{ACPA}}(G)$, which we showed to have an upper bound of 3. □

As stated above, the situation that three events can be processed arises at most once per YAWNS-based lookahead window. All remaining events are processed in sets of at most two events. In Figure 5.7, we illustrate an extreme case where three events can be processed by ACPA in all but the first execution on the example of an artificial precedence graph. There are at most $e_{\text{global}}(G)$ YAWNS lookahead windows and the lookahead windows are pairwise disjoint intervals. Hence,

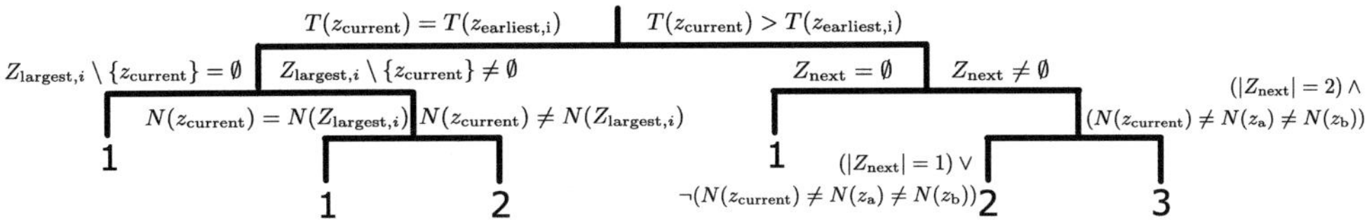

Figure 5.6: All cases of event visibility and node assignment when considering events for execution using ACPA on an arbitrary reduced precedence graph. Leaf nodes: number of events processed in the current execution.

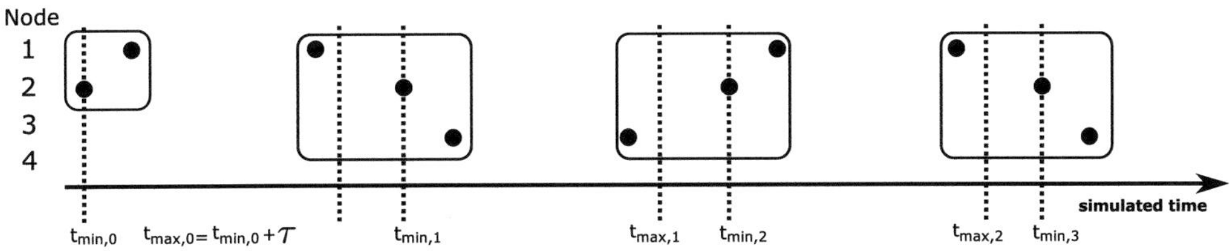

Figure 5.7: Processing of a reduced precedence graph using ACPA. Dashed lines indicate the positions of the YAWNS lookahead windows. Boxes indicate events that are processed by ACPA in a single execution. In this example, in all but the first execution, ACPA processes three events per execution.

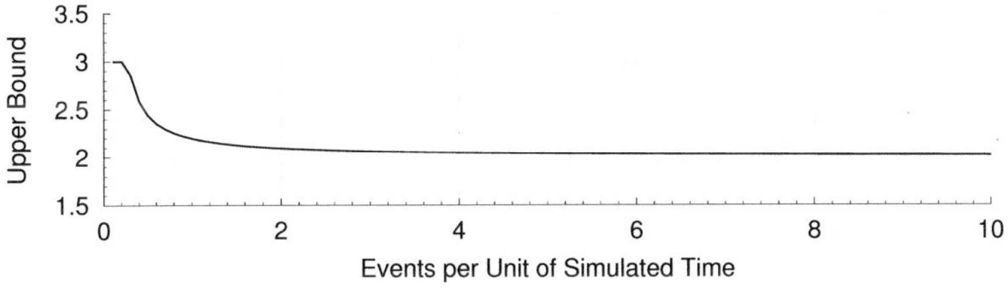

(a) $\tau = 10$, $t = 1\,000\,000$.

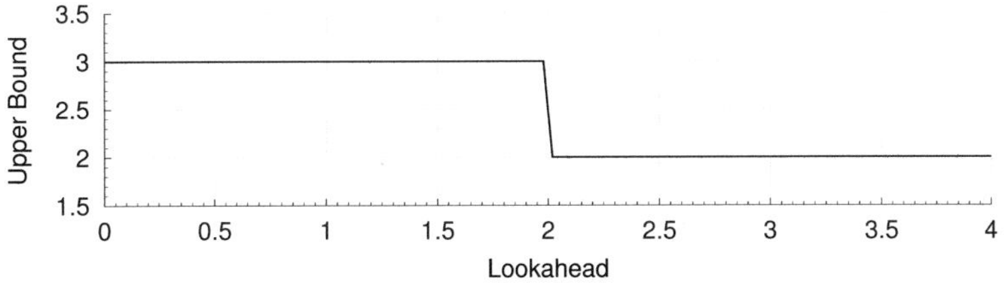

(b) $t = 1\,000\,000$, $e_{\text{global}} = 1\,000\,000$.

Figure 5.8: Upper bound of $X_{\text{YAWNS}}/X_{\text{ACPA}}$.

we can state an upper bound on the number of executions in which three events can be processed: $E_{\text{ACPA,three,max}}(G) = \lfloor \min(\{t/\tau + 1, e_{\text{global}}(G)/3\}) \rfloor$, where t is the number of units of simulated time covered by the precedence graph. In all other executions, two or fewer events are processed. A tighter lower bound on the *total* number of executions is then given by the term $E_{\text{ACPA,three,max}}(G) + \lceil \max(\{0, e_{\text{global}}(G) - 3E_{\text{ACPA,three,max}}(G)\})/2 \rceil$. In Figure 5.8, we plot the resulting upper bound for $X_{\text{YAWNS}}/X_{\text{ACPA}}$, varying e_{global} and the lookahead. We can see that with higher event densities in simulated time and with larger lookahead, the ratio approaches 2. In Section 5.4 we evaluate the concurrency of three network models implemented in popular network simulators to empirically study the deviation between ACPA and YAWNS by concrete examples.

5.3 Network Model Analysis

In this section, we study the concurrency of three network models. For each model, we first analyze the event patterns resulting from the communication patterns in the simulated network. Then, we determine the parameters required to analytically estimate the model's concurrency according to the estimation approach proposed in Section 5.2.3.

5.3.1 Peer-to-Peer Overlay Network

As our first example, we study the **Kademlia$_{\mathbf{A}}$** model (cf. Chapter 3). We analyze **Kademlia$_{\mathbf{A}}$** with reference to an implementation in the PeerSim network simulator[1]. The model abstracts from all OSI layers but the application layer, i.e., the physical topology is reflected by link latencies drawn from a random distribution. The application layer itself is modeled accurately in accordance with the BitTorrent DHT specification [LN08].

Event Patterns

There are two sources of traffic in Kademlia-based networks: communication triggered actively by users of the DHT, and routing table maintenance. The latter comprises both operations for refreshing routing table contents as well as operations for checking the responsiveness of specific peers.

The event patterns representing the communication activities in Kademlia are shown in Figure 5.9. The building block fundamental to all communication in Kademlia is the remote procedure call (RPC), a sequence of three events representing the following interaction: [i]. Peer 1 sends a request; [ii]. Peer 2 receives the request and creates a response; [iii]. Peer 1 receives the response.

So-called *lookups* are used to perform storage and retrieval operations. Each lookup consists of a sequence of RPCs where step [iii] generates a new request until the lookup terminates. A parameter α specifies the number of concurrent RPCs during a lookup. Lookups with $\alpha > 1$ can be regarded as a superposition of multiple sequences of RPCs.

We can now easily determine the number of events associated with a lookup: one initial event triggers the lookup, and each subsequent RPC is reflected by two events: a request and its response. If the number ρ of RPCs per lookup is known, the total number of events per lookup

[1] `http://peersim.sourceforge.net/`

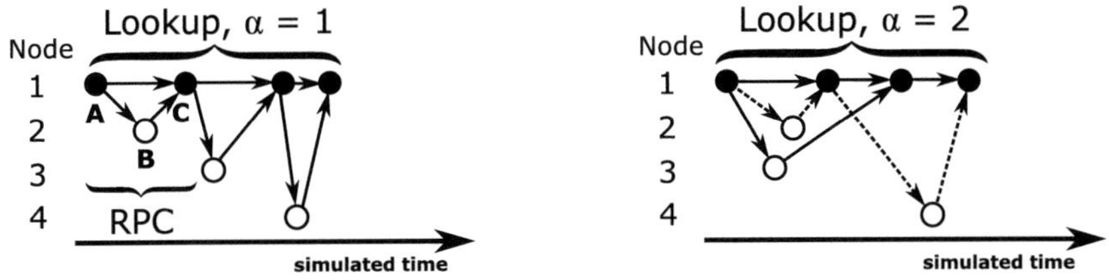

Figure 5.9: Event patterns in **Kademlia$_A$**: lookups are composed of α overlapping sequences of RPCs. Node 1 performs a lookup with $\alpha = 1$ and $\alpha = 2$.

is $e_{per\_lookup} = 2\rho + 1$, independently of α. Of these, $\rho + 1$ events pertain to the peer performing the lookup, and ρ events pertain to other peers.

The remaining traffic in **Kademlia$_A$** is created by pings triggered if the responsiveness of a peer is to be checked. If a peer's routing table is fully populated and a peer becomes aware of a new remote peer, peers of unknown responsiveness in the routing table are checked using ping RPCs. The receiver of a ping request may then recursively trigger new pings to further peers. When gathering the inputs to the analytical model, we consider the events created by lookups in detail, while treating ping events as uniformly distributed among the simulated nodes.

Concurrency in **Kademlia$_A$** results from two independent scenario parameters: λ independent lookups running concurrently, and α concurrent RPCs performed during each lookup.

Analytical Concurrency Estimation

In the following, we describe how, based on key metrics of **Kademlia$_A$**, we determine the inputs required for the analytical concurrency estimation.

We differentiate between two categories of peers: *active* peers that are currently executing a lookup, and *passive* peers that respond to incoming requests only. In **Kademlia$_A$**, the number λ_{user} of concurrent lookups is a scenario parameter. Further, the generation of user-initiated lookups is distributed uniformly over the peers in the simulated network. The average number λ_{rt} of additional concurrent lookups created for routing table maintenance can be gathered from a sequential simulation run of the given configuration and subsequently be included in our consideration: $\lambda = \lambda_{user} + \lambda_{rt}$. Then, given n peers in the network, the proportion of active peers is: $n_{active} = 1 - (1 - \frac{1}{n})^{\lambda}$. The absolute numbers of active and passive peers are thus $n_{active} = n \times n_{active}$ and $n_{passive} = n - n_{active}$. Given the average number ρ of RPCs per lookup, each lookup creates $2\rho + 1$ events. Hence, a lookup of duration d creates an average of $(2\rho + 1)/d$ events per unit of simulated time. Since each lookahead window cover $\tau + 1$ timestamps, the total number of events generated by all concurrent lookups within a single lookahead window is:

$$e_{lookups} = (\tau + 1) \times \lambda \times \frac{2\rho + 1}{d}$$

We additionally consider the number k of ping RPCs per unit of simulated time generated for checking the online status of peers, each generating two events, to obtain the total number of events per lookahead window:

$$e_{\text{total}} = (\tau + 1) \times (\lambda \times \frac{2\rho + 1}{d} + 2k)$$

Now, we analyze the event counts for active and passive peers separately. In each lookup, active peers generate one initial event and one event for each RPC. The number of these events for all active peers is:

$$e_{\text{active,lookup}} = (\tau + 1) \times \lambda \times \frac{\rho + 1}{d}$$

Active peers also receive some of the requests generated in lookups of other peers. The number of request events for all active peers is:

$$e_{\text{active,request}} = (\tau + 1) \times \lambda \times n_{\text{active}} \times \frac{\rho}{d}$$

Finally, a proportion of ping events targets active peers:

$$e_{\text{active,ping}} = (\tau + 1) \times k \times n_{\text{active}}$$

Now, the total number of events expected to be generated per lookahead window for all active peers is:

$$e_{\text{active}} = e_{\text{active,lookup}} + e_{\text{active,request}} + e_{\text{active,ping}}$$

The remaining events pertain to passive peers:

$$e_{\text{passive}} = e_{\text{total}} - e_{\text{active}}$$

Using the estimated number of events for the two categories of active and passive peers, we can now determine the expected largest number m of events per lookahead window to be processed by a single peer in the simulation according to the analytical model described in Section 5.2.3. The estimated concurrency is then e_{total}/m.

Discussion

In the simulated network, each lookup creates a sequence of RPCs targeting a sequence of peers according to the dynamic contents of the routing tables of peers on the path to the target of the lookup. Nevertheless, in the analysis, we consider the events pertaining to each peer category as uniformly distributed among the peers in the respective category, ignoring the network topology created by the Kademlia protocol completely. In Section 5.4 we will see that nonetheless, our estimations are reasonably accurate, showing that the impact of the exact topology of the considered Kademlia-based network on the concurrency of the network model is relatively low. Instead, the concurrency is dominated by the raw message counts per peer category as well as by the overall network size.

5.3.2 TCP/IP in a Fixed Topology

Our second example is the **NMS** model (cf. Chapter 3). The model was selected for its strong impact of the network topology on concurrency.

The basic building block of the topology is the campus network depicted in Figure 5.10. A configurable number n_{cns} of campus networks is connected in a ring using links. Ellipses represent local area networks (LANs) with a configurable number n_{lan} of nodes each. To each of the LAN nodes, a TCP stream with a constant data rate of 500 kbps is transmitted by one of the nodes 1:2, 1:3, 1:4 or 1:5 of the neighboring campus network.

Since all messages pass through the nodes connecting individual campus networks, we study the effects of varying the bandwidth b between these nodes between 1 Mbps and 1 000 Mbps. In the following, we refer to the nodes connecting the individual campus networks as *hubs*. In addition, we differentiate between two types of bottlenecks: *network bottlenecks* are nodes that due to their position in the network and their limited bandwidth restrict the overall throughput in the network. *Simulation bottlenecks* are nodes for which disproportionally large numbers of events are processed per unit of simulated time, so that these nodes limit the concurrency of the simulation model.

Our experiments are based on a model implementation in the network simulator ns-3[2] version 3.21 (`nms-p2p-nix.cc`), which uses an accurate representation of the network and transport layer, whereas the lower layers are modeled by the fixed link latencies specified above. We apply the common approach of using a fixed lookahead value of 1ms that is applicable to all nodes in the network. It may be possible to extract larger concurrency with a dedicated lookahead value for each link at the cost of higher complexity of the synchronization scheme (e.g., [MB99]).

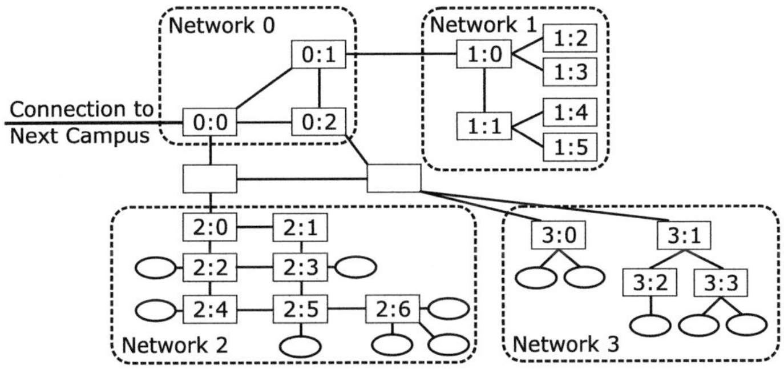

Figure 5.10: A campus network in the **NMS** network model.

A campus network in the **NMS** network model (Figure adapted from [PR11]).

Event Patterns

Since it is not always possible to transmit messages created by a simulated application instantaneously, in ns-3, creation of messages and their transmission is modeled separately. Hence, the transmission of a single message holding a payload via a linear sequence of nodes is reflected by the events and precedence relationships depicted on the left hand side of Figure 5.11: the sender generates one event for the message's creation (`SendPacket`), one for the message's successful transmission on the link layer (`TransmitComplete`), and one notifying the transport layer that a packet was sent (`NotifyDataSent`). Each node on the path to the receiver generates two events for reception (`Receive`) and successful forwarding (`TransmitComplete`) of the message. Finally, the receiving node generates two events representing reception: one for recep-

[2] `http://www.nsnam.org/`

tion on the link layer (`Receive`), and one for forwarding the message to the upper layers of the network stack (`ForwardUp`).

Additional messages are created by TCP on the receiver side. We use the New Reno implementation of TCP, wherein by default, for every second message, an acknowledgement is transmitted from the receiver to the sender. As depicted on the right hand side of Figure 5.11, each acknowledgement generates one event for the receiver of the payload (`TransmitComplete`), two events for each hop on the path to the sender (`Receive`, `TransmitComplete`) and two events for the original sender (`Receive`, `ForwardUp`).

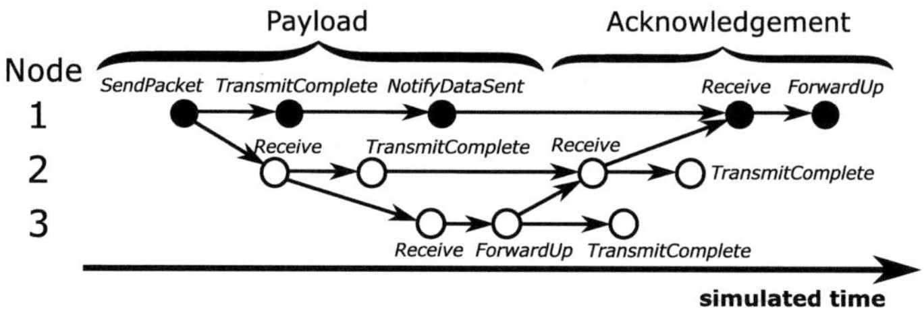

Figure 5.11: Event patterns in the **NMS** model: a single packet is transmitted from node 1 to 3 via node 2. Node 3 replies with an acknowledgement.

Analytical Concurrency Estimation

We estimate the number of events created in the simulation using the following parameters: r_{app} is the configured bitrate of each application that generates a TCP flow, and s_m is the size of each message including headers. In our example, TCP and IP each add 20 bytes of header data to a payload of 512 bytes. m_{app} is the message rate per flow. n_{fw} is the average number of forwarding nodes between a sender and a receiver. Using these values, the total event rate is given by the sum of the payload and acknowledgement event rates. This calculation can be repeated for each TCP flow to determine the total event rate of the simulation.

We model network bottlenecks by considering the number m_{tm} of messages actually transmitted per second according to the maximum message rate m_{hubs} of the hubs resulting from their configured bandwidth. Of course, in the general case, network bottlenecks must be identified first. For complex topologies, an approximation can be calculated using common flow algorithms. In the topology considered here, hubs with low bandwidth are obvious network bottlenecks. All other forwarding nodes handle substantially smaller numbers of events. Now, the total number e_{total} of events per TCP flow and simulated second in the steady-state can be estimated as follows:

$$m_{\text{app}} = r_{\text{app}}/s_m$$

$$m_{\text{tm}} = \min(m_{\text{hubs}}, m_{\text{app}})$$

$$e_{\text{payload}} = m_{\text{tm}}(2 + 2n_{\text{fw}} + 2) + m_{\text{app}}$$

$$e_{\text{ack}} = m_{\text{tm}}/2(1 + 2n_{\text{fw}} + 2)$$

$$e_{\text{total}} = e_{\text{payload}} + e_{\text{ack}}$$

The estimation is performed under the hypothesis that the combination of all TCP flows can be considered to fully saturate the capacity of network bottlenecks. Since TCP only approximates the channel capacity, in an actual simulation run, the average number of messages will be lower than our estimation. In Section 5.4, we evaluate how the deviation in event counts affects the accuracy of the concurrency estimation.

We now explicitly consider the event rates of two categories of nodes: hubs and senders. Each of the n_{cns} campus networks holds a single hub and four senders:

$$n_{\text{hubs}} = n_{\text{cns}}$$

$$n_{\text{senders}} = 4n_{\text{cns}}$$

Since each campus network contains both senders and receivers, the number of TCP flows crossing each hub is $2 \times n_{\text{lan}} \times n_{\text{cns}}$. The total event rate for the hubs is thus:

$$e_{\text{hubs}} = 2n_{\text{hubs}} \times \left(m_{\text{tm}} + \frac{m_{\text{tm}}}{2}\right)$$

Again, each forwarded message generates one event for reception and one for transmission and there is one acknowledgement for every other message. The event rate for the senders is:

$$e_{\text{senders}} = n_{\text{flows}} \times \left(m_{\text{app}} + 2m_{\text{tm}} + 2 \times \frac{m_{\text{tm}}}{2}\right)$$

As before, we make the hypothesis that e_{hubs} and e_{senders} events are placed in the lookahead window with approximately the same per-event probability for each hub and sender, respectively. Using our analytical model, we can now estimate the largest expected number of events in each lookahead window for a single node in either the hub or the sender group. The result m is the number of parallel event executions required to process a single lookahead window. The estimated concurrency is then e_{total}/m.

Discussion

From the analysis, we can gather relationships between properties of the considered network model and the model's concurrency: first, since parallel simulation progress is determined by the simulation bottlenecks, a large number of events for non-bottleneck nodes is beneficial for high concurrency. Hence, given the fact that each hop forwarding a message generates two events, longer path lengths increase concurrency. Second, m_{tm} decreases if there are network bottlenecks, whereas m_{app} is independent of network bottlenecks. Therefore, it is possible that the total event rate is dominated by events generated at senders, even though all traffic passes through the hubs. Because of this, there is an inverse relationship between network and simulation bottlenecks: *hubs that* ***do not*** *limit the message rate form simulation bottlenecks, but do not form network bottlenecks, whereas hubs that* ***do*** *limit the message rate form network bottlenecks, but do not form simulation bottlenecks.*

5.3.3 Wireless Ad-Hoc Communication

As a third example, we study the concurrency of the **Wireless$_A$** model (cf. Chapter 3). Due to the broadcast nature of the wireless medium and the avoidance of message collisions, we can express the concurrency directly based on an analysis of individual transmissions, without reliance on the statistical approach presented in Section 5.2.3.

In the scenario considered here, a configurable number of nodes are positioned randomly on a linear 100m road segment. The nodes broadcast at a configurable packet rate, each packet comprising 400 bytes of data including headers. Transmissions use a data rate of 6 Mbps over a wireless channel using a CSMA-based MAC layer, i.e., nodes check for activity on the channel and delay their transmissions if necessary.

Event Patterns

We study the event patterns in the described model by reference to ns-3. A single transmission comprises the following sequence of events (cf. Figure 5.12): given no ongoing transmission on the channel, a `SendPacket` event of the transmitting node represents the start of a transmission and creates a `Receive` event for each remaining node as well as a single `EndTxNoAck` event reflecting the completion of the transmission. For each receiver that detects the packet, the `Receive` event creates an `EndReceive` event. In total, a successful transmission is reflected by a minimum of $1 + (n - 1) + 1 = n + 1$ and a maximum of $1 + (n - 1) + 1 + (n - 1) = 2n$ events.

A CSMA-based MAC layer aims to reduce the probability of collisions. If the channel is busy, the initial `SendPacket` event creates a single `AccessTimeout` event that takes the role of a `SendPacket` at a later point in simulated time. In the following, we refer to `SendPacket` events only, since `AccessTimeout` events are handled identically. We refer to `SendPacket` events by which a busy channel is detected as `Probe` events.

There are two situations in which interactions between multiple transmission attempts affect concurrency: first, collisions occur in case two nodes start sending at the same time. Second, a `SendPacket` event can detect a busy channel and delay the new transmission, so that no `Receive` events are created until the next attempt. The occurrence probabilities of both situations depend on the channel load. Our concurrency estimation disregards overlapping transmissions, but does consider `Probe` events.

Analytical Concurrency Estimation

To estimate the concurrency in the model analytically, we need to be aware of the lookahead that will be available in a simulation run. Simulations of wireless networks are well-known to exhibit only small amounts of fixed lookahead. Due to the broadcast nature of wireless networks, transmissions pertain to all nodes in proximity of the sender, and due to the speed-of-light propagation of radio waves, the time delta between transmission and reception is quite small. Hence, a fixed lookahead value considering the minimum latency between any two nodes of the network can be insufficient for high concurrency. The literature proposes the use of model knowledge regarding OSI layers 2 and above to enable larger lookahead values [LN02, PVM09]. If it is known at simulation runtime

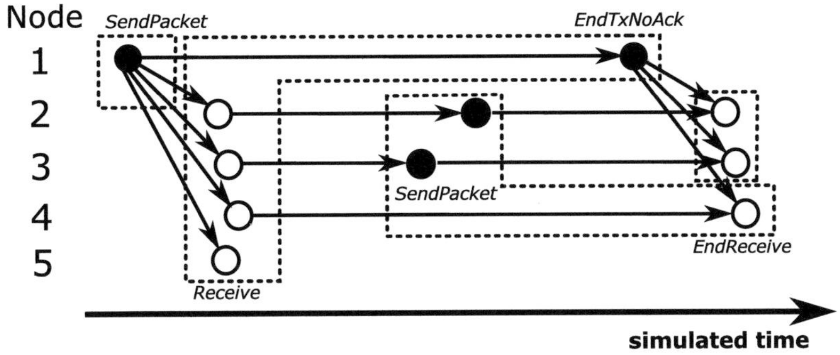

Figure 5.12: Concurrency of a single transmission in **Wireless$_A$**.

that according to the current state of, e.g., the MAC or application layer of the nodes, new events up to a certain point in time can be ruled out, the lookahead can be extended up to this point.

For the analysis, we consider the case where model knowledge provides sufficient lookahead to cover all events that have no pending precedence relationships. Figure 5.12 depicts the event patterns in the model, grouping concurrent events. The initial `SendPacket` event creates $n-1$ `Receive` events as well as a single `EndTxNoAck` event. Since execution of the `SendPacket` event triggers the creation of all other events, it cannot be executed in parallel with any further events. Now, all `Receive` events can be executed in parallel together with the `EndTxNoAck`, n events in total. Next, all remaining `SendPacket` events are executed concurrently with `EndReceive` events of nodes that execute no `Probe` events and receive the current packet successfully.

We now consider the number of parallel event executions required to process the `Probe` events. Since events for each node must be executed in timestamp order, up to n events can be executed at the same time. For a given simulation run of T transmissions with p_t `Probe` events during transmission t, the average number of event executions required to process all `Probe` events is $r_p = \frac{1}{T}\sum_{t=1}^{T}\lceil\frac{p_t}{n}\rceil$, the value of which can be determined from a sequential simulation run. Let s be the average ratio of nodes successfully receiving a frame, and let p be the average number of probe events during each transmission. We estimate the model's concurrency by dividing the number of events per transmission by the number of executions required. The estimated concurrency is:

$$C_{\mathrm{est}} = \frac{1+(n-1)+1+s(n-1)+p}{3+r_p} = \frac{n+1+s(n-1)+p}{3+r_p}$$

Discussion

The simplicity of the analysis reflects the simplicity of the event precedence relation: the available concurrency results from the independent reception events evenly distributed among all receivers. Since, contrary to the previous two network models, a statistical estimation of event counts is not necessary, we can estimate the ACPA concurrency directly without estimating YAWNS concurrency first.

5.4 Evaluation

In this section, we first evaluate the sensitivity of the previously analyzed network models' concurrency to scenario parameters. This analysis is performed by analyzing precedence graphs from sequential simulation runs using ACPA. The precedence graphs were created by modifying ns-3 and PeerSim to output for each event an ID, a timestamp, the node assignment and the creating event's ID. The ACPA results serve as reference values to validate our proposed estimation approach. Subsequently, we compare the ACPA results with YAWNS and finally with the results obtained analytically using the proposed estimation approach, i.e., without reliance on precedence graphs. The ACPA and YAWNS results were generated using a C++ implementation of the algorithms described in Section 3. The calculations required by the analytical estimation model were performed using an R script.

5.4.1 Sensitivity Analysis

We first study the sensitivity of **Kademlia**$_{\mathbf{A}}$ to the number n of peers in the network, the number λ_{user} of concurrent user-initiated lookups, and the number α of concurrent RPCs per lookup. To set a fixed λ_{user} accurately, we require an estimate of the average lookup duration d, which can be gathered from a brief initial simulation run. Then, the rate at which lookups must be generated to achieve the desired number λ_{user} of concurrent lookups follows Little's law and is λ_{user}/d.

For runs with $\lambda_{\text{user}} = 100$ and $\lambda = 1\,000$, we triggered the generation of precedence graphs after 1 000s of simulated time to allow the network to reach a steady state. Using ACPA according to Section 5.2, we analyzed events executed within 10s of simulated time. However, since the results differed only slightly with shorter runs, we configured the computationally expensive runs for $\lambda_{\text{user}} = 10\,000$ with only 300s of warm-up time. Since link latencies in milliseconds are drawn from a uniform distribution on $\{10, 11, \ldots, 200\}$, a fixed lookahead value of 10ms was used. In Figure 5.13, we can see that, as expected, larger numbers of concurrent lookups result in larger concurrency. Furthermore, larger α provides an increase in concurrency. In both figures, we can see that concurrency is limited by the network size. Disregarding the costs of inter-processor communication during simulation, many of the considered parameterizations suggest a simulation on a hardware platform that enables the parallel execution of hundreds of events.

For the sensitivity analysis of the **NMS** model, we used 60s of warm-up time. Since the results were virtually independent of the considered amount of simulated time, it was sufficient to analyze events executed within 1s of simulated time. The results in Figure 5.14 show the sensitivity of the model's concurrency to scenario parameters. When varying the number n_{cns} of campus network and the hub bandwidth for a fixed number n_{lan} of 16 LAN nodes, we can see that since campus networks communicate only with their direct neighbors, larger numbers of campus networks do not increase the amount of traffic handled by individual hubs. Hence, irrespective of the hub bandwidth, there is a linear relationship between the number of campus networks and the ACPA concurrency. The concurrency does not simply increase with larger hub bandwidth: even though a hub bandwidth of 1 000 Mbps allows for far fewer messages transmitted per unit of simulated time than a bandwidth of 10 Mbps, the larger number of messages crossing the hubs limits the concurrency of the simulation.

When varying the number of LAN nodes and the hub bandwidth for a fixed number of 16 campus networks, we can see that with 2 LAN nodes, only 2 000 kbps of traffic cross each hub, i.e., there is a network bottleneck in the run with 1 Mbps only. Accordingly, the results with hub bandwidths of 10

Mbps and above are nearly identical. For 4 and more LAN nodes, the magnitudes of the results do not simply follow the hub bandwidth. Instead, the resulting concurrency depends on three factors: the rate of message generation by the senders, the rate at which the messages pass through the network as dictated by the hub bandwidth, and the total number of message flows. With 1 000 Mbps, the concurrency is nearly independent of the LAN node count. The reason is that, since there are no network bottlenecks, each doubling of the LAN node count doubles the total number of messages per unit of time, but at the same time doubles the number of messages at each hub, i.e., twice the original number of events is processed in twice the number of executions. Hence, the resulting concurrency remains nearly unchanged. When disregarding the costs of communication during a simulation run, the concurrency with 32 campus networks suggests simulation on a hardware platform that allows parallel execution of up to about 200 events.

Finally, the sensitivity of the concurrency of **Wireless$_A$** to the beacon rate and the number of nodes was analyzed using precedence graphs covering 10s of simulated time after a warm-up time of 30s. Figure 5.15 shows that the concurrency increases close to linearly with the number of nodes in the network. For extremely large channel loads, collisions increase the concurrency substantially. Further, slight differences in concurrency for lower beacon rates are caused by varying numbers of events representing transmission attempts. In the considered parameter combinations, we measured concurrency values below 100 even for large node densities. Due to the limited spatial extent of 100m of the network, larger node counts lead to unrealistically large channel load. Parallel execution on many-core devices should hence be considered when studying scenarios with larger spatial extent that support larger numbers of nodes under realistic channel loads.

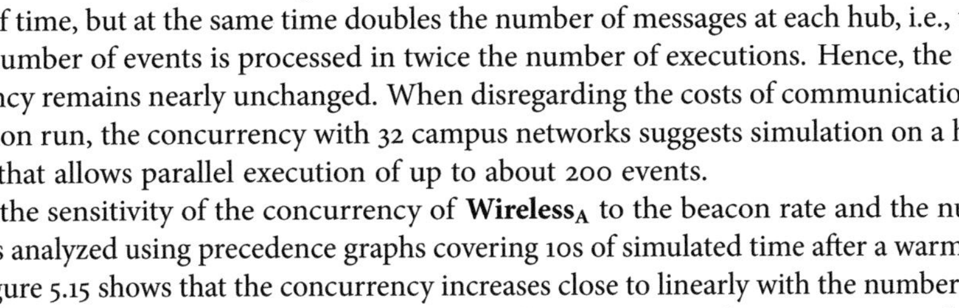

(a) $\alpha = 8$, varying λ_{user}.

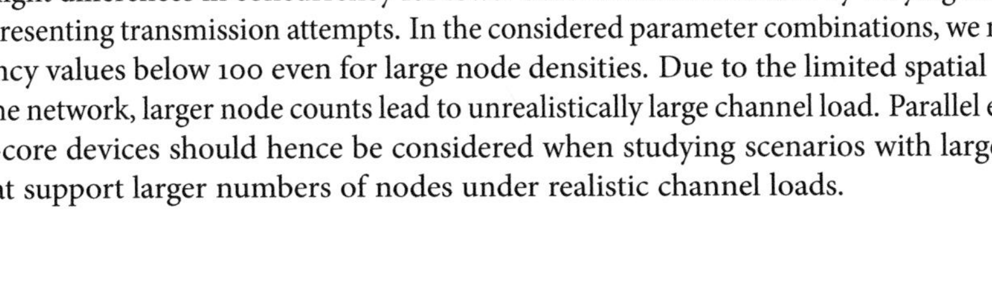

(b) $\lambda_{\text{user}} = 10\,000$, varying α.

Figure 5.13: Sensitivity analysis of **Kademlia$_A$**.

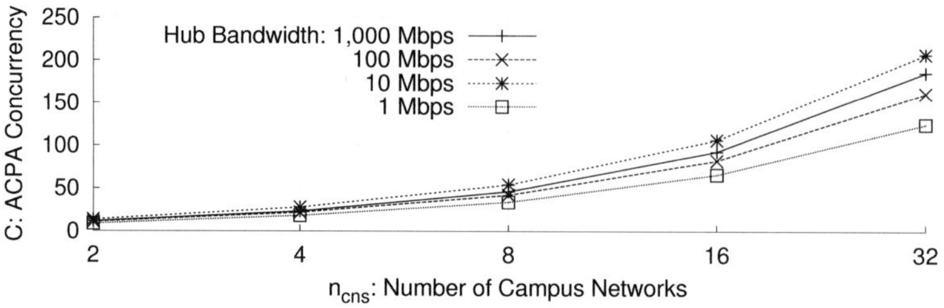

(a) Varying the number n_{cns} of campus networks.

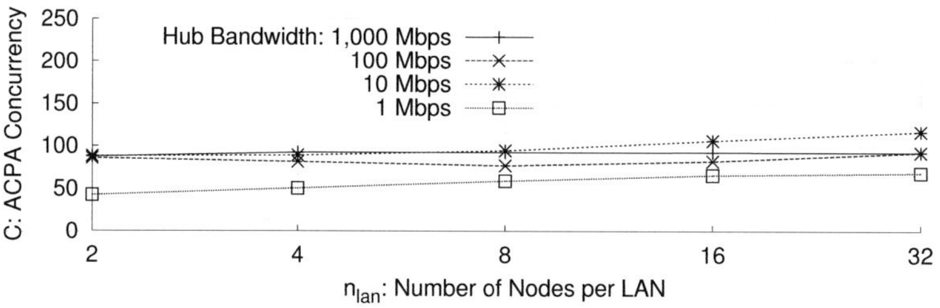

(b) Varying the number n_{lan} of nodes per LAN.

Figure 5.14: Sensitivity analysis of the **NMS** model

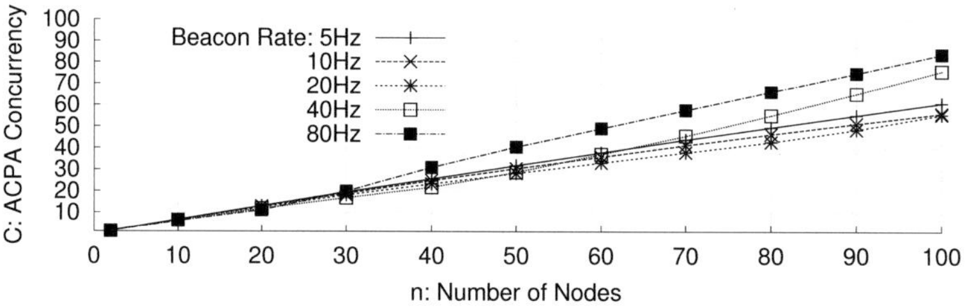

Figure 5.15: Sensitivity analysis of **Wireless$_{\text{A}}$**, varying the number of nodes and the beacon rate.

5.4.2 Validation of Estimations

In the following, we evaluate the accuracy of the proposed concurrency estimation approach. To this end, two questions are addressed:

Question A: *Are the concurrency values determined by an automated analysis of precedence graphs using YAWNS and ACPA sufficiently close to use these methods interchangeably?*

Our analytical model estimates the results of YAWNS. However, since ACPA determines the largest possible concurrency, we use ACPA as our reference method.

Question B: *Does our analytical model estimate ACPA concurrency of the considered network models with sufficient accuracy?*

A correspondence between the estimation and the ACPA results indicates that our network model analysis captured the key influencing factors for the models' concurrency.

We first consider question A and focus on the results for the **Kademlia$_A$** and **NMS** models, since the concurrency of **Wireless$_A$** was estimated directly with reference to ACPA. The parameters of the **Kademlia$_A$** model were varied as follows: $n \in \{1\,000; 10\,000; 100\,000\}$, $\lambda_{user} \in \{100; 1\,000; 10\,000\}$, $\alpha \in \{1; 2; 4; 8; 16; 32\}$. In addition, we configured the probability of packet loss as 0%, 25%, 50% and 75%. The **NMS** model was configured as follows: $n_{cns} \in \{2; 4; 8; 16; 32\}$, $n_{lan} \in \{2; 4; 8; 16; 32\}$, $b \in \{1; 10; 100; 1\,000\}$ Mbps.

Figure 5.16 compares the results of YAWNS and ACPA. We can see that YAWNS determines lower concurrency values than ACPA. The deviation increases slightly with larger concurrency. However, even for very large concurrency values, the YAWNS-based results are never below a factor of 0.6 of ACPA. We consider the correspondence sufficiently close to evaluate the parallelization potential of network models.

Now, we address question B and compare the analytical estimate with the ACPA results (cf. Figure 5.17). For **Kademlia$_A$**, an underestimation between the analytical model and ACPA can be observed in many cases. However, the model captures ACPA sufficiently so that, apart from few outliers, the estimation lies within a factor of 0.5 and 1.5 of the reference value over a vast range of model parameters and concurrency values. Similarly, the results for the **NMS** model show a close correspondence between the analytical estimate and ACPA results. Here, a repeating pattern emerges in the plotted results: our network model analysis assumed a full utilization of the channel capacity in the simulated network. With decreasing hub bandwidth, the simulated network deviates increasingly from full utilization, leading to an overestimation of concurrency. The proposed analytical estimation approach is applied under the hypothesis that events can be considered as being uniformly distributed among the nodes of each of the identified categories. If the assumption of a uniform distribution of events to nodes holds, we expect a binomial distribution of the number of events assigned to each node in each lookahead window. Since this section already shows the validity of the concurrency estimations of our analytical model, we limit our illustration of the validity of our hypothesis of approximately uniform distribution to two example scenarios. We determined the appropriate parameters for the binomial distribution according to the observed number of events per lookahead window, and the number of nodes in the considered node category. Figure 5.18 compares the expected binomial distribution with the number of events per node of the *active* category (cf. Section 5.3.1) actually observed in an exemplary simulation run of **Kademlia$_A$**. We can see that in the considered scenario, the simulation results are matched closely by the binomial distribution. Figure 5.19 compares the expected binomial distribution with the number of events per node of the *hub* category (cf. Section 5.3.2) in a run of the **NMS** model. Here, a deviation in the distributions is caused by the fact that in the network model, groups of two events each are scheduled with only a small delta in simulated time. Hence, in almost all cases, an even number of events is assigned to an individual node in each lookahead window. Still, we can see that in these examples, the binomial distribution approximates the measured results well.

For validation of the estimations for **Wireless$_A$**, we varied the number of nodes in the network between 2 and 100. Figure 5.20 relates the estimated concurrency C_{est} to the results from ACPA of precedence graphs. For small networks, the estimation is nearly identical to the ACPA results. The estimation becomes too pessimistic only in cases of extreme channel load, where collisions, which are not considered by the analytical estimate, are frequent. The largest deviation was measured in a scenario with 100 nodes and a beacon rate of 80Hz. In this case, the estimation amounts to 73.5% of the concurrency determined using ACPA.

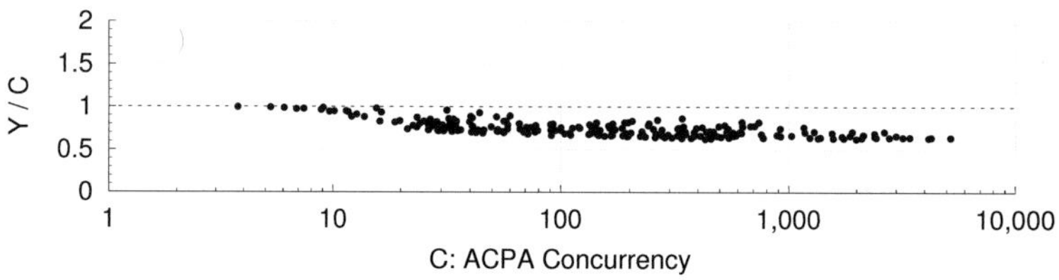

(a) **Kademlia**$_{A}$ model

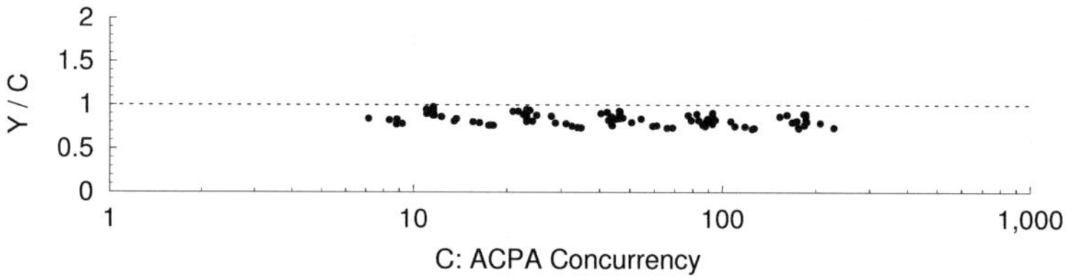

(b) **NMS** model

Figure 5.16: Comparison of YAWNS (Y) with ACPA concurrency (C).

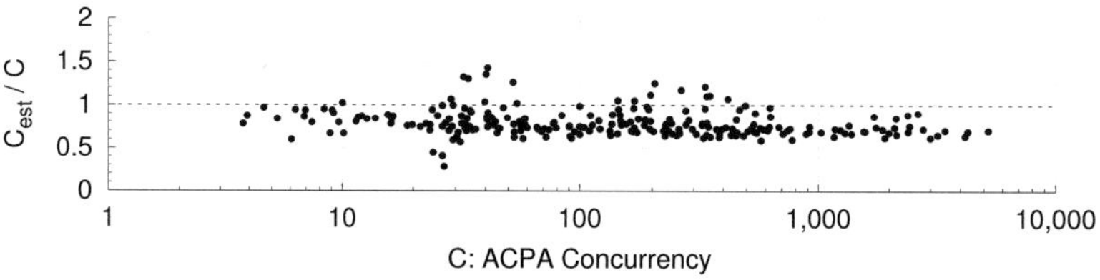

(a) **Kademlia**$_{A}$ model.

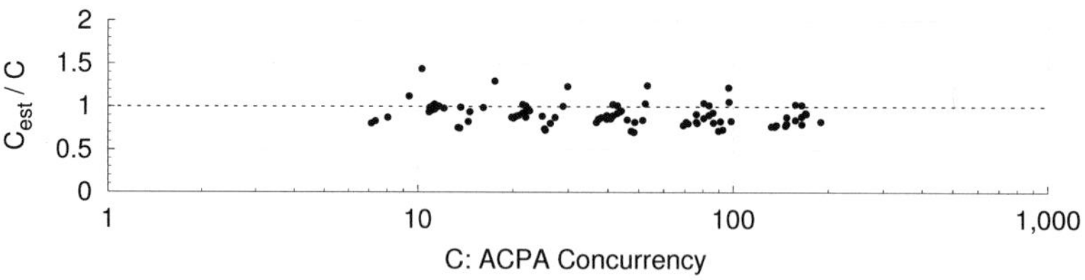

(b) **NMS** model.

Figure 5.17: Comparison of analytical estimate (C_{est}) with ACPA concurrency (C).

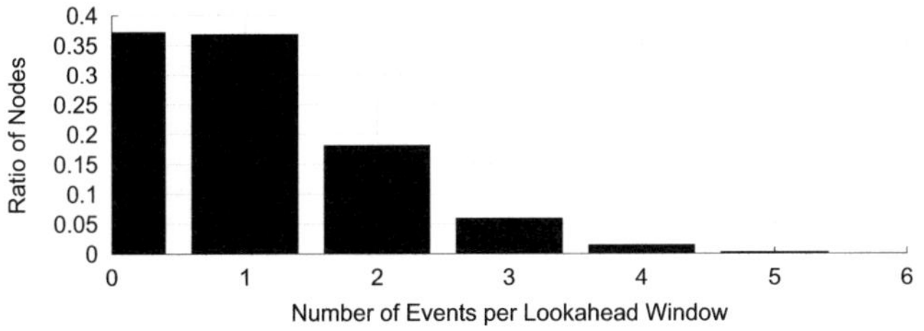

(a) Binomial distribution B(296, 1/300)

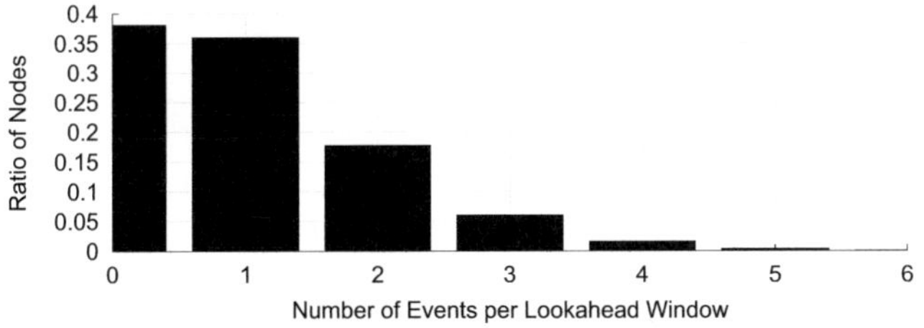

(b) Results from simulation run.

Figure 5.18: Expected and observed distribution of the number of events per node in the *active* category in each lookahead window for a run of **Kademlia$_A$** with $n = 1\,000$, $\lambda_{\text{user}} = 300$, $\alpha = 8$, and 0% packet loss.

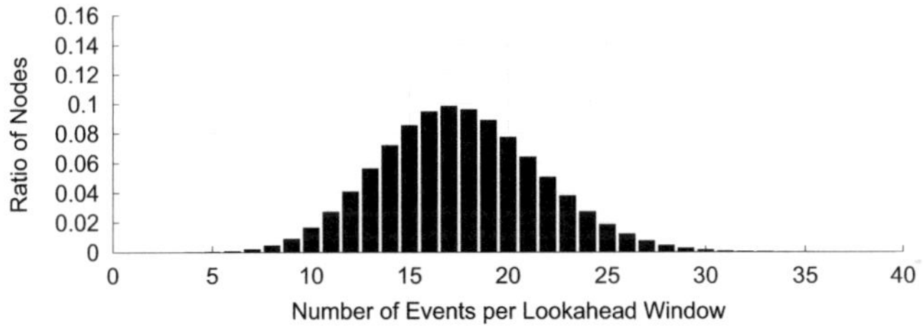

(a) Binomial distribution B(281, 1/16)

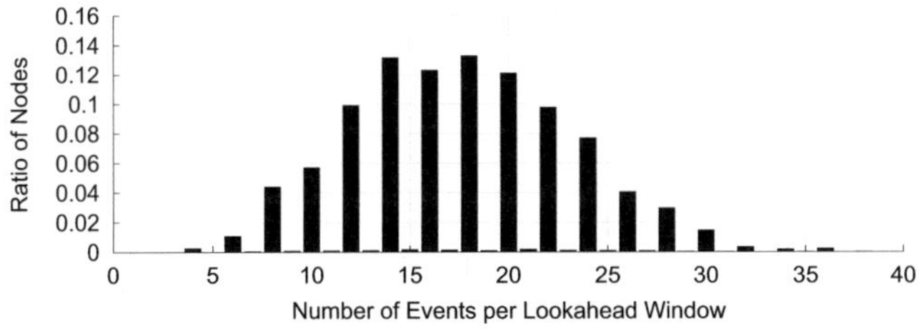

(b) Results from simulation run.

Figure 5.19: Expected and observed distribution of the number of events per node of the *hub* category in each lookahead window for a run of the **NMS** model with 16 campus networks, 1 node per LAN, and 1Gbps of hub bandwidth.

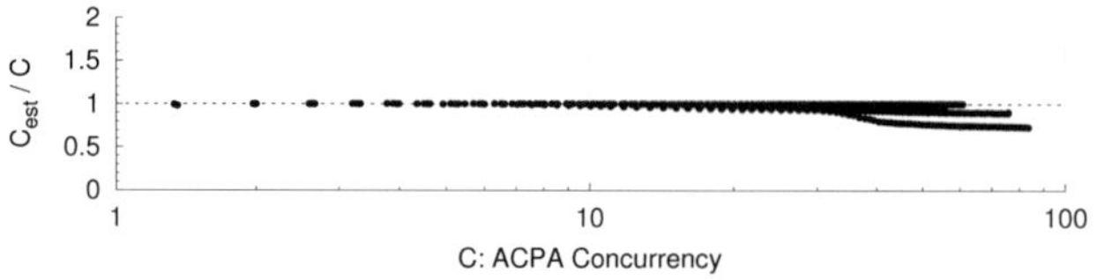

Figure 5.20: Comparison of our analytical estimate (C_{est}) with ACPA concurrency (C) of **Wireless$_\mathbf{A}$**.

5.5 Towards a Consideration of Variable Event Processing Times

The analytical estimation model proposed in the previous section assumes identical processing times for all events in the simulation. This assumption holds true for simulators where a new event execution commences only after all processors have finished the previous execution. In this section, we show how the analytical estimation model can be refined to consider variable event processing times. Subsequently, we present measurements of event processing times of three concrete network models. Finally, we discuss the effects of variable event processing times on concurrency estimations.

5.5.1 Refined Concurrency Estimation Model

Previously, the estimation result was the ratio $C_{\text{est}} := e_{\text{total}}/m$ of the expected total number of events in a lookahead window and the expected maximum events in a window pertaining to a single simulated node. Now, our aim is to determine $S_{\text{est}} := r_{\text{sequential}}/r_{\text{parallel}}$, where $r_{\text{sequential}}$ and r_{parallel} are the expected amounts of wall-clock time required to process the events in a lookahead window sequentially and in parallel. We make the simplifying assumption that the processing times of individual events are stochastically independent. Now, we follow the same reasoning as before: in YAWNS, when simulating one node on each processor, the amount of wall-clock time required to process a lookahead window is the largest processing time associated with any single node. Let $c_1(t), t \in \mathbb{N}_0$ be a discrete probability density function expressing the probability that a single event requires t units of wall-clock time to be processed. The distribution $c_1(t)$ can be gathered from measurements in a sequential simulation run of the network model. Then, the expected sequential processing time is:

$$r_{\text{sequential}} = e_{\text{total}} \sum_{t=1}^{\infty} t c_1(t).$$

To determine the expected parallel processing time r_{parallel}, we require the probability density function $f_i(k)$ describing the probability that a single node of category i executes k events in the lookahead window. As in the previous section, $f_i(k)$ can be determined based on the binomial distribution. In addition, we require the distribution function $c_k(t)$ that describes the probability that a node requires t units of wall-clock time to execute k events. While $c_0(t) = 0$, for $k \geq 2$, $c_k(t)$ is the k-th convolution power of $c_1(t)$:

$$c_k(t) = (\underbrace{c_1 * c_1 * \ldots * c_1 * c_1}_{\text{k times}})(t),$$

where * is the convolution operator. Applying the law of total probability, the probability that a single node of category i requires t units of wall-clock time is:

$$g_i(t) = \sum_{k=0}^{\infty} f_i(k) c_k(t).$$

Then, using the cumulative distribution function G_i of each probability density function g_i, the probability that all nodes of category i have processing times $\leq t$ is $H_i(t) = G_i(t)^{n_i}$. As in the previous section, we now consider all of the c node categories:

$$H(t) = \prod_{i=1}^{c} H_i(t).$$

Finally, using the probability density function h of the cumulative distribution function H, the expected largest processing time of any node and thus the parallel processing time for the lookahead window is:

$$r_{\text{parallel}} = \sum_{t=1}^{\infty} t h(t).$$

Now, an estimate of the speedup through parallelization assuming no overheads for communication between processors is given by

$$S_{\text{est}} = r_{\text{sequential}} / r_{\text{parallel}}.$$

5.5.2 Impact of Variable Event Processing Times

In this section, we study the effects of considering measured event processing times of the considered network models on the estimation results. To this end, we first present measurement results of the processing time distributions and compare estimation results under the assumption of fixed per-event processing times with estimation results of the refined estimation model.

Figure 5.21 shows the distribution of processing times of *individual events* in example configurations of the **Kademlia**$_{\mathbf{A}}$ and **NMS** model. All measurements were performed on a single core of an Intel Xeon E5-2670 processor. In ns-3, we measured the event processing times by accessing the accurate cycle counter available in recent Intel CPUs [Pa010]. In PeerSim, the Java method `System.nanoTime()` was used. In both cases, we aimed to minimize the runtime overhead of the measurements by storing the results in a pre-allocated array and performing the output of the measurements only after the termination of the simulation run. We now compare the estimation results of the basic analytical estimation model with the results of the refined estimation model that considers the per-event processing time distribution. To gather the individual estimates, we measured the per-event processing time distribution in a sequential run of each of the configurations and subsequently applied the refined analytical model of Section 5.5.1. We study the ratio between the speedup estimate of the refined estimation model and the concurrency estimate of the basic analytical model, i.e., $S_{\text{est}}/C_{\text{est}}$. We perform the comparison for the **Kademlia**$_{\mathbf{A}}$ and **NMS** network models only, since the concurrency estimation of **Wireless**$_{\mathbf{A}}$ does not rely on the statistical approach of Section 5.2.3. Due to the consistent and recurring sequences of event types in **Wireless**$_{\mathbf{A}}$, considering variable processing times would require a consideration of individual events in order of occurrence.

Table 5.2 lists S_{est}/C_{est} for a set of configurations of **Kademlia$_A$**. Considering all of our measurements, the largest deviation (S_{est}/C_{est} = 0.011) between the basic and refined analytical model was observed with 100 000 peers, λ_{user} = 100, α = 4 and 50% timeouts. The lowest deviation (S_{est}/C_{est} = 0.466) was observed with 1 000 peers, λ_{user} = 1 000, α = 1 and 0% timeouts. Table 5.3 lists S_{est}/C_{est} for a set of configurations of the **NMS** network model. The largest deviation (S_{est}/C_{est} = 0.086) was observed with 16 campus networks, 32 nodes per LAN and a hub bandwidth of 1Mbps. The lowest deviation (S_{est}/C_{est} = 0.963) was observed with 2 campus networks, 16 nodes per LAN and a hub bandwidth of 1 000Mbps.

The results show that considering variable event processing times can significantly lower the estimation results, demonstrating that the real-world simulation performance must in some cases be expected to be much lower than suggested by the plain concurrency results. However, a full and realistic consideration of event processing times requires a consideration of different types of events and their individual processing time distributions, as well as their order of occurrence in the simulation. While a more detailed modeling enables the consideration of further factors such as overheads for physical communication between processors, the efforts required by such an estimation must be weighed against the costs of enabling direct performance measurements through an actual parallelization of the model.

5.6 Discussion

The proposed estimation approach requires the identification of simulation bottlenecks and a classification of nodes according to the number of assigned events. However, it may not always be possible to determine these properties without executing the simulation. Depending on the network model, a sequential run is required to approximate the required statistics. For instance, a brief sequential simulation run of **Kademlia$_A$** was performed to approximate the average lookup duration. In the cases considered here, such an estimation was sufficient to achieve a reasonable level of estimation accuracy. Since the statistics gathered from simulation runs represent characteristics of the simulated network, the analytical approach still enables an understanding of the relationships between network properties and concurrency. In contrast, critical path analysis determines the concurrency without exposing its causes.

The concurrency values determined by both ACPA and the proposed estimation approach disregard the costs induced by communication between the processors executing the simulation. Also, since an unlimited number of processors is assumed, the results can be considered to be determined under a trivial partitioning strategy of assigning a single simulated node to each processor. In general, even disregarding the significant hardware resources required by such a partitioning strategy, there will be unacceptably large communication overheads. An optimal number of processors must be determined according to the network model, the synchronization algorithm and the costs for communication between processors in the given hardware environment. Still, the raw concurrency of the network model provides an upper bound on the average number of events processed per execution using conservative synchronization under the assumption of fixed event processing times and fixed lookahead. This upper bound cannot be exceeded in conservative parallel simulations even through future improvements in synchronization algorithms or using novel hardware platforms.

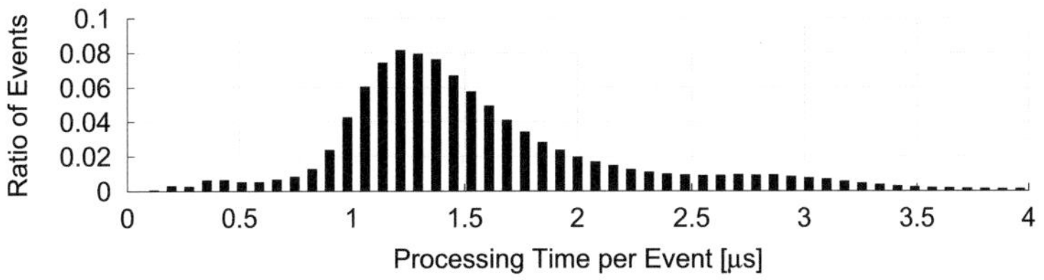

(a) **Kademlia$_A$**: 100 000 peers; λ_{user} = 100; α = 4; 50% timeouts.

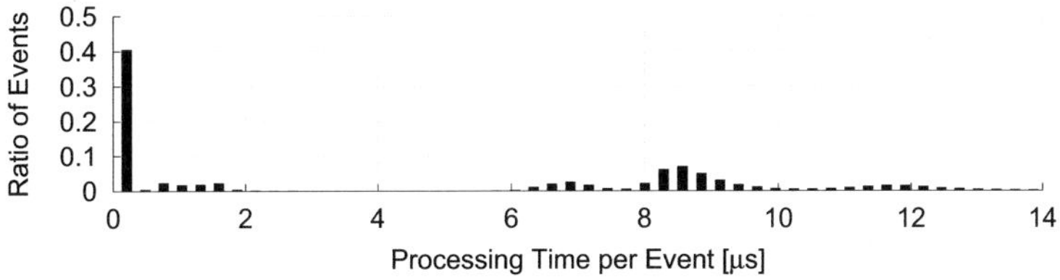

(b) **NMS** model: n_{cns} = 2; n_{lan} = 16; b = 1000Mbps.

Figure 5.21: Distribution of per-event processing time.

	λ_{user}		
#Peers	100	1 000	10 000
1 000	0.248	0.411	0.415
10 000	0.111	0.165	0.252
100 000	0.023	0.056	0.032

Table 5.2: Ratio between refined and basic estimations for **Kademlia$_A$** with α = 8 and 0% timeouts.

		Hub Bandwidth [Mbps]			
#CNs	$\frac{\#\text{Nodes}}{\text{LAN}}$	1	10	100	1 000
2	2	0.533	0.891	0.924	0.923
8	8	0.470	0.788	0.897	0.887
16	4	0.152	0.290	0.404	0.403

Table 5.3: Ratio between refined and basic estimation results for the **NMS** network model.

5.7 Conclusions

We presented an analytical model to estimate and understand the concurrency of network simulation models based on a modest amount of knowledge of the network model and information from sequential simulation runs. To show the soundness of the estimation approach, we proved an upper bound on the deviation between results obtained using the well-known synchronization algorithm YAWNS and critical path analysis: when assuming fixed event processing times and fixed lookahead, the concurrency determined using YAWNS is at least 1/3 of the concurrency determined using critical path analysis. A sensitivity analysis and investigation of event patterns showed the factors determining the concurrency of three network models and the differences in their potential for parallelization. The analytical approach estimates concurrency with high accuracy over a broad range of scenario parameter settings. For the models **Kademlia$_A$** and **NMS**, we showed that the concurrency can be estimated accurately even when abstracting from the network topology to a large degree. The concurrency of **Wireless$_A$** was shown to scale in proportion to the number of nodes in the network. The model **Kademlia**$_{\mathbf{A}}$ exhibits particularly large concurrency, potentially enabling parallel execution of up to thousands of events.

Finally, we refined the analytical model to assess the impact on the estimations when considering variable event processing times. Depending on the measured event processing time distribution and the scenario configuration, we observed up to about one order of magnitude deviation from the results under the assumption of fixed event processing times. However, since a refined model requires either the introduction of additional assumptions or extensive measurements, the proposed basic estimation model seems to provide a reasonable tradeoff between estimation effort and accuracy.

6
Second-Order Network Simulation

In the previous section, we studied upper bounds on the parallelism of an idealized parallel or distributed simulation run, assuming no costs for communication and synchronization between logical processes and identical computation time for all events. However, these aspects must be considered if the aim is to accurately predict the performance to be expected in a real-world simulation run. In this chapter, we describe an evaluation approach that enables realistic performance predictions of parallel and distributed simulation runs based on information gathered from a sequential execution of the network model under study.

The approach serves two purposes: first, the performance predictions enable simulationists to decide whether the parallelization of an existing sequential network model will yield a sufficient performance benefit to justify the required development effort. Second, the approach allows for variation of properties of the network model and the envisioned execution network, so that the predictions can guide network model optimization and hardware selection.

The core idea of the approach is to regard the envisioned parallel or distributed simulation as a generic application. From this perspective, it is clear that the well-known set of performance prediction approaches of measurements, analytical modeling, and simulation, can be applied. However, in general, the complexity in the runtime interactions between a simulator, an execution platform and a network model move accurate performance predictions out of the reach of analytical methods. In case measurements are infeasible as well, e.g., since a parallel variant of the network model does not exist, simulation can be applied instead, similarly to performance prediction approach for general applications [BM02, ZKK04, BKR07, HMS+09, RHB+11, BRM12]. When considering performance predictions of parallel and distributed simulations, the resulting evaluation approach is a *simulation of a parallel or distributed simulation*. We refer to this kind of nested simulation in the context of network simulations as *second-order network simulation*.

In the remainder of this section, we describe in detail the model components and execution procedure of a second-order network simulator. Subsequently, we generate predictions for two of the network models introduced in Chapter 3 in order to evaluate the accuracy of the performance predictions by comparison to parallel and distributed simulation runs of the network models on physical hardware. The description of the prediction approach is based on [AH13].

6.1 Methodology

In this section, we describe the methodology used by SONSim, our implementation of the second-order simulation approach, to obtain performance predictions. Based solely on information gathered from an existing sequential simulator and simple network measurements, SONSim predicts the performance of a parallel or distributed implementation of the simulator, enabling decisions on whether parallelization of a simulation will provide a performance benefit.

6.1.1 Modeling Levels

Figure 6.1 illustrates the modeling levels involved in second-order simulation. The original computer network to be evaluated using simulation is referred to as the *network under study* (NuS). Creating a simulation model of the network under study produces a *first-order model*, which can be implemented in a sequential, parallel or distributed *first-order simulator*. Since we are interested in the performance of the first-order simulator, we repeat the modeling step to arrive at a *second-order model*, which describes the behavior of the first-order simulator. The second-order model can be implemented in a *second-order simulator* that is used to conduct performance evaluations of the first-order simulator.

The network under study operates with respect to wall-clock time t_{NuS}, for which a prediction t'_{NuS} is produced by the first-order simulator. Performing the first-order simulation itself requires an amount of wall-clock time t_{1st}, for which a prediction t'_{1st} is produced by the second-order simulator.

We contrast the ***network under study*** with the network a parallel or distributed first-order simulator is executed in, which in the following we refer to as the ***execution network***.

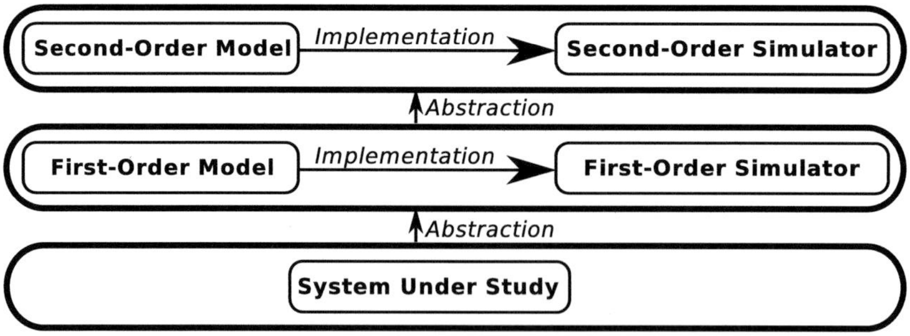

Figure 6.1: Levels of abstraction in modeling of simulations.

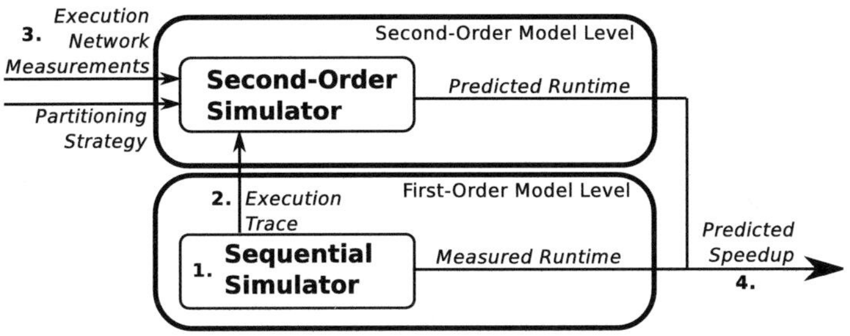

Figure 6.2: Data flow during performance prediction.

6.1.2 Prediction Workflow

The following sequence of activities is performed to obtain performance predictions (cf. Figure 6.2).

1. The existing sequential first-order simulator is executed multiple times for a given scenario to determine the average sequential runtime as a reference value for speedup calculation.

2. The sequential first-order simulator is instrumented to perform time measurements of the execution of individual event types and to generate an *execution trace*. The execution trace contains the sequence of event executions including event timestamps and the mapping of individual events to nodes of the network under study in the first-order simulation, as well as the sequence of events being created during simulation. The instrumented sequential simulator is executed to obtain the execution trace. We note that to avoid overheads, the sequential run in step 1. is performed without tracing.

3. As a basis for predicting the network overhead involved in the parallel or distributed simulation, we measure the average time required for individual message transfers in the execution network.

4. Finally, after supplying the execution network measurements, a partitioning of the first-order network model and the execution trace to the second-order simulator, a performance prediction for the parallel or distributed first-order simulation is generated.

6.1.3 Model Components

In this section, we describe the entities constituting the first-order and second-order models used by SONSim. Consistent with the discrete-event modeling approach, networks under study are commonly reflected by first-order models as follows:

- **System objects** represent the nodes in the network under study.
- **Events** model transmissions and receptions of packets by individual nodes.
- **Logical processes** run on nodes of the execution network, each storing a number of system objects and executing events pertaining to these system objects.

Applying the same modeling pattern again, we represent the state and the behavior of the parallel or distributed simulation in a sequential *second-order* simulation as follows:

- **System objects** represent the logical processes of the first-order simulation.
- **Events** model activities performed by individual logical processes: execution network operations and execution of first-order events.
- Since the second-order simulator itself is executed sequentially, only a single **logical process** is executed on the physical hardware.

To be able to predict the runtime of first-order simulations, a model of the operations executed by each logical process of a first-order simulator is required. A sequential discrete-event simulator operates in a simple loop: all events to be executed are stored in a priority queue. In each step, the event with the lowest timestamp is executed and removed from the queue. If the execution of the event triggers the creation of further events, the newly created events are added to the queue.

Parallel and distributed execution extends the basic sequential discrete-event logic in the following ways according to the null message algorithm (cf. Section 2.1): as long as safe events are available, these events are executed in non-decreasing timestamp order. If the executed events create new events, these are enqueued in the local future event list or sent to a remote logical process. If no safe events are available, a null message is broadcasted to all remote logical processes and the logical process blocks until a message is received from a remote logical process. If a null message is received, the logical process returns to checking for safe events. If an event is received, the event is enqueued before checking for safe events. Once all logical processes' future event lists are empty, the simulation terminates. The simulated time with respect to t'_{1st} until termination is the predicted runtime of the first-order parallel or distributed simulation.

6.1.4 Hardware Measurements

In the second-order simulation, the operations required by first-order logical processes to execute the parallel or distributed simulation are derived from a model of each logical process' behavior. However, to estimate the time required to perform the simulation, the costs of the individual operations with respect to t_{1st} must be estimated. Measurements in the execution network can be performed to determine values that approximate the individual costs. Two types of measurements are required: first, the costs for executing events of different types and for event management tasks are measured either by applying code profiling tools to the sequential simulator implementation, or by instrumenting the code with timing calls. Second, the costs of communication between LPs via shared memory or a network are measured by micro-benchmarks that repeatedly perform the communication tasks in question in the execution network to be used for the envisioned parallel or distributed simulation. For instance, the tool SKaMPI [RSPM98] measures the costs of individual message passing operations.

6.1.5 Second-Order Simulator Operation

In this section, we describe the states and behavior of a second-order simulation. SONSim operates by executing second-order events in timestamp order until no events are left in the queue. Each second-order event may extend an LP's position in t'_{1st} according to the time measurements used as input to SONSim. On termination of the second-order simulation, the final position in t'_{1st} represents SONSim's prediction of the first-order simulation runtime.

When supplied with an execution trace of a first-order simulation, measurements of the execution network, and a partitioning of the model, the second-order simulator loads the execution trace and translates all initial first-order events to the second-order events required to reflect the first-order events' execution.

The event types in the second-order simulation follow the states depicted in Figure 6.3. Each state can be associated with a cost in the predicted runtime with respect to t'_{1st}. The cost is modeled by representing each state using two second-order events: a *start* event reflects the point in t'_{1st} at which the state is entered. A *finish* event reflects the point in t'_{1st} a transition into a subsequent state is performed. Hence, the delta in t'_{1st} between the *start* and *finish* event associated with a state models the time spent by a logical process in that state. Each first-order logical process holds four main data structures that represent the logical process' state:

- **EventMap** is a timestamp-ordered queue representing the logical process' future event list. Each entry in the EventMap corresponds to a node in the precedence graph that is provided to SONSim in the form of an event trace. The processing of events contained in the EventMap is modeled by a time delta in t'_{1st} according to the previously measured processing time for the event's type.

- **EnqueueFifo** is a "first in, first out" queue that holds events to be inserted in a first-order logical process' EventMap. Events are inserted into the EnqueueFifo whenever a locally executed event creates further events, and whenever an event is received from a remote logical process.

- **SendFifo** is a "first in, first out" queue that holds events to be transferred to remote logical processes.

In the following, we describe the tasks performed by a first-order logical process in each of its states. We also describe the conditions under which the transitions between states are taken. The transitions that are not annotated in Figure 6.3 are taken unconditionally once the time delta associated with the respective state has expired.

- **CheckSafeEvent**: if the EventMap is non-empty and the earliest event in the EventMap is safe to execute, the event is removed from the EventMap and the LP transitions to the state ExecuteNextEvent. If all logical processes' EventMaps are empty, the LP transitions to the state Finished. If the EventMap is non-empty but does not hold any safe events, the LP transitions to the state SendNullMessage.

- **ExecuteNextEvent**: since the execution of first-order events is modeled solely by a delta in t'_{1st} and does not require the actual execution of a first-order event handler, ExecuteNextEvent handles only the management of events that are newly created by the currently executed event, according to the event trace. The time delta is determined according to the measurements performed for the first-order event's type. Each newly created event is handled as follows: if the new event is to be executed by the local LP, it is inserted into EnqueueFifo. If the event is to be executed by a remote LP, the event is inserted into SendFifo. In both cases, the LP subsequently transitions to the state SendEvents.

- **SendEvents**: for each event in SendFifo, the LP schedules a second-order event that inserts the event into the target LP's ReceiveFifo. Each second-order event is delayed by a time delta in t'_{1st} that is determined according to the estimated time required to send all previous first-order events. Finally, the LP transitions to the state EnqueueEvents.
- **EnqueueEvents**: each event in EnqueueFifo is inserted in the LP's EventMap. The total time spent in the state is determined according to the measured cost of enqueuing a single event and the total number of events to be enqueued. Subsequently, the LP transitions back to the state CheckSafeEvent.
- **SendNullMessage**: a new EOT is calculated according to the null messages previously received from the remote LPs. If the EOT is increased in this process, null messages holding the new EOT are inserted into the receiveFifos of all remote LPs. The total time delta is determined by the costs of sending a single null message and the number of remote LPs. Now, the LP transitions to the state ReceiveMessage.
- **ReceiveMessage**: the LP removes the first message from ReceiveFifo. If the message is a null message, a new EIT is calculated taking into account the null message's timestamp, and the LP transitions to the state CheckSafeEvent. If the message contains an event, the event is inserted into EnqueueFifo and the LP transitions to the state EnqueueEvents. The time delta spent in the state is determined according to the measured cost of receiving a message.
- **Finished**: each LP outputs performance statistics such as the number of executed events and sent null messages.

A second-order simulation run provides two key pieces of information: first, it estimates the *runtime of the envisioned parallel or distributed simulation* when using the configured execution network hardware, simulation model and partitioning. Comparing this value to the measured sequential runtime, the benefit of parallelization can be evaluated. Second, the run returns a *parallel or distributed simulation schedule* that allows for examination of the first-order logical processes' interactions during execution.

Second-order simulation can be considered a generalization of critical path analysis: if the costs of network operations are configured to be zero and only one simulated node is assigned to each logical process, the results represent the raw concurrency of the model given only by the dependencies between events.

6.2 Performance Predictions

In this section, we study the expected performance of parallel and distributed runs of the models studied analytically in Chapter 5. Subsequently, we evaluate the accuracy that is achieved by the approach by comparison with parallel and distributed simulation runs on physical hardware.

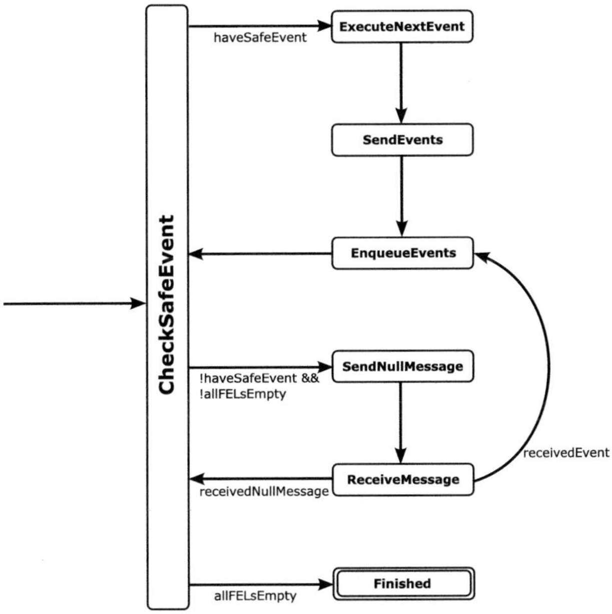

Figure 6.3: Finite state machine description of the LP behavior in SONSim.

The predictions are generated using SONSim, our implementation of the second-order simulation approach. SONSim is implemented in CPUDES, a lightweight discrete-event framework we developed from scratch. CPUDES is a C++ application that provides the basic components required to implement arbitrary discrete-event models both for sequential and for parallel and distributed simulation. Communication between logical processes is performed using the Message Passing Interface (MPI) [SOHL+98].

6.2.1 Experiments

In Chapter 5, we analyzed three network models to determine upper bounds on the average number of events executed in parallel. Here, we apply SONSim, a concrete implementaton of the second-order simulation approach, to study the expected performance gains under more realistic circumstances, i.e., using a limited number of logical processes and given the overheads incurred by communication and synchronization.

Measurements of the individual steps performed during a sequential simulation as well as estimations of the costs of transferring events between processors are required to perform estimations. For the experiments targeting **Kademlia**$_B$ and **PHOLD**, we used the CPU profiling tool from gperftools[1], a set of development tools provided by Google. We identified the operations with the largest contribution to total simulation runtime through profiling of sequential simulation runs. In

[1]`https://code.google.com/p/gperftools`

CPUDES, the relevant costs are the time required for enqueuing an event in the local future event list and the time required for executing the handler corresponding to an event's type.

Communication costs between processors were measured using a simple MPI benchmark tool created from scratch. The tool transfers a large number of messages of the size of the data associated with events in the envisioned parallel or distributed simulation are transferred between two processes using MPI. The average time required for sending (using the MPI primitive *MPI_Send*) or receiving (*MPI_Recv*) is measured and used as a fixed estimate of the cost of the respective operation.

6.2.2 Evaluation

We validate the estimations by comparing our performance predictions with the runtime measured in actual distributed simulation runs of the considered network models, focusing on **Kademlia$_B$** and **PHOLD**. All measurements were performed in a cluster of processing nodes with Intel Xeon E5-2670 processors running at 2.6 GHz, interconnected using OpenMPI[2] to communicate via an InfiniBand 4X QDR interconnect. We used up to 16 processing nodes, each processing node handling one logical process.

In the evaluation of **Kademlia$_B$** model, the parameters were varied as follows: the number of logical processes was set to 2, 4, 8, and 16. The number of simulated peers was set to 131 072, 262 144, and 524 288. The number of concurrent lookups was set to 100 and 1 000. The simulation terminated after 60s of simulated time with 100 concurrent lookups, and 120s with 1 000 concurrent lookups. Simulated nodes were assigned randomly to the logical processes. Figure 6.4 shows the evaluation results for the **Kademlia$_B$** model. While the estimations follow the general trend of the measurement results, there is some deviation: SONSim underestimates the simulation runtime for the runs with 1 000 concurrent lookups and overestimates the runtime with 100 concurrent lookups. We expect the reason for the deviation to be the limited accuracy in modeling network overheads. The smallest and largest ratio between SONSim's estimation and the measured runtime was 0.55 and 1.68, respectively.

To explore the limits of SONSim's estimation accuracy, we additionally estimate the performance of simulations of the **PHOLD** benchmark model. **PHOLD** can be considered a "worst-case" network model with respect to estimation accuracy: if no artificial computational overhead is added, the execution of each event in a **PHOLD** simulation comprises only the generation of a single pseudo-random number and the creation and possible transfer of a single new event. Low computation times per event strengthen the impact of network overheads on the simulation runtime. Since SONSim includes only a basic model of the costs of network transfers, large deviations between the estimated and measured simulation performance must therefore be expected. The parameters were varied as follows: the rate parameter λ of the exponential distribution of inter-event time was set to 0.001, 0.01, 0.1, and 1.0. The number of logical processes was set to 2, 4, 8, and 16. To vary the total runtime of the simulation, the total number of executed events was set to 102 400 000. To show the effect of large network overheads, the ratio of events targeting remote logical processes was set to 0.5 and 1.0. A fixed lookahead of 10 ms was used. The simulation was initialized with a population of 1 024, 5 120 and 10 240 events. Figure 6.5 shows the evaluation results for the **PHOLD** model. As expected, the results deviate strongly from the measurements: in many cases, SONSim significantly underestimates the distributed simulation runtime. The smallest and largest ratio between SONSim's

[2] `http://www.openmpi.org`

estimation and the measured runtime was 0.29 and 1.10, respectively. The deviation increases with larger runtime of the simulation runs on physical hardware. The reason is that in lower-performance runs, network overheads, which in SONSim are estimated using a constant cost per message, have particularly large impact. We repeated the experiment with an artificial processing time of 100μs per event. The artificial processing time is introduced based on the accurate cycle counters available in recent Intel CPUs [Pa010]. The total number of events was set to 614 400. Figure 6.6 shows that with the larger processing time per event, the performance prediction is highly accurate. The largest and lowest ratio between the estimation and the measured runtime was 1.01 and 0.94.

We conclude that in cases of extremely fine-grained computations and extremely frequent inter-processor communication, SONSim's estimations must be viewed as only rough indications of the distributed simulation performance that can be expected on physical hardware.

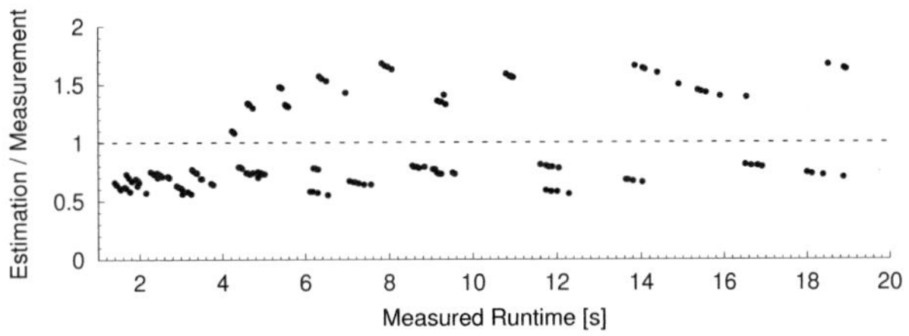

Figure 6.4: Accuracy of runtime estimations of the **Kademlia$_B$** model.

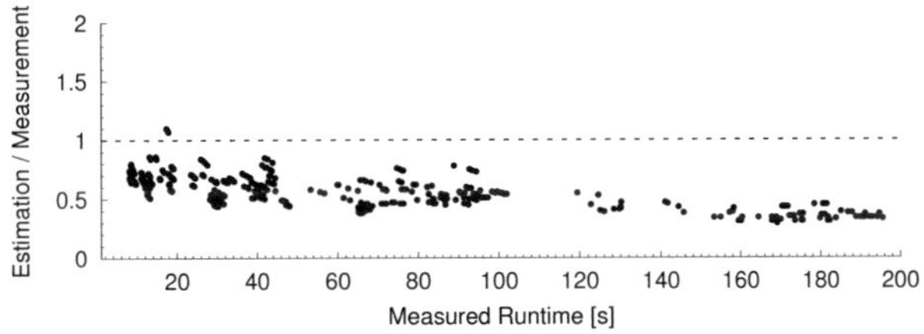

Figure 6.5: Accuracy of runtime estimations of the **PHOLD** model.

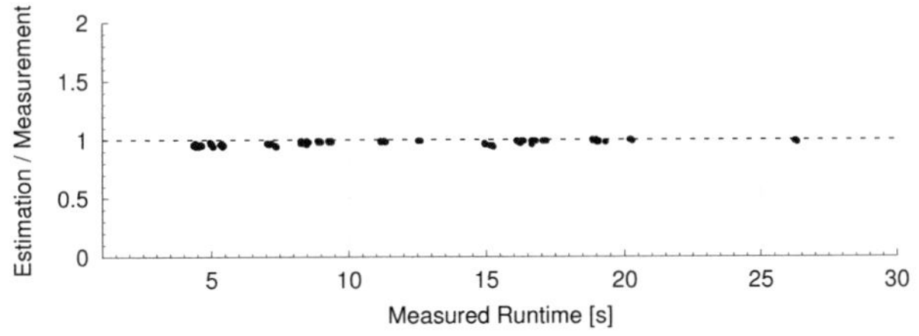

Figure 6.6: Accuracy of runtime estimations of the **PHOLD** model with an artificial processing time of 100μs per event.

6.3 Discussion

The validation results for the **Kademlia$_B$** model showed that SONSim produced a reasonably accurate performance prediction. Strong deviations can be observed for the **PHOLD** model, whose execution requires only extremely fine-grained computations. Hence, the costs of communication between processors dominate the simulation runtime. Since we apply a comparatively simple model of the execution network that estimates the costs of MPI operations using constant values, effects such as network congestion are not considered. A closer modeling of the communication between logical processes may enable more accurate performance predictions, while increasing the complexity in interpreting the results.

The second-order simulation considers the precedence relationships between events and estimates the costs of event executions, inter-processor communication and synchronization based on measurements. Hence, on the one hand, the performance of the targeted execution network can be modeled in high detail. On the other hand, the results apply specifically to the modeled execution network, whereas more generic approaches such as concurrency estimations provide results that apply independently of a specific execution network.

7
Identifying Concurrency – Conclusions

In this part of the thesis, we presented two approaches for evaluating the potential of discrete-event network models for parallelization. An analytical evaluation approach was shown to accurately estimate the concurrency of network simulations. The estimation determines the number of cores than can be utilized assuming no overheads for inter-processor communication. Contrary to established automated "black-box" methods, the proposed approach enables insights into the causes of the determined concurrency. The estimation results can be used to guide model optimizations with respect to concurrency and to select a suitable execution platform for the simulation. To show the soundness of the estimation approach, we proved an upper bound on the deviation between results obtained using the well-known synchronization algorithm YAWNS and critical path analysis: when assuming fixed event processing times and fixed lookahead, the concurrency determined using YAWNS is at least 1/3 of the concurrency determined using critical path analysis. Further, by applying the analytical approach to three network models implemented in well-known existing network simulators, we showed that a high accuracy in concurrency estimation can be achieved.

Since the complex interactions between a parallel or distributed simulator realization and the network model defy a full performance prediction using purely analytical means, we additionally presented a simulation-based tool to estimate the parallel and distributed simulation performance under more realistic conditions. A second-order network simulator performs a simulation of an envisioned parallel or distributed simulation and allows researchers to vary properties of the execution hardware and the envisioned simulator realization to determine the effects on performance. We described the components of the second-order simulation model and its execution procedure and provided performance prediction results for two network models. An evaluation of the results showed a strong dependence of the prediction accuracy on the amount of computation per simulation event.

Part III
Harnessing Concurrency

8 Harnessing Concurrency – Introduction

This second part of the dissertation is concerned with the efficient execution of network simulations on modern hardware platforms. We consider two types of hardware platforms: clusters of interconnected symmetric multiprocessor (SMP) systems and graphics processing units (GPUs). Clusters of SMP systems are typically available to researchers through a shared batch system. We show that the large combined memory capacity of a cluster of SMP systems can be utilized to enable simulations of peer-to-peer networks at the scale of 10 million nodes, more than an order of magnitude beyond commonly used sequential simulators for peer-to-peer network models. Some previous works have considered discrete-event simulations of peer-to-peer networks a problem that benefits at most marginally from parallelization due to fine-grained computational tasks and frequent fine-grained communication between nodes in the network [DLTM08, QRT12]. We show that in the case of networks based on the Kademlia protocol, which forms the basis of one of the largest public peer-to-peer networks, a distributed simulation achieves a reduction of simulation runtime by a factor of 6.0 and reductions in memory usage per logical process that increase close to linearly with the number of logical processes. A key requirement for substantial runtime reduction is a suitable partitioning strategy. We analyze and compare the effects of two partitioning schemes and show that a partitioning strategy based on the simulated nodes' routing table structure reduces the simulation runtime considerably, whereas a partitioning strategy based on the simulated nodes' locations can increase the efficiency of the synchronization between logical processes. Distributing the simulation enables the execution of large-scale scenarios, but occupies substantial amounts of hardware resources relative to the achieved runtime reductions.

In order to enable runtime reductions without allocating large amounts of computational resources, we consider the use of commodity GPUs for parallel simulation. Modern GPU architectures employ hundreds or thousands of cores to efficiently execute highly data-parallel computational tasks. Originally, the GPU hardware architecture evolved to handle the demanding graphics processing tasks required for realistic rendering of three-dimensional scenes in the context of video games, computer-assisted design and simulation. Today, GPUs are established as coprocessing devices that are used by a host computer's CPU to offload computational tasks with large amounts of data parallelism. Even though modern GPUs and the application programming interfaces provided by manufacturers enable general-purpose programmability, the GPU hardware architecture is subject to design decisions that make GPUs suitable for an efficient execution of different classes of computations compared to CPUs. We study how GPUs can be used to accelerate computationally expensive network simulations on the example of two network models: we first consider a low-level network model of wireless communications. Executing the model requires expensive signal processing steps that are inherently data-parallel. Accordingly, it is clear that GPUs can be employed to accelerate these signal processing steps. However, the performance of the resulting hybrid CPU-GPU-based simulator depends on the amount of overhead incurred by the communication between graphics memory and host memory. We measure the impact of optimizations to the hybrid CPU-GPU-based architecture that aim to reduce the overhead for CPU-GPU interaction and show that mechanisms from traditional CPU-based parallel and distributed simulation are required to achieve significant runtime reductions.

To further reduce the need for interaction between CPU and GPU, we propose a fully GPU-based simulator that performs all steps of a discrete-event network simulation on a commodity GPU. In contrast to hybrid CPU-GPU-based approaches, the fully GPU-based simulation enables high-performance simulations of models with particularly fine-grained computations. We propose a novel event management scheme that efficiently utilizes the GPU's resources by aggregating the simulated nodes into logical processes. Dynamically varying the number of simulated nodes in the logical processes enables the simulator to weigh the utilization of the GPU's computational resources against event management overheads. Hence, the best configuration depending on the hardware, the network model and the scenario can be selected dynamically at simulation runtime.

Applying the simulator engine to execute a model of a Kademlia-based peer-to-peer network, we show that the model contains sufficient implicit data parallelism to enable a simulation speedup of up to 19.5 compared to a sequential CPU-based execution and event rates of up 6.8×10^6 events per second of wall-clock time, while relying on a single commodity GPU. For the PHOLD benchmark model, we achieve a speedup of 27.5 and event rates up to 39.3×10^6 events per second of wall-clock time.

9
CPU-Based Distributed Simulation of Kademlia-Based Networks

In this section, we focus on the simulation of large-scale peer-to-peer networks. Some previous works suggested that simulations of peer-to-peer networks exhibit only limited speedup by parallel and distributed execution [DLTM08, QRT12]. On the example of networks based on the Kademlia protocol, we have seen in Chapter 5 that a network model of a Kademlia-based network contains substantial concurrency. In this section, we study the degree to which the concurrency can be exploited using CPU-based distributed simulation. In such an environment, the costs of communication between logical processes are a core concern. In Chapter 10, we will consider parallel simulations on a many-core device using shared memory for communication between logical processes.

In parallel and distributed simulations, an event is transferred from one logical process LP_a to a remote logical process LP_b whenever the simulated node that created the event resides in LP_a, while the simulated node handling the newly created event resides in LP_b. The probability of this situation can be reduced by choosing a partitioning strategy that aims to minimize the probability of interacting simulated nodes to reside in separate logical processes. In this section, we analyze two partitioning strategies on the example of distributed simulations of Kademlia-based networks: communication overhead can be reduced substantially by a partitioning strategy that follows the simulated nodes' routing table structure. A partitioning strategy based on the simulated nodes' geographical locations can instead improve the potential for efficient synchronization between logical processes. We propose metrics that allow us to expose remaining potentials for increases in the efficiency of the synchronization mechanism.

Our performance measurements demonstrate that distributed simulations of Kademlia-based networks can benefit sufficiently from distributed simulation both with respect to runtime as well as to memory utilization to enable simulations at the network's real-world scale of 10 million nodes. We investigate the network model **Kademlia**$_\mathbf{A}$ (cf. Section 5.3.1) implemented in the network simulator PeerSim that we extended with support for parallel and distributed simulation based on the message passing interface (MPI [SOHL+98]). We apply conservative synchronization according to the null message protocol (cf. Section 2.1.1).

The remainder of this chapter is based on [AJH14].

9.1 Related Work

A previous effort of extending PeerSim for distributed simulation was presented by Dinh et al. [DLTM08] in 2008 for networks based on the Chord protocol. As in our work, synchronization is achieved using the Null Mesage Algorithm. While memory usage per LP is reduced substantially, the authors report simulation slowdown factors of 83 and more compared to a sequential implementation. In the same year, the authors presented performance measurements of the same simulator for the Chord and Pastry networks [DTM08], reporting a super-linear speedup factor of more than 100 using 64 LPs. A partial explanation for the large speedup can be gathered from the enormous computational load incurred by their network model: a runtime of over two weeks is reported for a *sequential* simulation of a static network of 524 288 peers generating a fixed amount of traffic. While the performance of simulations of Chord and Kademlia cannot be compared directly, an indication of the computational intensity of their model is given by the runtime of 399s for identical parameters in our own sequential implementation. If the computational load of a simulation is very large, overheads for communication and synchronization incurred by distributing the simulation have only marginal impact, even though the absolute runtime remains large.

Lin et al. presented a simulator engine for peer-to-peer networks that uses a synchronous master-worker synchronization scheme [LPGZ05]. As limited scaling was observed using strict synchronization, the authors relax the synchronization requirements and ensure that simulated results are not affected substantially by determining bounds within which event timestamps may be altered during simulation. Simulations of networks based on the XRing protocol achieved speedup factors of up to 5.4 using 32 workers. A similar architecture was proposed by Quinson et al. for simulations of the Chord protocol, achieving a speedup factor of up to about 1.45 using 24 threads [QRT12]. The authors identify the low computational granularity and the difficulty of partitioning networks exhibiting the small-world property, i.e., low hop counts separating peers, as particular challenges in distributed simulation of peer-to-peer networks. Arguing that the resulting overheads cannot be amortized using traditional synchronization approaches, the authors propose a synchronous master-worker architecture for multicore systems. In contrast to this argument, for Kademlia-based peer-to-peer networks, our results show that distributing the simulation using the classical null message algorithm (cf. Section 2.1) can substantially reduce the simulation runtime. Furthermore, we measure remaining efficiency potentials that can possibly be exploited with future optimizations.

9.2 Partitioning Schemes

Kademlia is a peer-to-peer protocol that generates a logical topology aiming to maintain low hop counts between arbitrary peers in the network. Hence, distributed simulations using a random partitioning strategy result in large numbers of simulated messages that cross logical process boundaries an require physical communication between logical processes. For this reason, we propose a partitioning scheme that aims to reduce the number of logical process interactions. However, in addition to the physical exchange of messages between logical processes, the partitioning strategy can also affect the waiting times and number of physical messages required for synchronizing the simulation: if each logical process is aware of large periods of simulated time that can be covered before a simulated message originating from a remote logical process will be received, large amounts of time can be spent executing events instead of handling synchronization. Therefore, we additionally propose and numerically analyze the effect of a partitioning strategy that aims to increase the utilization of lookahead (cf. Section 2.1).

In the following, from the perspective of a given peer, we refer to peers simulated on different LPs as *remote peers* and events targeting remote peers as *remote events*. Accordingly, peers simulated on the same LP are referred to as *local peers* and events targeting local peers are referred to as *local events*.

When simulating physical networks, a suitable partitioning can usually be found on the basis of the physical proximity of the simulated peers by assigning spatially close peers to the same LP. If closely located simulated peers are connected through high-throughput links and interact frequently (e.g., in a LAN), while distant peers interact less frequently over a low-throughput connection (e.g., through a WAN), remote events are infrequent and the overhead for exchanging messages between LPs is low. In addition, as link latency tends to increase with spatial distance [AKK10], in a simulation using a location-based partitioning scheme, the minimum link latency of simulated messages sent across LP boundaries tends to be larger than the minimum latency of messages simulated within an LP, allowing for a large fixed lookahead value. Therefore, for simulations of physical networks, location-based partitioning can jointly reduce remote events and synchronization overheads.

In contrast, peer-to-peer overlay networks superimpose an application-level logical topology onto the underlying physical network. Finding a suitable partitioning for simulations of overlay networks is complicated by the fact that the logical topology of the overlay network does not necessarily reflect the physical proximity relationships between peers. Hence, contrary to simulations of physical networks, there is a tradeoff between minimization of the number of remote events through a partitioning based on the logical topology of the network, and maximization of latencies, and hence lookahead, associated with remote events through location-based partitioning.

9.2.1 ID-Based Partitioning

First, we focus on reducing the physical exchange of messages between LPs. To this end, we need to be aware of the communication patterns arising from the topology of the simulated network. The traffic induced by two of the sources of traffic in the Kademlia network, bootstrapping and routing table maintenance, is concentrated around the initiating peer's ID (cf. Section 5.3.1). We can exploit the resulting locality by partitioning the ID-space into segments of equal size and assigning one partition to each LP (cf. Figure 9.1).

We show that ID-based partitioning results in low amounts of overhead for communication between LPs: *For each doubling of the number of LPs, only a maximum of k additional peers in a peer's routing table come to reside on a remote LP, where k is the maximum number of peer IDs each bucket in a peer's routing table can hold, usually 8.*

Each peer's routing table can be viewed as a binary tree [MM02] where leaf nodes are k-buckets and edges are annotated with the ID prefix handled by the leaves of the corresponding subtree (cf.

Figure 9.2). The splitting mechanism described in Section 5.3.1 is the only way the depth of the tree is ever increased. We use α to denote the ID of the peer owning the routing table. Consider the leaf node pertaining to α at depth i of the binary tree. The leaf node corresponds to a k-bucket holding peers with a common prefix of length i. The splitting mechanism replaces a leaf node containing α with a new subtree consisting of two edges: an edge e_s with a leaf node corresponding to IDs with a common prefix of length $i + 1$ shared by α, and an edge e_n with a leaf node for a prefix of the same length *not* shared by α. In consequence, when following the edges pertaining to α's prefix, on level i of the tree, there is either a leaf node containing α, or there are two edges: one edge leading to an arbitrary number of nodes pertaining to IDs with prefix length i shared by α, and one edge leading to only a single node pertaining to IDs with prefix length i *not* shared by α. Doubling the number of LPs from 2^i to 2^{i+1} mirrors the splitting mechanism and can be regarded as dividing two halves of the subtree at depth i between two LPs. With $2^0 = 1$ LP, the k-buckets pertaining to all nodes of the tree are handled by the local LP. When doubling the number of LPs, there are two cases: if the subtree at depth i is a leaf node, peers in one half of the corresponding k-bucket's ID range are assigned to a remote LP, while peers in the other half remain local. If the subtree at depth i has two edges, the peers of the single leaf node below e_n are assigned to a remote LP, while all other nodes in the subtree remain local. All nodes below e_s remain on the local LP. Hence, as each k-bucket holds a maximum of k peers, only a maximum of k peers become remote in each doubling of the LP count.

In Section 9.3.1, we show through measurements that the inter-LP communication indeed increases only by a roughly constant amount when doubling the number of LPs.

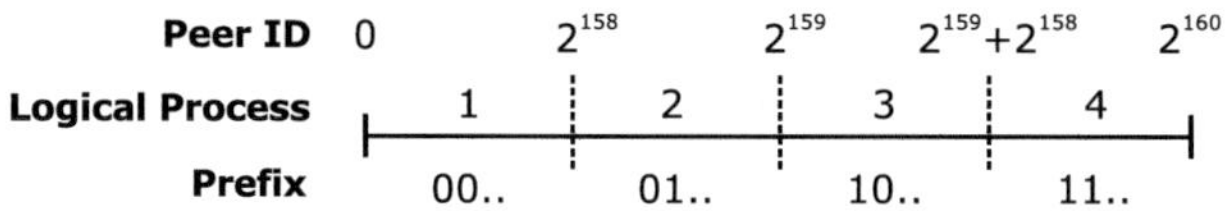

Figure 9.1: Example of ID-based partitioning of a simulated network into 4 logical processes. Each logical process contains peers with IDs sharing a common prefix.

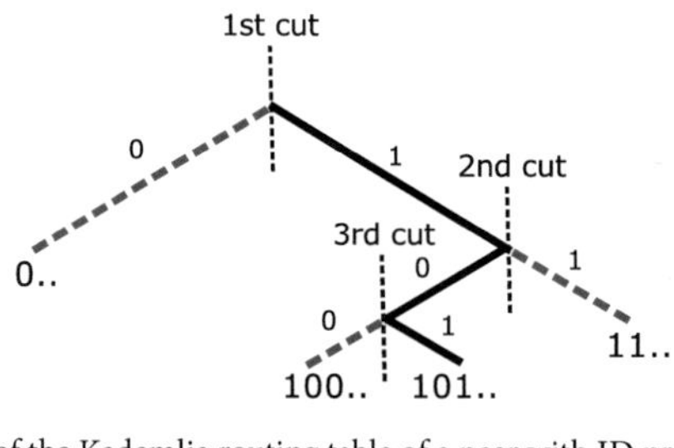

Figure 9.2: Binary tree structure of the Kademlia routing table of a peer with ID prefix 101. Dashed lines denote edges leading to leaf nodes not sharing the peer's prefix. Each doubling of LPs leads to a cut that displaces the peers in a single leaf node of the routing table to a remote LP.

9.2.2 Location-Based Partitioning

We will now focus on increasing the maximum lookahead value available in the simulation. A location-based partitioning can increase the average spatial distance between remote peers compared to local peers. As there is a strong relationship between physical distance and link latency [AKK10], an increase in distance between communicating remote peers will be reflected by an increase in link latencies. Hence, with dynamic lookahead calculation, more local events will be safe to execute on average, potentially reducing idle times.

In our location-based partitioning scheme, peers are assigned to LPs according to the peers' spatial position. We compare three strategies: assignment based on ranges of latitudes or longitudes, and an assignment to regions with small diameter and equal area (cf. Figure 9.3). To find appropriate regions on the earth's surface, we used the MATLAB implementation of the algorithm proposed by Leopardi [Leo06].

For a network model that follows the real-world distribution of peers across the earth's surface [JAH11], the partitioning scheme would need to consider the given distribution both to achieve load balance between LPs and to maximize distances between remote peers. Here, we follow simplifying assumptions to be able to demonstrate the fundamental effects of the partitioning scheme. Based on the assumptions of a perfectly spherical earth and peers being distributed uniformly on the earth's surface we numerically examine the average spatial distance between peers exchanging messages across LPs. For each chosen number of partitions, we calculate the average distance between points residing in different partitions, picked at random on the surface of a sphere.

For picking points on the surface of a sphere, we use a method by Marsaglia [Mar72]: we generate V_1 and V_2, both uniformly distributed on $(-1, 1)$, and reject all pairs where $S = V_1^2 + V_2^2 \geq 1$. Using the remaining pairs, the cartesian coordinates of points distributed uniformly on the unit sphere are given by $(2V_1\sqrt{1-S}, 2V_2\sqrt{1-S}, 1-2S)$. Given two such points, and after conversion to spherical coordinates ϕ_1, λ_1 and ϕ_2, λ_2, the distance on a sphere of radius r is given by $d = r\psi$, with $\psi = cos^{-1}(cos\phi_1 cos\phi_2 cos(\lambda_1 - \lambda_2) + sin\phi_1 sin\phi_2)$ (e.g., [BB93]). The numerical results with 95% confidence intervals are listed in Table 9.1. The average distance between two points for a single partition is 10 000 km, corresponding to the expected distance between points on the surface

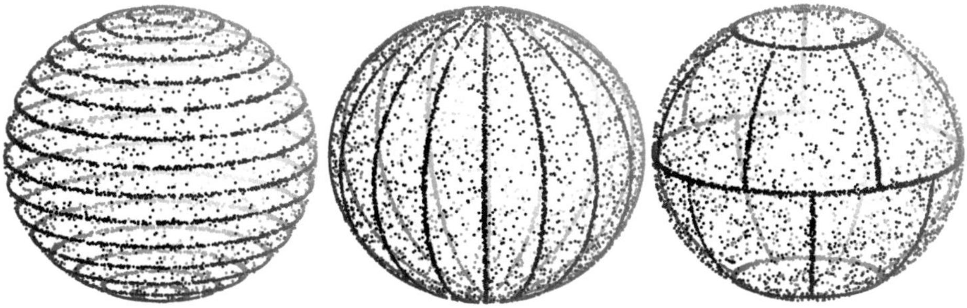

Figure 9.3: In the location-based partitioning scheme, peers are assigned to ranges of latitudes ("discs", left) or longitudes ("slices", middle), or to regions of small diameter and equal size (right) on the earth's surface.

	Average Distance [km]		
#Part.	By Latitude	By Longitude	By Regions
2	11895.2 ± 2.4	11895.7 ± 2.4	11895.4 ± 2.4
4	10685.5 ± 2.5	11263.4 ± 2.4	10954.7 ± 2.5
8	10341.4 ± 2.6	10653.3 ± 2.5	10808.4 ± 2.5
16	10166.9 ± 2.6	10325.1 ± 2.6	10465.0 ± 2.5
32	10084.2 ± 2.7	10158.8 ± 2.7	10254.6 ± 2.6
64	10040.3 ± 2.7	10078.1 ± 2.7	10132.5 ± 2.6

Table 9.1: Average distance between remote peers using location-based partitioning.

of a sphere with 40 000 km circumference. The same mean distance is achieved by partitioning schemes not considering peer locations, regardless of the number of partitions. The largest benefit is achieved for two LPs: remote link latencies are increased by about 19%. When increasing the number of partitions, each partition becomes smaller and the results asymptotically approach those for a single partition. For large numbers of LPs, partitioning the earth into regions of small diameter gives the largest benefit of the three schemes.

In all cases, for 2 and more LPs, the minimum latency is given for communication between peers at the shared border of two partitions and is hence constant for all three location-based partitioning schemes. Therefore, the lookahead must be calculated dynamically to benefit from the location-based optimization scheme. The overall effect on simulation runtime depends on the communication costs between LPs: since peer IDs are chosen independently from locations, location-based partitioning does not follow the simulated network's logical topology. Consequently, the number of messages exchanged between LPs is as large as with a random partitioning.Since further, our implementation of the null message algorithm in the distributed PeerSim variant supports only fixed lookahead values, we focus on the ID-based partitioning scheme in comparison with a random partitioning.

9.3 Simulator Evaluation

In this section, we evaluate the effects of the partitioning schemes introduced in Section 9.2 through performance measurements of our distributed simulator implementation. The simulator performance is studied for simulations of networks of 1 and 10 million peers. Simulation runs were performed on up to 16 machines equipped with 16 Intel Xeon E5-2670 cores each and connected using InfiniBand 4x QDR. To be able to fully exploit each machine's memory resources, each LP uses all 16 cores of one machine. Each LP uses one core each for simulation and communication. The remaining cores are available to the Java runtime environment to perform garbage collection. The sequential simulator used as a reference for speedup calculation utilizes 16 cores in the same fashion. The sequential implementation is highly optimized and simulates a network of one million peers for one simulated hour in about 1.5h of wall-clock time. Results are stated as averages of three runs with 95% confidence intervals.

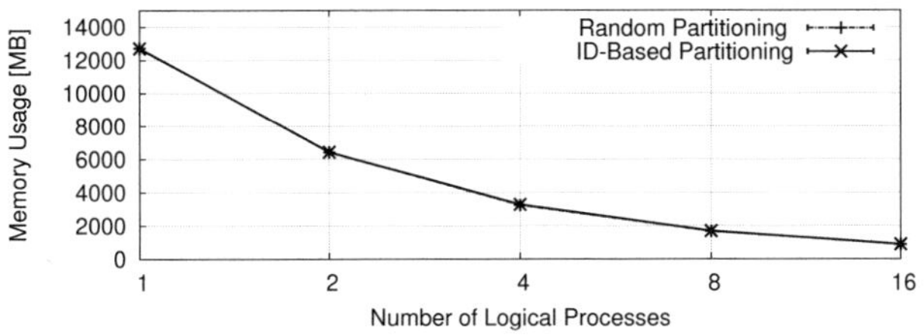

Figure 9.4: Memory usage per LP for a network size of 1 million peers, varying the number of logical processes and the partitioning scheme.

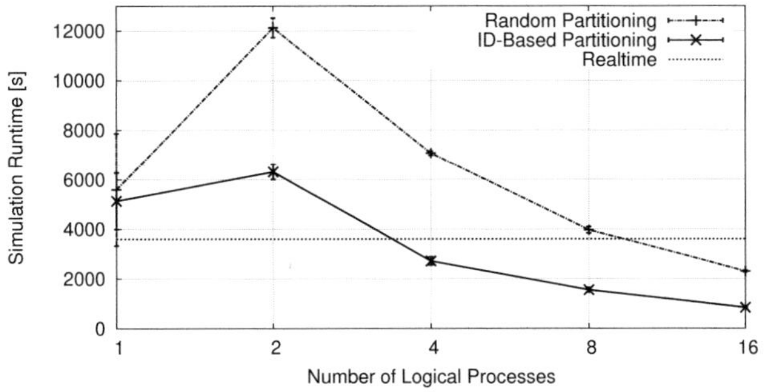

Figure 9.5: Simulation runtime for a network size of 1 million peers, varying the number of logical processes and the partitioning scheme.

9.3.1 Performance

We study the performance of the simulator for two different partitioning schemes. Our focus is on the ID-based partitioning scheme that promises high performance by considering the simulated network's topology. We contrast the results with a random partitioning scheme that does not consider peer IDs and therefore incurs the same amount of overheads as the proposed location-based partitioning schemes assuming fixed lookahead.

Figure 9.4 shows the memory usage per LP for simulation runs using ID-based and random partitioning, for networks of 1 million peers over the course of one simulated hour. Memory usage was reduced close to linearly with the number of LPs, from 12713 MB to 883 MB when moving from 1 to 16 LPs, a factor of 14.4. The choice of partitioning scheme had no marked impact on memory usage.

Simulation runtime (cf. Figure 9.5) was reduced substantially as well. For two LPs, the overheads for synchronization and physical message exchanges were not amortized by the distributed computation. This is an effect of null messages being sent by each LP only after executing all available safe events. Each LP frequently waits for the next null message from the remote LP before computation may proceed. Starting with 4 LPs, simulations using ID-based partitioning proceeded faster than wall-clock time. Highest performance was achieved using 16 LPs with ID-based partitioning, reducing simulation runtime by a factor of 6.01 compared to sequential runs. The simulation runtime was 843s, compared to 2301s for random partitioning.

In order to demonstrate the simulator's scalability, we performed an additional simulation run for a network with the size of the BitTorrent Mainline DHT [JAH11] of 10 million peers over the course of one simulated hour using ID-based partitioning on 16 LPs. The simulator required 14966s (about 4.2h) of wall-clock time to simulate a total of about 8.24×10^9 requests. Each of the 16 LPs used about 9450 MB of memory.

To explore the basis of the benefit of ID-based partitioning in the simulations for 1 million peers, Table 9.2 lists the percentage of simulated messages that were exchanged between local peers and thus did not require physical communication between LPs. With the random partitioning, the percentage of local messages was roughly halved when doubling the number of LPs. With the ID-based partitioning, the percentage of local messages was reduced by a roughly constant amount of about 8% for each doubling of LPs, supporting our analysis in Section 9.2.1. Location-based partitioning (cf. Section 9.2.2) does not consider peer IDs and must hence be expected to create as many remote events as the random partitioning.

We studied the distributed simulation performance more closely by instrumenting the simulator to measure the proportion of runtime spent in the following simulation states:

- *Execute Event*: a safe event is being executed.
- *Forward Event*: an event is sent to a remote LP.
- *Handle Message*: an incoming message is parsed, and if the message contains a remote event, it is added to the local queue.
- *Send Null Message*: a null message is sent to a remote LP.
- *Idle*: the LP waits for local events to become safe to execute. The *Idle* state includes the overheads incurred by the time measurements.

LPs	Random	ID-Based
1	100	100
2	45.67 ± 0.04	91.11 ± 0.01
4	22.24 ± 0.14	83.00 ± 0.03
8	11.11 ± 0.09	75.27 ± 0.03
16	5.82 ± 0.06	67.69 ± 0.06

Table 9.2: Percentage of messages to local peers [%] depending on the partitioning scheme.

	1 LP	2 LPs	4 LPs	8 LPs	16 LPs
Execute Event	98.19 ± 0.47	56.32 ± 4.65	55.82 ± 2.53	50.68 ± 2.58	47.38 ± 1.85
Forward Event	N/A	3.00 ± 0.66	6.13 ± 1.70	7.24 ± 1.64	8.32 ± 1.55
Handle Message	N/A	15.31 ± 1.17	22.28 ± 1.86	19.56 ± 2.72	17.53 ± 2.73
Send Null Message	N/A	0.01 ± 0.00	0.06 ± 0.01	0.22 ± 0.02	0.80 ± 0.08
Idle (incl. Overhead)	1.81 ± 0.47	25.37 ± 3.83	15.72 ± 6.03	22.30 ± 4.41	25.97 ± 5.14

Table 9.3: Percentage of time spent in the different execution states during simulation runtime.

Table 9.3 lists the proportion of time after initialization that was spent in the different states for simulations with ID-based partitioning. We can see that with increasing numbers of LPs, the time spent executing events decreased. As expected, the time spent on exchanging events between LPs increased only moderately with larger LP count. Null message sending overhead increased super-linearly, yet only accounted for a small proportion of the simulation runtime. In all distributed runs, a large amount of time was spent in the idle state. For 1 LP, the idle state was comprised completely of time measurement overheads, which accounted for less than 2% of the simulation runtime, indicating that in the distributed runs, the time spent in the idle state was indeed dominated by waiting for local events to become safe.

9.3.2 Synchronization Efficiency

In the previous section, we have seen that in large distributed simulations, the logical processes spent a significant proportion of time waiting for events to become safe to execute. In this section, we analyze the efficiency of our implementation of the null message algorithm. To this end, we propose two novel variants of existing metrics that determine the efficiency of conservative synchronization.

A logical process in a parallel or distributed simulation using Null Message Algorithm alternates between two states: waiting for local events to become safe, and the execution of safe events. The identification of safe events is performed based on information received from remote logical processes, either via shared memory or a network. In the commonly used null message algorithm, each logical process sends messages containing its earliest output time (*EOT*), which is the earliest possible timestamp of an event created by the EOT's sender for the LP that receives the EOT.

Safe events are determined according to the metrics used by Bagrodia et al. [BT00]:

- *Lookahead (τ)*: the lowest possible delta between the timestamp of the event to be executed next by an LP and the timestamp of any locally created event to be executed on a remote LP (cf. Section 2.1).

- *Earliest Input Time (EIT)*: for each LP, the EIT is the earliest possible timestamp of an event that can be received from any remote LP.

- *Earliest Output Time (EOT)*: for each LP, the EOT is the earliest possible timestamp of the next locally created event to be executed on a remote LP. In the Null Message Algorithm, *null messages* containing the EOT are exchanged between LPs. If t_{i+1} is the timestamp of the next locally scheduled event, the EOT can be calculated as $\text{EOT} = \min(\text{EIT}, t_{i+1}) + \tau$ (cf. Figure 9.6). The EIT can be determined from the minimum of all other LPs' EOT.

In the distributed PeerSim implementation, each LP progresses through simulated time as follows: local events are executed in non-decreasing timestamp order until the earliest local event has a timestamp larger than the EIT. Then, the LP determines the local EOT and, in case the EOT has changed compared to the most recently broadcasted value, sends a new null message to all remote LPs. The LP blocks until a message is received from a remote LP. Then, the above process is repeated.

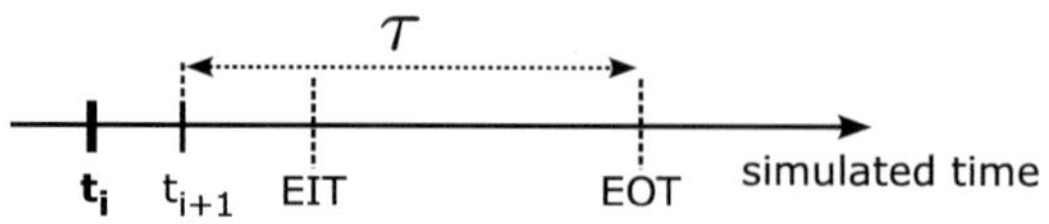

Figure 9.6: An LP determines its EOT by considering the timestamps of the earliest possible incoming remote event and of the next locally scheduled event. If the earliest of these events will trigger the creation of a remote event, given the lookahead τ, the lowest possible timestamp of the new event is $\text{EOT} := \min(\text{EIT}, t_{i+1}) + \tau$.

High simulation performance is achieved when logical processes spend a large proportion of wall-clock time executing events instead of waiting. Since only events covered by the current EIT are safe to be executed, the EIT should therefore be as large as possible. There are two aspects affecting the EIT of a logical process: the first aspect is the calculation of the remote logical processes' EOTs. In network simulations, frequently the lookahead value used for EOT calculation is the minimum link latency in the network. However, by exploiting knowledge of the network model it can be possible to determine larger lookahead values (cf. Section 2.3.1). The second aspect is the time at which EOTs are sent and received by the logical processes. Consequently, a number of strategies have been proposed in the literature to decide when null messages are sent during simulation [BS88].

Considering the timeline of a logical process LP_A depicted in Figure 9.7 in a distributed simulation using two LPs. The *EIT distance* is the delta between the current EIT and the LP's current point in simulated time. LP_A is currently idle, waiting for its EIT of $t_0 + 100ms$ to advance beyond any of the locally scheduled events so they become safe to execute (1.). Now, LP_B updates its EOT to $t_0 + 200ms$ and LP_A can start executing local events (2.). Finally, LP_A receives a remote event from LP_B with a timestamp of $t_0 + 250ms$ (3.). As we can see, at 1. it would have been possible for LP_A to start executing local events right away without violating timestamp order. Recall that the EOT is a lower bound on the timestamp of any event which may be created for a remote LP. An obvious question is then: *how tight is this lower bound?* We can consider the unnecessarily large waiting time of LP_A as an effect of the insufficient *quality* of the EOT calculated by B. We introduce the term *EOT quality* and define it intuitively as follows: **the EOT quality is the average proportion of simulated time until an actual remote event is received that is covered by a previously received EOT**. An EOT quality of 100% corresponds to perfect synchronization between LPs, i.e., LPs are able to exactly predict the timestamp of the next incoming remote event and can execute all prior safe events immediately. This situation is established artificially in performance evaluations using the Ideal Simulation Protocol [JB96, BT00] (cf. Section 2.2). In contrast, an EOT quality of 0% will not allow the simulation to progress at all. As we are interested in the average quality of the EOT over the course of a simulation run, we sample the EOT distance periodically during simulation runtime by storing remote EOT distances received in the most recent null messages. When the next remote event by each remote LP is received, the stored EOT distance is divided by the distance of the remote event's timestamp from the reference point in simulated time. In our example, the quality of EOT_B at 1. is $100ms/250ms = 40\%$. The EOT quality indicates how efficiently the lookahead available in the simulation model using a given partitioning scheme is determined *and communicated* to other LPs. A related metric is the lookahead ratio introduced by Fujimoto [Fuj88] and a similar metric proposed by Preiss et al. [PL90], the null message inverse lookahead ratio (NILAR). The lookahead ratio relates the average time increment between an LP's events to the lookahead, without

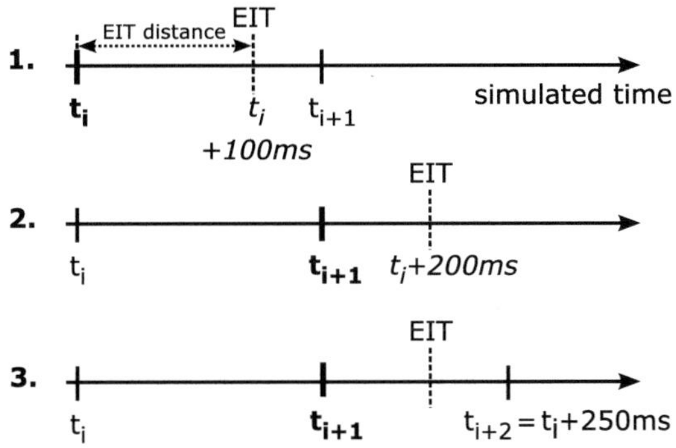

Figure 9.7: Chronological sequence of activities performed by LP_A as an example for waiting times due to synchronization. LP_A waits for its EIT to advance (1.) before executing further events (2.). At $t_i + 250ms$, a remote event arrives from LP_B (3.).

considering null messages. The NILAR applies the same idea to the lookahead used in null messages. Both metrics are determined from the perspective of the LP *sending* events and null messages. However, our aim is to study the reasons for idle times in the distributed simulation. Since an LP is idle whenever there are no safe events according to the EOTs received from other LPs, the EOT quality is calculated from the perspective of an LP *receiving* an EOT and sampled over wall-clock time. This way, in addition to considering the lookahead calculation itself, the EOT quality takes into account the efficiency of the null message sending strategy.

We will now give a more formal definition of the EOT and EIT quality metrics. Given the current wall-clock time τ and the current position t_i in simulated time, we define the *EOT distance* as the delta between the last EOT received from the remote logical process LP_r and the current position in simulated time: $d_{\mathrm{EOT}}(\tau, LP_r) = \mathrm{EOT}(\tau, LP_r) - t_i(\tau)$. Sampling the EOT quality at τ in wall-clock time in a logical process LP_l is comprised of the following steps.

1. LP_l's current position in simulated time $t_i(\tau)$ is stored together with all current EOT distances $d_{\mathrm{EOT}}(\tau, LP_r)$.

2. For *each* remote logical process LP_r, when the next remote event with timestamp t_{r,LP_r} is received, the corresponding EOT quality is calculated as

$$Q_{\mathrm{EOT}} = \frac{d_{\mathrm{EOT}}(\tau, LP_r)}{t_{r,LP_r} - t_i(\tau)}$$

In simulations with more than two LPs, another metric becomes useful: EIT quality is the proportion of simulated time until a remote event is received that is covered by a previous EIT. The EIT quality shows the effect of aggregating the remote LPs' EOTs. Sampling is performed as follows.

1. LP_l's current position in simulated time $t_i(\tau)$ is stored together with the current EIT distance $d_{\mathrm{EIT}}(\tau) = EIT(\tau) - t_i$.

2. When the next remote event with timestamp t_r is received from *any* of the remote LPs, the EIT quality is calculated as

$$Q_{\text{EIT}} = \frac{d_{\text{EIT}}(\tau)}{t_r - t_i(\tau)}$$

The proposed metrics are based on two previous works: the *lookahead ratio* was introduced by Fujimoto [Fuj88], while a similar metrics, the null message inverse lookahead ratio was proposed by Preiss et al. [PL90]. The metrics are calculated from the perspective of the LP *sending* future events and are averaged over a number of samples taken at the point when a null message is sent.

In contrast, our proposed metrics take the perspective of the *receiver* of future messages. The receiver perspective allows us to determine how efficiently the lookahead is communicated among the LPs, i.e., to what extent the parallelism extracted from a simulation model by a given LP can actually be utilized by the other LPs. In addition, we sample at a fixed rate in wall-clock time to capture whether synchronization messages arrive frequently enough to maintain a sufficiently accurate knowledge of the remote LPs' progress.

To investigate the previously identified idle times in the distributed simulations of the Kademlia-based network, we sampled the EOT and EIT quality once every second of wall-clock time. The measurement results are listed in Table 9.4. On average, a maximum of 39.43% of the simulated time up to the next remote event was covered by a received EOT. As the EIT is calculated as the minimum of all received EOTs, even less time was covered by the EIT, with a decrease in quality for larger numbers of LPs. For 16 LPs, the measured EIT covered only 9.92% of the simulated time until the next remote event was received. There are two possible causes for low EOT and EIT quality: either the LPs do not communicate their EOT frequently enough, or the lookahead calculation does not exploit the concurrency in the simulation model sufficiently. To determine which of the explanations applies, we maximized the null message sending frequency by sending null messages on each change of the EOT, instead of only when there were no local safe events. With more frequent null messages, we achieved an EOT and EIT quality of 46.88% for simulations using two LPs. Simulation runtime decreased from 6315s to 5340s. Idle time decreased from 25.37% to 18.48%. However, for all simulations using more than two LPs, the overheads of a more frequent broadcasting of null messages increased the simulation runtime compared to the less eager strategy.

In addition to varying the null message sending frequency, the EOT and EIT quality can also be increased by improving the lookahead calculation. In our simulation model implementation, link latencies in milliseconds are drawn from a uniform distribution on the interval $\{10, 11, \ldots, 200\}$. We therefore use 10 ms as the fixed lookahead, which covers only a small proportion of the available maximum lookahead in the model. We expect that applying methods for dynamic lookahead calculation could further improve simulation performance.

LPs	Q_{EOT} [%]	Q_{EIT} [%]
2	32.30 ± 2.20	32.30 ± 2.20
4	39.43 ± 0.45	26.94 ± 4.61
8	31.33 ± 3.38	17.89 ± 1.79
16	23.96 ± 5.26	9.92 ± 0.56

Table 9.4: EOT and EIT quality when varying the number of LPs.

9.4 Conclusions

In this section, we showed, contrary to some previous results from the literature, that simulations of peer-to-peer networks can benefit substantially from distributed simulation. On the example of a large-scale peer-to-peer network based on the Kademlia protocol, we observed substantial runtime reductions and near-linear reductions in memory usage per execution node. A simple partitioning strategy based on the Kademlia routing table structure was shown to strongly reduce the communication overhead between execution nodes, while a partitioning strategy based on the geographical position of simulated nodes increases the available lookahead. Considering the low increase in lookahead with larger numbers of logical processes and the need for dynamic lookahead calculation with the geographical approach, a partitioning based on the routing table seems clearly preferable. In the context of future work, studies of further peer-to-peer network protocols could clarify whether the achieved performance gains are specific to the Kademlia protocol, or whether similarly efficient partitioning strategies can be found for other peer-to-peer networks as well.

When considering the achieved speedup of 6.0 when using 16 logical processes, it must be noted that each logical process occupies a full execution node with 16 processor cores each. Hence, the efficiency of the distributed simulation, i.e., the speedup achieved in relation to the number of allocated cores, is relatively low. Therefore, while the distributed simulation enables simulation of large-scale networks beyond the limitations in the typical memory capacity of individual execution nodes, the reduction in runtime through distributing the simulation must be weighed against the substantial increase in the required hardware resources.

10
GPU-Based Parallel Simulation

Traditional CPU-based conservatively synchronized parallel and distributed simulations can be subject to limitations in the number of logical processes: in parallel simulations using shared memory, only the typically small number of available processor cores in a single execution node can be used. In distributed simulations, the large costs associated with physical communication between execution nodes can cause highest efficiency to be achieved with modest numbers of logical processes. In addition, considering the frequently comparatively low runtime reductions of discrete-event simulations in comparison with highly parallelizable scientific codes, it can be difficult to justify the use of large numbers of execution nodes for a network simulation study.

Modern many-core devices are comprised of hundreds or thousands of cores with access to shared memory. Hence, many-core devices promise to enable parallel simulations that exploit a much larger portion of the concurrency of a given model, while allowing for comparatively low-latency interaction between cores. The most prominent example of many-core devices are graphics processing units (GPUs), which compared to CPUs achieve enormous performance improvements with respect to highly data-parallel computations. However, for computational tasks that display limited parallelism or contain highly divergent code paths, CPUs tend to outperform GPUs. Hence, it is important to select a suitable hardware platform for simulation depending on the properties of the simulation model.

There are two fundamental approaches to GPU-based acceleration of discrete-event simulations: *hybrid CPU-GPU-based* approaches executing some or all of the simulated events on a GPU, but rely on a CPU to handle the event management logic. In contrast, *fully GPU-based* approaches perform both the event execution as well as the event management on the GPU. Hybrid CPU-GPU-based simulation has multiple advantages compared to fully GPU-based approaches:

- Only parts of the simulation model must be developed on the GPU. Although the facilities for programming on GPUs have improved in the past years, the efforts required to achieve an efficient and correct model implementation may still exceed the efforts required for implementation in a familiar CPU-based environment. In case a CPU-based implementation of a model already exists, it is possible to create a GPU formulation of only the most computationally expensive parts of the model.

- Since hybrid approaches can make use of the computational and memory resources of the host system as well as of additional nodes in a cluster, the memory limitations of a GPU can easily be overcome to achieve larger simulation scale.

However, by design, hybrid approaches require data transfers between CPU and GPU memory. If only a small amount of computation is performed in between data transfers, the significant costs of data transfers limit the performance gains through parallel processing. For instance, the PCI Express 3.0 x16 bus that is commonly used for the data transfer between CPU and GPU has a maximum theoretical throughput of about 15.75 GB/s. If this throughput is achieved, even if latency is not considered, a simulation model that requires a transfer of 100 MB of data after each GPU-based computation can perform at most about 160 such computations per second. For comparison, the maximum memory throughput between the onboard graphics memory of an NVIDIA GTX 660 Ti and the GPU itself is about 144 GB/s. Hence, fine-grained computational tasks may benefit strongly from reductions in the frequency of CPU-GPU interactions. In fully GPU-based simulations, the CPU-GPU-interaction can be restricted to the initialization and termination phases of a simulation run.

In this chapter, we study the use of GPUs for the acceleration of simulations on the example of the network models **Wireless$_B$**, **Kademlia$_C$** and **PHOLD**. Since the modeled networks differ substantially in their structure and behavior, we present fundamentally different simulator architectures suitable for models comprised of coarse-grained and fine-grained computational tasks.

The remainder of the chapter is structured as follows: first, we give an introduction into the use of GPUs for general-purpose computations. Subsequently, we propose and evaluate hybrid CPU-GPU-based architectures that exploit the data parallelism in detailed wireless network simulations. Finally, we present a fully GPU-based simulator that reduces overhead by executing all parts of the simulation on a commodity GPU and that dynamically balances the degree of parallelism and associated overheads at runtime. The descriptions of the hybrid and fully GPU-based simulators are based on [AMH11] and [AH14].

10.1 General-Purpose Computation on Graphics Processing Units

In the past two decades GPUs have found widespread use in order to handle the enormous computational demands of rendering three-dimensional graphics, most prominently in the context of video games. Graphics processing tasks frequently involve performing the same operation on enormous numbers of pixels or vertices and are hence massively parallel tasks. The GPU hardware is optimized to handle *data-parallel* tasks, i.e., independent but identical operations performed on large numbers of data elements. Today, GPUs are increasingly capable of general-purpose computations and are used to accelerate computational tasks in audio processing [SVS11], biology [DYB10], medicine [JLL⁺10], cryptography [SG08], and astronomy [HHSS08].

In this section, we briefly illustrate the heritage of general-purpose computation on GPUs by giving an overview of the steps performed by a GPU when rendering a three-dimensional scene. Subsequently, we introduce the programming model used when developing GPU code and the limitations incurred by the GPU's architecture.

10.1.1 The Graphics Pipeline

Traditional GPUs employed a fixed-function graphics pipeline to handle the computational stages required for rendering a three-dimensional scene on a two-dimensional display. Luebke et al. [LH07] give an overview of the computational stages required for rendering:

1. **Transformation:** To support hierarchical scenes, each object can be described with respect to a local coordinate system. In the first computational stage, the GPU transforms the each objects' coordinates to place all objects in a global coordinate system.
2. **Lighting:** Lighting is applied to each triangle, commonly requiring operations on vectors that represent the triangle's position and alignment in relation to the light sources and the viewer of the scene.
3. **Camera Simulation:** The triangles are projected onto the two-dimensional display using matrix-vector multiplication.
4. **Rasterization:** In this stage, the visible triangles overlapping each pixel are determined for each pixel independently.
5. **Texturing:** Images are placed on objects to increase the realism of the scene. To determine the color of a pixel to be drawn on screen requires, at minimum, one access to the image in graphics memory.
6. **Hidden Surfaces:** When drawing each pixel to the display, a depth buffer allows the GPU to determine which of the triangles overlapping a given pixel is the closest to the viewer and should hence determine the color of the pixel.

A defining characteristic of each of the stages is their large degree of data parallelism, i.e., the large number of identical operations performed on different elements of data independently. Initially, the rendering stages were implemented in GPUs in a pipeline of fixed-function components. Since the computational demands on the various parts of the pipeline can vary immensely, GPUs have since evolved to employ general-purpose processors, so-called *unified shaders*. Unified shaders are able to be assigned any of the steps required for rendering depending on the current computational demands, enabling a higher utilization of the GPU.

Initially, researchers leveraged the processing capabilities of GPUs by transforming non-graphical problem into graphical problems. Once the required computations had been performed, the results were transformed back into the problem domain. However, today's GPUs support general-purpose computations directly and can be programmed in high-level programming languages. Some early limitations, such as substantial performance degradations on random accesses to graphics memory and huge costs of independent branching between cores, have since been lifted. Still, GPU acceleration provides the largest benefits when applied to problems that are highly data-parallel.

10.1.2 NVIDIA CUDA

In this section, we give a brief overview of the technical details relevant for development targeting GPUs. In the remainder of the chapter, we will repeatedly refer to technical details of NVIDIA CUDA devices. Hence, we base our overview on NVIDIA CUDA terminology and hardware. The terminology used in the OpenCL and AMD APP contexts is largely analogous and is subject to similar hardware constraints. The description of the hardware and programming model is based on the CUDA programming guide[1].

A CUDA hardware device contains a number of streaming multiprocessors (SMs), each comprising a number of CUDA cores. Computational tasks are organized in thread blocks that are assigned to SMs by a hardware scheduler. Threads are executed in groups of 32 called warps that operate in lockstep, i.e., all threads of a warp execute the same instruction in parallel. If there is branching in the code executed by threads within a single warp, the individual branches are processed sequentially.

Threads have access to various types of memory. Here, we briefly describe the types of memory used in our work. A set of low-latency registers is available to each thread. Thread interactions within a warp can be performed in a low-latency shared memory region. Larger amounts of data can be held in global memory, which has the largest access latency: on recent NVIDIA graphics card models, an access to global memory requires 200-400 clock cycles, whereas executing a single instruction requires about 11 cycles. Accesses to global memory are performed in 256 bit transactions and are cached in a low-latency memory region. Hence, consecutive access to neighboring elements of data results in frequent cache hits. Further, if neighboring threads access neighboring data elements in parallel, the number of transactions can be reduced significantly. The large effects of memory access patterns makes the arrangement of data in graphics memory a common focus of performance optimizations.

Further, the hardware scheduler aims to hide memory access latencies by exchanging active warps in case of memory accesses. Of course, efficient latency hiding requires sufficiently large numbers of threads. Typically, GPU programs schedule many more threads than the number of hardware threads of the GPU.

GPU programs, so-called kernels, are executed using API calls from the CPU context. Kernel input and output data is transferred over the PCI-E bus. As the data transfer bandwidth of the PCI-E bus is significantly lower than the bandwidth between the GPU and graphics memory, frequent data transfers can limit the performance of CUDA programs. Additional overhead is incurred by the exchange of the execution control between the GPU and the CPU. An overlapping of computations with memory transfers and subsequent kernel launches can be applied to ameliorate this issue.

CUDA hardware is classified by its compute capability (CC), a version number indicating a device's feature set. To allow for interaction between computations of different threads, barrier primitives synchronize memory accesses between threads of *the same block*. Devices starting with CC 3.5 additionally support memory access synchronization between threads of *multiple blocks* through so-called dynamic parallelism. Devices prior to CC 3.5 support only **API-based** inter-block synchronization: when returning the control flow from the GPU to the CPU, all previous writes to graphics memory are guaranteed to be visible to all threads during future kernel executions. Hence, a need for frequent synchronization of memory accesses is reflected by repeated control flow

[1] `https://docs.nvidia.com/cuda/cuda-c-programming-guide/`

exchanges between the GPU and the CPU. Xiao et al. presented a method enabling **software-based** inter-block synchronization from GPU code independently of dynamic parallelism [XF10]. When calling a new barrier function, a global variable is incremented atomically by each block until all blocks wait at the barrier. Then, the barrier function terminates and the threads of all blocks can access any data written to memory prior to the barrier call. To avoid deadlocks, only as many thread blocks as there are SMs can be scheduled with this method, allowing for up to $\#SMs \times 1024$ threads with CC 2.0 and above. Without software-based synchronization, it is possible to schedule up to 65535^3 blocks for CC 2.0, and up to $(2^{31} - 1)^3$ blocks for devices with CC 3.0.

10.2 Related Work

A number of previous works considered the use of GPUs for the acceleration of discrete-event simulations. In the following, we distinguish between two categories of approaches: *hybrid CPU-GPU simulators* use the CPU for event management, but transfer some or all events to the GPU for execution. In contrast, *fully GPU-based simulators* perform both event management and event execution on the GPU. In the following, we also briefly discuss works applying GPU-based simulations outside the discrete-event modeling paradigm. Approaches applicable to discrete-event simulations are analyzed in more detail to enable a comparison with our proposed approach.

10.2.1 Hybrid CPU-GPU-Based Simulation

In 2007, Xu et al. [XB07] presented a hybrid CPU-GPU platform for high fidelity network modeling. Events are aggregated by a CPU-based scheduler for parallel execution on a GPU. Substantial speedup is achieved for a fluid-based model of TCP that requires the solving of differential equations and a model of adaptive antenna arrays for wireless communication. However, contrary to our experiments, no clear benefit was observed for an implementation of the Viterbi algorithm for error correction, possibly due to limitations in the computational capabilities of GPUs at the time the study was conducted.

Park et al. proposed a hybrid CPU-GPU-based simulation approach that relaxes the synchronization with respect to simulated time by allowing events within a range of timestamps to be executed in parallel [PF08]. The authors note the significant adverse impact of data transfers between graphics and host memory on the simulation performance. The approach was later refined for fully GPU-based simulation. We discuss the fully GPU-based variant of the simulator in detail in the next section.

Bai et al. studied the use of GPUs for raytracing in the context of wireless network simulation [BN08]. The authors combine multiple CPUs and GPUs to further increase performance.

In the context of his diploma thesis, Andelfinger ported three computationally expensive signal processing algorithms to a GPU in order to accelerate a sequential CPU-based wireless network simulator [And11]. In Section 10.3, we build on this previous work by proposing and comparing architectures for an efficient coupling between a CPU-based sequential simulator and a GPU.

In 2012, Kunz et al. [KSGW12] proposed a hybrid CPU-GPU simulator focusing on parameter studies. Their approach exploits concurrency on the level of independent events within each *individual* parametrization of a simulation, as well as on the level of independent events across *multiple* parametrizations. The events to be executed on the GPU are selected by a CPU-based scheduler. Events are sorted according to their event types to reduce divergent code paths within each warp. Their use of parallelism across multiple simulation runs can be considered to increase the "throughput" in receiving simulation results, i.e., the number of simulation results obtained per unit of wall-clock time. In contrast, our work aims to reduce the "latency" in receiving simulation results, i.e., the time until a particular simulation result is obtained. The latter may be of particular interest in early exploratory phases of a simulation study, where iterative changes are made to the network model and scenario.

In 2013, Zou et al. [ZLC+13] proposed techniques for time-stepped epidemic simulations on GPU clusters, while still executing some parts of the model on CPUs. Low-latency shared memory on the GPU is utilized to implement a software-based caching mechanism.

Romdhanne et al. [BR13] proposed master-worker schemes for large-scale network simulations using heterogeneous platforms comprised of CPUs and GPUs. A CPU-based master process dispatches events to the available processing elements depending on the current computational load.

Raghav et al. [RRM+15] presented mechanisms to execute simulations of heterogeneous hardware using a hybrid CPU-GPU approach. While a model of a general-purpose CPU is executed using a CPU-based emulator, a many-core coprocessor is simulated using a GPU. A proposed synchronization scheme reduces the frequency of the costly interactions between the CPU and the GPU.

10.2.2 Fully GPU-Based Simulation

In addition to executing events in parallel on a GPU, fully GPU-based simulators perform all event management tasks on the GPU. Hence, no significant CPU-GPU interaction is required during a simulation run, enabling GPUs to efficiently execute simulations models with particularly fine-grained computations.

In the following, we cover existing works targeting the GPU-based execution of three classes of simulation models: models that can efficiently be executed using fixed increments in simulated time, discrete-event models in the context of simulation-based verification of electronic design, and discrete-event models of networks. While the approaches targeting the first two model categories cannot be easily applied to general discrete-event simulations, we analyze the approaches from the third category with respect to the time complexity of the proposed mechanisms in comparison with our proposed approach.

Simulations Using Fixed Time Increment

Some GPU-based simulators focus on models that can efficiently be executed using state changes at fixed increments in simulated time. While fixed-increment simulations can be considered a special case of discrete-event simulation [Law14], events may be highly dispersed in simulated time, so that fixed-increment approaches consider many time steps that do not affect the modeled system's state. In such cases, parallelized fixed-increment approaches must be expected to only expose a small proportion of the concurrency that is present in the model.

In 2008, Perumalla et al. studied the challenges and opportunities of agent-based simulations on GPUs, noting the substantial impact of the locality of agent interactions on the simulation performance [PA08]. The authors proposed mechanisms to efficiently perform operations commonly used in agent-based simulation models on GPUs. Depending on the considered models, the authors achieved a simulation speedup of up to multiple orders of magnitude in comparison with a CPU-based sequential implementation.

In 2008 and 2009, Perumalla et al. presented GPU-based approaches to simulate vehicular mobility models, enabling large-scale simulations comprised of millions of vehicles and achieving simulation progress substantially faster than real-time [Per08, PAYS09].

In 2010, Aaby et al. presented a latency-hiding scheme that replicates parts of a grid of interacting simulated entities to multiple processing elements of a multi-GPU cluster or CPU-based multi-core cluster [APS10]. Their latency-hiding scheme performs some computations redundantly across processing elements to reduce the frequency of synchronization between processing elements.

In 2012, Seok et al. [SK12] proposed a GPU-based execution scheme for cellular models formulated in the discrete-event systems specification (DEVS) formalism [ZKP00]. The insertion of new events in each cell's buffer is performed as follows: each thread is mapped to one cell and iterates over all other cells that can affect the current cell. If an event targeting the current cell is found, the event is delivered to the current cell. This event insertion mechanism requires no explicit mutual exclusion operations. However, the approach applies to models where each event creates at most a single new event, which is not generally the case in discrete-event models. Further, since the approach does not utilize model lookahead, only events that share the earliest timestamp in the simulation are executed in parallel in each iteration.

In 2013, Jin et al. studied the use of multi-GPU systems for time-stepped simulations of information propagation over complex networks [JTL+13]. Due to the large costs of synchronization between multiple GPUs, the benefit of utilizing more than one GPU depends strongly on the simulated network.

Simulations in Electronic Design

Simulation is an important building block in the verification of electronic designs, e.g., in the context of developing embedded systems. Models of electronic designs can benefit substantially from CPU-based parallel discrete-event simulation approaches (e.g., [ADM94]). We discuss some of the works from this field that considered the use of GPUs for simulation.

Although many models of electronic designs can be considered to follow the discrete-event modeling approach, GPU-based parallel simulation approaches perform optimizations that rely strongly on the properties specific to the structure and behavior of models of electronic designs. Hence, only some of the ideas from these approaches can be applied directly to general discrete-event simulations.

A number of previous works have considered the use of GPUs for accelerating discrete-event simulations in the context of electronic design automation. An overview of existing approaches is given by Nanjundappa in [NKPS12]. Some authors have focused on partitioning strategies in order to maximize the opportunities for parallel processing on GPUs [VCBF12, BCB+13]. Vinco et al. make use of the fact that in some simulations using the system description language SystemC it is possible to determine a static parallel scheduling strategy prior to a simulation run, rendering the use of a synchronization algorithm at simulation runtime unnecessary.

A GPU-based simulation approach using variable lookahead was presented in the context of hardware verification [ZWD11, QD11]. In this approach, LPs represent logic gates. Similarly to the null message algorithm (cf. Section 2.1), each LP can have a different lookahead window. The properties of the considered simulation model of logic gates enables simplified LP interactions: each logic gate has a number of input pins. Since due to the model's properties, events arrive at each input pin in non-decreasing timestamp order, each LP simply selects the earliest event at any of the input pins to determine the lower bound on the local lookahead window. Contrary to this case, general discrete-event models provide no guarantees of a particular ordering of events arriving at an LP.

In general, the discussed works exploit the specific properties of models of hardware designs to maximize performance. Hence, the approaches are not directly applicable to the general case of discrete-event simulation.

Discrete-Event Network Simulations

Some authors previously considered the use of GPUs to execute discrete-event network simulations. A number of the approaches from this category can be compared directly with our proposed approach. Still, in some cases, assumptions are made about the simulation model that limit the efficiency or applicability in the general case.

The need for explicit synchronization of accesses to graphics memory by separate GPU threads makes synchronous algorithms a natural approach when implementing parallel discrete-event simulation on GPUs. In line with this observation and our proposed approach, most previous works propose event management and synchronization mechanisms closely related to the YAWNS algorithm (cf. Section 2.1).

Ideally, large numbers of events are executed in parallel in each iteration of the algorithm, one event per GPU thread. The key distinction between the different approaches lies in the way the next per-node event is identified, which is reflected by fundamentally different layouts of the event data in graphics memory.

In most cases, the performance benefits of GPU-based simulation approaches have been evaluated on the example of the PHOLD benchmark model (cf. Section 3.4) and closed queuing network simulations. In both model types, the total number of events in existence remains constant over the course of the simulation. Since each event e_1 creates exactly one new event, the new event can simply be stored in the previous memory location of e_1. However, when considering arbitrary models, events can create zero or arbitrarily many new events. Then, the placement of a new event in graphics memory cannot be determined in this simple fashion. Instead, an unused memory location to store the new event must be determined dynamically. In case multiple GPU threads can create events at the same time, event placement poses a particular challenge, since a unique location must be found for each event.

In 2006, Perumalla [Per06] discussed possible realizations of a fully GPU-based discrete-event simulator. The proposed execution method skips unnecessary time steps of a time-stepped execution by advancing the current simulation time to the lowest timestamp among all queued events. More generic approaches to DES on GPUs are discussed, yet could not be implemented due to limitations in the opportunities for addressing input and output memory elements using the GPU hardware of the time. The proposed approach exhibits high speedup for a diffusion model compared to a CPU-based implementation, although only the concurrency given by events with identical timestamps is exploited.

In 2010, Park et al. presented a fully GPU-based simulation framework that reduces the frequency of synchronization by considering all events within a configurable tolerance interval in simulated time as occurring simultaneously and by processing these events in parallel [PF10, PF11]. Based on queuing theory, the authors provide upper bounds for the introduced statistical error when simulating queuing networks. If the approach is applied to a model that provides a non-zero lookahead τ, the tolerance interval can be set to τ to accomplish a synchronization scheme similar to YAWNS and without statistical error. Park et al. propose the use of a single unsorted future event list (FEL) that holds all events.

In the previously discussed works, FELs are represented by linear arrays in graphics memory. In contrast, He et al. proposed a generic parallel priority queue for many-core architectures, enabling fine-grained parallel insertion and deletion by the threads of a GPU [HAP12], citing discrete-event simulations as a potential use case. The proposed queue enables combined insertion and deletion of multiple values. Since the authors achieve large speedup compared to a sequential priority queue implementation on a CPU, their approach might be an interesting subject for future research in discrete-event network simulations on GPUs. Since events cannot be executed based on their timestamp alone but must also be executed in per-node timestamp order, the question whether the parallel priority queue should be partitioned according to the events' node assignment might be of particular interest.

In 2013, Tang et al. proposed a synchronous conservative synchonization algorithm for fully GPU-based simulation [WYF13, TY13] similar to the YAWNS algorithm (cf. Section 2.1). The frequency of parallel reductions to determine a new lookahead window is reduced by evaluating the system state after each event execution. If some events from a set of candidate events become safe through the previous event execution, these events can be executed without calculating a new lookahead window. The authors compare their approach with two basic variants: calculating a new lookahead window after each execution, and calculating a new lookahead window only once there are no events left in the lookahead window. The latter approach corresponds with the YAWNS algorithm. Events are stored in a global unordered FEL that is segmented into columns. For each execution, each thread is assigned to a unique column according to a stochastic function. The assignment avoids the need for explicit mutual exclusion when inserting new events. Further, the stochastic nature of the column assignment avoids uneven utilization of columns if there are imbalances in the event counts of different simulated entities. Finally, the assignment function aims to increase the efficiency of memory accesses by assigning threads of the same block to neighboring columns.

Also in 2013, Sang et al. proposed a simulator based on procedures provided by NVIDIA's Thrust library of parallel algorithms [SLRK13]. The authors focus on closed queuing networks, i.e., event locations in memory can be reused without further considerations. Their approach uses a global FEL on which parallel reductions are performed to determine the current lookahead window. Now, a stream compaction operation (e.g., [HLJ+13]) is performed to collect the safe events in a target array. Stream compaction is performed in two steps: first, the new index of each element in the target array is determined using a parallel prefix sum operation. Then, the events are transferred to their target index. If more than one event arrives at a simulated service facility, a pre-defined order is used to determine which event is executed. If the service facility is busy, newly arrived events are inserted into a local waiting queue in non-decreasing timestamp order.

The approach does not consider simulations comprised of varying numbers of events and hence does not address general discrete-event simulations.

Li et al. [LCT13] proposed an optimistic fully GPU-based simulator using an "event-parallel" approach: all events of the simulation are executed at the same time, irrespective of their timestamps and causal relationships. In subsequent steps, the simulator checks for violations of the correctness of the simulation and iteratively cancels and re-executes events to achieve a complete and correct simulation. Since all events must be created prior to executing the simulation, the approach seems not to be easily applicable to general discrete-event simulations.

In 2014, Zhen et al. proposed a simulation kernel for joint CPU-GPU-based simulation of large-scale agent-based simulations using a GPU-based event management mechanism [ZGGB14]. In their execution scheme, each agent in the simulation holds a local FEL. Hence, during the parallel reduction to determine the minimum timestamp of the simulation, only the earliest timestamp of each agent must be considered. Atomic operations are used to synchronize accesses when scheduling events for the agents. Subsequently, each thread inserts the events of a single agent into the agent's sorted FEL.

In 2015, Swenson presented an event management scheme for fully GPU-based simulation that uses a global sorted FEL [Swe15]. Their approach is evaluated with respect to the PHOLD model, allowing each new event to occupy the memory location of the event it is created by. Hence, the issue of efficiently identifying memory locations for new events, a solution for which is required to support general discrete-event simulations, is not addressed by their approach.

10.3 Hybrid CPU-GPU-Based Simulation of Wireless Networks

The most common approach to apply GPUs to general computations is to utilize the GPU as a coprocessor of the host CPU. The sequential portion of an application is executed on a CPU, while highly data parallel computations are executed on a GPU. An advantage of the coprocessing approach is given by the possibility to apply both the CPU and the GPU to computations that can be executed most efficiently by the respective component. A disadvantage is given by the costs of the frequent switches of control between the CPU and the GPU, and of the required data transfers between host memory and graphics memory, both of which can limit the performance increases compared to a solely CPU-based execution.

10.3.1 Proposed Simulator Architectures

In this section, we consider the GPU-as-coprocessor approach for detailed simulations of wireless networks as a base case for parallel simulation using GPUs. This type of simulations requires computationally expensive signal processing steps that exhibit large degrees of data parallelism and are therefore well-suited for GPU-based acceleration. We consider the network model **Wireless**$_{\mathbf{B}}$ introduced in Section 3.3. Our focus is on a suitable coupling of the CPU-based portion and the GPU-based portion of the simulation, so that large performance gains compared to a sequential

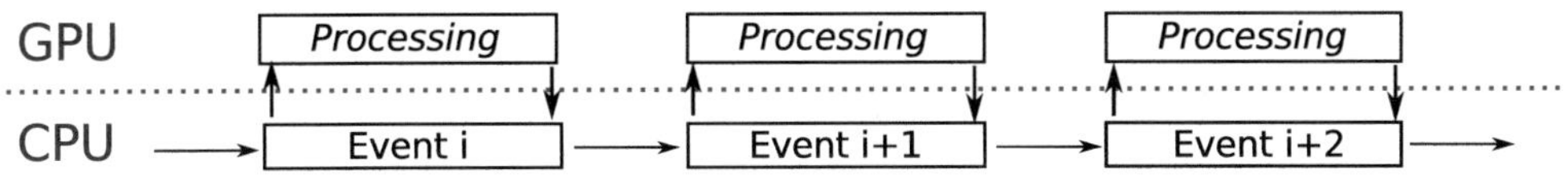

(a) Base architecture.

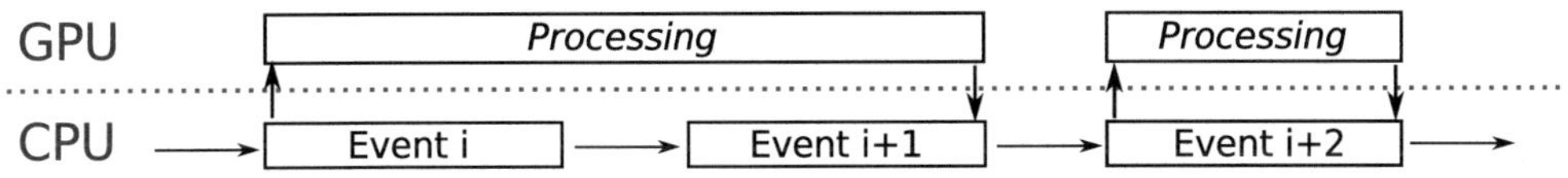

(b) Event aggregation.

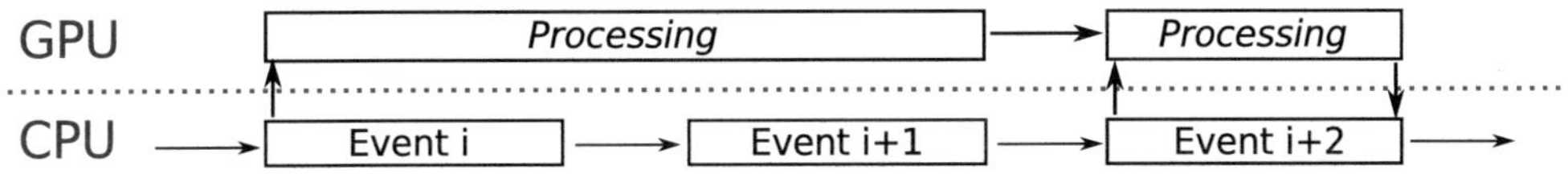

(c) Event aggregation and memory reuse.

Figure 10.1: Hybrid CPU-GPU-based simulation architectures

execution are achieved without requiring deep modifications of an existing CPU-based simulator architecture. We show that if a basic coprocessing approach is extended by classical parallel simulation mechanisms, substantial performance gains are achieved.

A basic approach for a hybrid CPU-GPU-based discrete-event simulation of such models is depicted in Figure 10.1a. Events are processed sequentially on the CPU. For time-consuming data-parallel tasks, input data is transferred to the graphics card's memory. Once the GPU finishes parallel processing of the task, the output data is transferred back to the host computer's main memory. This process is repeated for all data-parallel tasks associated with the event. A second and more efficient approach is based on the aggregation and parallel execution of identical tasks that belong to different but independent events (cf. Figure 10.1b). With this approach, multiple data transfers and context switches are reduced to only one transfer and one context switch. This approach can be optimized even further if the output of one event serves as the input of the next event, or if subsequent events operate on the same input data. Additional data transfers can then be avoiding by reusing data that has been transferred to the graphics card at an earlier stage (cf. Figure 10.1c).

10.3.2 Evaluation

As a basis for a performance evaluation, we used three computationally expensive signal processing algorithms that were ported for GPU-based execution in a work outside the scope of this dissertation [And11]. Here, we present the results of a subsequent study [AMH11] that compares the performance of different architectures for GPU-based coprocessing.

The considered algorithms are a simulation of channel effects using a Rayleigh fading model [Pro01], frame synchronization using autocorrelation of the wireless signal, and error correction using the Viterbi algorithm [Vit67]. For each considered algorithm, we measured the achieved speedup by execution on a ATI Radeon HD 5870 graphics card with 1600 cores compared to a sequential execution on a single core of an AMD Phenom II X6 1035T CPU. The algorithms are part of the **Wireless$_B$** model and operate on simulated packets with a payload of 500 bytes each. To analyze the conditions under which significant speedups can be observed, we vary the number of packets processed in parallel between 1 to 100, corresponding to 1 to 100 receivers. Figure 10.2 illustrates the speedup factors achieved by the parallelization. Across all three algorithms it is evident that speedups are marginal when only a small number of packets is processed in parallel. The benefit of GPU-based signal processing is increases substantially in case larger numbers of packets are processed in parallel. For instance, when processing 100 packets in parallel, we observed speedup factors of 59.1 for the computation of Rayleigh fading channel effects, 44.3 for frame synchronization and 27.0 for Viterbi decoding.

From the results, we conclude that a substantial speedup can be achieved using GPU-based signal processing. However, we identify a maximization of the amount of input data processed per GPU work cycle as a prerequisite for optimal performance.

To evaluate and compare the performance of the three simulator architectures of Section 10.3.1, we developed a simple hybrid CPU-GPU-based simulator that executes a synthetic benchmark model approximating the behavior of the **Wireless$_B$** model (cf. Section 3.3) by a chain of three simulation events associated with a single frame transmission and the corresponding receptions in a wireless network. Each event triggers one of the three signal processing algorithms, during which each algorithm uses the output of the previous algorithm as its input.

Figure 10.3 depicts the speedup achieved when implementing the GPU-based simulation architectures compared to a sequential execution on a CPU. The basic hybrid simulation yields a speedup factor of 1.5 independent of the number of receivers. This demonstrates the impact of overheads involved in frequent crossing of the CPU-GPU boundary. The event aggregation yields an overall speedup factor of 30.9 for 100 receivers. Elimination of redundant data transfers by memory reuse further increases the total speedup factor to 69.6 for 100 receivers.

10.3.3 Discussion

The results exposed substantial differences in the performance of the different architectures. Due to the overhead of the interaction between the host system and the GPU, a naïve coprocessing approach is insufficient to achieve a significant reduction in runtimes compared to a sequential CPU-based execution. Instead, it is necessary to consider multiple events in parallel to leverage inter-event parallelism as well as intra-event parallelism. Now, in order to maintain the correctness of the simulation, it is necessary to apply mechanisms of parallel simulation: for instance, a conservative synchronization approach can be used wherein a fixed lookahead value is determined according to the speed-of-light propagation of the wireless signal. Previous works have suggested the use of dynamic lookahead to unlock larger amounts of parallelism in wireless network simulations [PVM09].

All of the proposed architectures proposed in this section rely on the CPU for event management and to execute inherently sequential events. Hence, repeated switches of control and data transfers between CPU and GPU are necessary during simulation. Since the incurred overheads must be amortized by the acceleration in the execution of events, the proposed architectures are suited for simulations of network models with high data parallelism and large computational costs within individual events.

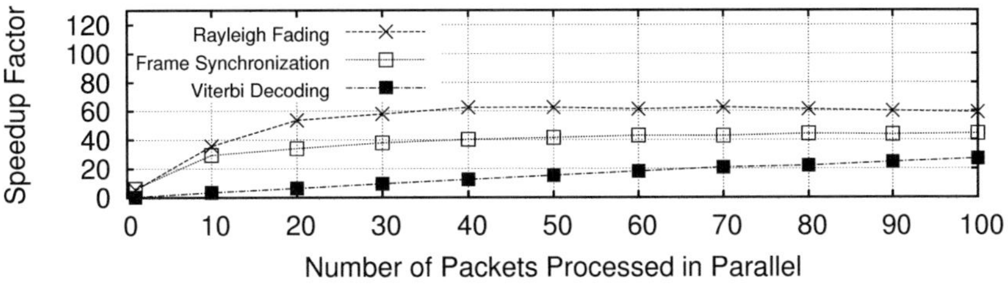

Figure 10.2: Speedup achieved by GPU-based parallelization of individual signal processing algorithms compared to sequential execution on a CPU.

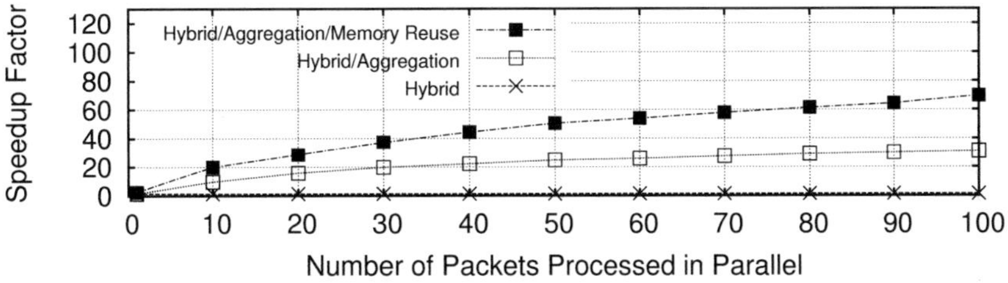

Figure 10.3: Speedup of the proposed hybrid CPU-GPU-based architectures when compared to sequential execution on a CPU.

10.4 Fully GPU-Based Parallel Simulation of Kademlia-Based Networks

In the previous section, we studied the GPU-based acceleration of simulation of network models with high per-event computation times and large data parallelism. Now, we investigate a suitable GPU-based simulator architecture for the peer-to-peer network **Kademlia**$_\text{C}$ described in Section 3.1, where each event is associated with only up to a few microseconds of computation time and where individual events contain no data parallelism. While we showed in Chapter 5 that the network model contains enormous amounts of concurrency, the small computational granularity and the high degree of communication between arbitrary simulated nodes creates a need for particularly low simulation overheads. In the following, we propose a fully GPU-based simulator architecture that avoids most of the control switch and data transfer overheads of a GPU-as-coprocessor approach. The fundamental architecture is depicted in Figure 10.4: significant CPU-GPU interaction is required only during initialization of the simulation and for retrieving the simulation results. The simulator design requires two main considerations: first, an efficient event management mechanism is required. Since the sequential performance of individual GPU cores is substantially lower than the performance of individual CPU cores, and access to graphics memory is optimized for high bandwidth instead of low latency, data structures used for CPU-based simulation may be

Figure 10.4: Fully GPU-based simulation.

inefficient on a GPU. Second, contrary to existing fully GPU-based simulation approaches, the proposed simulator architecture aggregates sets of simulated nodes into logical processes instead of considering each simulated node individually. We show that the aggregation substantially increases the simulation performance. However, the question of a suitable number of simulated nodes per logical process arises. On the one hand, smaller logical processes expose larger amounts of the network model's concurrency, but may leave many GPU threads idle if large workload imbalances exist between threads. Further, the costs of event management increase with larger numbers of logical processes. Hence, a balance must be found between the exploitation of concurrency of the network model and the resulting overheads.

10.4.1 Proposed Simulation Approach

The main challenge in parallel simulation is the synchronization between LPs. As in the YAWNS algorithm (cf. Section 2.1), the proposed simulator enforces timestamp order by alternating between two tasks:

1. *Selection*: from all events remaining to be executed, the simulator selects the set of *safe* events that can be executed without the possibility of causing a future violation of timestamp order.

2. *Execution*: the selected events are executed, potentially creating new events.

The steps are repeated until a termination criterion, e.g., the execution of a configured number of events, is satisfied. Executing these steps on a many-core GPU is associated with a number of challenges (C1-C4):

C1. Inter-block synchronization of memory accesses is required frequently during simulation runtime. However, on the GPU, synchronization of memory accesses between thread blocks is a costly operation.

C2. Dynamic allocation of memory from the GPU context is expensive, suggesting the use of statically allocated memory regions. However, if transfers between graphics and main memory are to be avoided, the limited amount of memory available must be managed so that it can hold the shifting simulation state.

C3. Graphics memory is optimized for high throughput instead of low access latency.

C4. The number of active threads required for efficient utilization of the GPU depends both on the GPU device itself and on the program to be executed and cannot be easily determined prior to the program's runtime.

We address C1 by comparing the performance of two different approaches to memory access synchronization in our simulator implementation. In the *fully GPU-based* variant, this is reflected by a call to the software-based synchronization method. In the *API-based* variant, a return of the control flow to the CPU and a separate kernel launch are required for synchronization. Challenge C2 is addressed by using a statically allocated memory region to hold FELs, and by adapting FEL sizes at runtime if size limits are exceeded. Challenge C3 is addressed by representing FELs using a simple data structure that does not require scattered memory accesses. To address C4, we employ performance measurements that allow the simulator to balance the number of active threads with simulation overheads at runtime.

Execution Procedure

Initially, a fixed number of simulated nodes is assigned to each LP. Initial events pertaining to the simulated nodes are created and inserted into their respective LP's FEL. Now, the simulation proceeds in a round-based fashion as shown in Algorithm 4. Simulation steps that require subsequent inter-block synchronization in every loop iteration are marked with **[S]**.

Algorithm 4: Execution procedure of the GPU-based simulator engine.

```
repeat
    determineLookaheadWindow() [S]
    repeat
        numEventsCurrentIteration ← selectSafeEvents()
        handleSafeEvents() [S]
        checkQueueOverflow()
        numEventsTotal ← numEventsTotal + numEventsCurrentIteration [S]
    until numEventsCurrentIteration < minEventsPerIteration
    insertNewEvents() [S]
until numEventsTotal ≥ finalNumEvents
```

In the following, we describe each of the steps of the execution procedure in detail.

determineLookaheadWindow(): We determine the events that are safe to be executed according to YAWNS (cf. Section 2.1): first, we determine the minimum timestamp $t_{\min}$ in any of the LPs' FELs. All events in the lookahead window $\{t_{\min}, t_{\min} + 1, \ldots, t_{\min} + \tau\}$ are safe, since any new event created by a safe event will have a timestamp larger than or equal to $t_{\min} + \tau$.

For each LP, the event at the LP's FEL head is selected and a *parallel reduction* is performed to find the lowest timestamp of all selected events: in each iteration, a number of concurrent threads calculate the minimum of two remaining elements of input data each. Hence, given n_{LPs} and a sufficiently large number of threads, determining the global minimum requires on the order of $\mathcal{O}(\log(n_{\text{LPs}}))$ iterations. If the number n_{threads} of threads is smaller than the number of LPs, the parallel reduction is repeated $\lceil n_{\text{LPs}}/n_{\text{threads}} \rceil$ times to cover all LPs' earliest events.

The following three steps address the execution of safe events and are repeated until fewer than a configured number of safe events remain. Each step is repeated $\lceil n_{\text{LPs}}/n_{\text{threads}} \rceil$ times, handling t LPs during each repetition.

selectSafeEvents(): Each thread selects an LP's earliest safe event, if any. If there is no event in an LP's FEL or the earliest event is not safe, the thread remains idle during the current repetition. Assuming a sufficiently large number of threads, this step is performed in constant time, i.e., requiring on the order of $\mathcal{O}(1)$ operations.

handleSafeEvents(): All threads that have selected a safe event call the event handler defined by the network model, passing the selected event as an argument. Each event has a type field and a memory region for event data. The model behavior is specified in the event handler function, which can in turn delegate event handling of different event types to specified functions.

If new events are to be created, the event handler calls the simulator function enqueueEvent(). Any new event is appended to the target LP's FEL. In graphics card memory, FELs are represented as ring buffers located in memory regions of equal size. Figure 10.5 shows the insertion of new events into a single LP's FEL. The FEL head is denoted by a circle, while the tail is denoted by a square. In enqueueEvent(), new events are appended in an unsorted fashion. As multiple threads may create new events for the same LP concurrently, the target LP's FEL tail is advanced atomically before storing the new event at the new tail position, eliminating the possibility of race conditions. In case no parallel accesses are performed, appending a new event requires constant time, i.e., on the order of $\mathcal{O}(1)$ operations. Otherwise, the accesses are serialized.

checkQueueOverflow(): When simulating only small numbers of peers in each LP, the limited amount of memory available on the graphics card restricts the number of events that can be contained in a single LP's FEL. If load imbalances in the simulated network lead to an overflow of any LP's FEL, excess events are stored in a temporary buffer of fixed size shared by all LPs. The FEL overflow is resolved by doubling the number of simulated network nodes, e.g., peers, per LP and thus combining the capacities of neighboring FELs until all events fit into their respective LP's FEL (cf. Section 10.4.1). The check for a queue overflow is performed by a constant-time access to an overflow flag.

insertNewEvents(): As a last step before a new lookahead window is determined, the events enqueued during the handleSafeEvents() step of the current round are inserted into FELs in timestamp order (cf. Figure 10.5). In each iteration, each thread handles the insertion of all new events assigned to a single LP. First, a binary search is performed to locate the target position of the new event in the sorted FEL. Then, to store the new event, all events with larger timestamps are moved by one position. Given an FEL that can hold at most $e_{\max,\mathrm{LP}}$, insertion of an event requires on the order of $\mathcal{O}(e_{\max,\mathrm{LP}})$ operations. Since each access to the memory region that holds the FEL is translated to a 256 bit read whose result is stored in a low-latency cache, the access to multiple consecutive events leads to frequent cache hits.

Figure 10.5: During event execution, newly created events are appended to the target LP's FEL in an unsorted fashion. In a subsequent step, the new events are inserted into the FEL in non-decreasing timestamp order.

Adaptation of Logical Process Size

In the simulator configuration, there is a tradeoff regarding the number of simulated network nodes assigned to each LP. Low numbers allow the simulator to expose a large proportion of the concurrency of the network model, but may lead to i) many idle threads if LPs' FELs do not contain safe events in most rounds, ii) large costs for aggregation of all FELs' minimum timestamps for advancing the lookahead window. On the other hand, large numbers of nodes per LP limit the exploitable concurrency and increase the overhead for insertion of events into FELs, as the number of events in each FEL increases with larger LPs.

An optimal LP size depends on a number of factors: the dependencies between events as given by the network model, the event density in simulated time, as well as hardware characteristics such as the number of hardware threads available, the number of active threads required to exhaust the graphics card's memory bandwidth, and the costs for FEL management. Network model properties can vary during runtime and typically cannot be easily predicted prior to a simulation run, since determining the network model's runtime behavior is usually the main goal of the simulation study itself. Hence, for high performance, the simulator should be able to adapt to the conditions of the network scenario at runtime.

LPs are resized as illustrated in Figure 10.6. First, each GPU thread aligns the FEL of one LP to the first element of the reserved memory area. Then, if the number of nodes per LP is to be increased, events of all LPs with index $2k + 1$ are appended at the tail of LPs with index $2k$. Now, the LP count is halved and insertNewEvents() is called to insert the new events into the sorted FELs. This way, both the number of nodes assigned to each LP and the maximum number of events in each LP's FEL is doubled. If the number of nodes per LP is to be halved instead, each thread iterates over the events of one FEL, separating events into two FELs, one for a new LP with index $2k$, and one for a new LP with index $2k + 1$. As timestamp order has already been established by previous simulation rounds, events can be copied to their new position in the existing order. Halving the number of nodes per LP halves the maximum size $e_{\mathrm{max,LP}}$ of each FEL as well. If an existing FEL holds more than $e_{\mathrm{max,LP}}/2$ events for one of the new lists it is to be split to, an overflow would occur. Hence, prior to a decrease in the number of nodes per LP, a check is performed to guarantee that the new FELs will not exceed the memory bounds reserved for each ring buffer.

At runtime, each time the adaptation process is triggered, LPs are resized to handle one peer each. Then, the simulator iterates over LP sizes up to a configured limit, for each LP size resuming simulation and measuring the number of events executed per second of wall-clock time. Once measurements for all configured LP sizes have been performed, LP size is adapted according to the largest measured number of events per second until the next adaptation is triggered, e.g., after a fixed number of executed events.

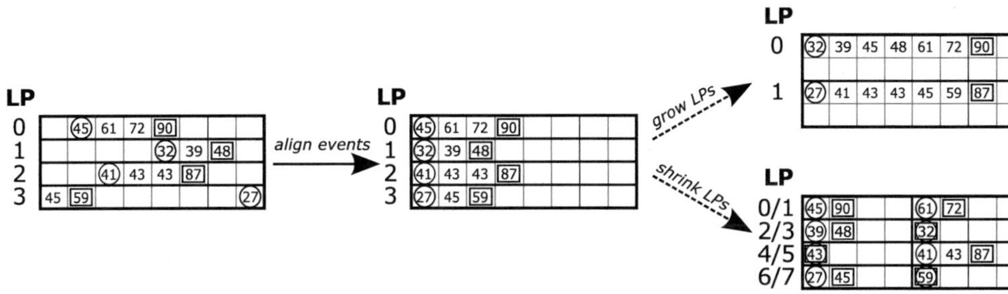

Figure 10.6: To resize LPs, FELs are aligned to the start of their respective memory area boundaries and subsequently relocated according to the new boundaries.

Model Implementation

For the performance evaluation of the GPU-based simulator, we implemented CUDA versions of the **PHOLD** and **Kademlia$_C$** models. In both cases, only minor changes were required in comparison with the CPU-based code used as a basis for performance comparison. Both models were developed in a reference CPU implementation first, and subsequently ported to the GPU. No efforts were made to maximize GPU utilization by explicitly exposing data parallelism or to increase memory access efficiency through reordering of data structures. Executing the model on the GPU required two minor modifications: first, in the sequential simulator, global variables used to gather statistics about the simulated network can be accessed directly from the event handling code. In the parallel case, multiple threads may attempt to modify global variables concurrently. We achieve consistency by replacing write accesses to global statistics variables with calls to corresponding atomic operations provided by CUDA. Second, random numbers are required to generate lookups and to determine link latencies in the simulated network. In the sequential case, random numbers are drawn from a single random number stream, leading to a deterministic simulation and identical simulation results between runs when using the same random number seed. In the parallel case, it is not sufficient to employ a single random number stream, since different random numbers will be assigned to different threads depending on timing. Even though a maximum of only a single event is executed for each LP concurrently at any time during simulation, it is also insufficient to assign one random number stream to each LP, as the size of LPs is adapted during runtime and may differ between runs. Since the memory footprint of each random number stream is low, we can create one random number stream for each simulated node. The same approach is used in case of the **PHOLD** model.

Apart from the changes for accessing global variables atomically and the separation of random number streams, the network model code is identical between the CPU and the parallel GPU-based variants.

10.4.2 Evaluation

In this section, we first compare the time complexity of the simulation tasks using the GPU-based simulation approaches from the literature and our proposed approach. Subsequently, we present performance measurement results in comparison with CPU-based sequential and parallel simulation runs.

Time Complexity

In the following, we study the time complexity of the steps that are repeatedly executed in fully GPU-based simulations according to the approaches proposed in the literature and discussed in Section 10.2. We then compare the results with our own approach.

In [PF10], Park et al. describe their approach on the example of a queuing network simulation where tokens are processed and passed between stations. The following steps are repeated until a termination criterion is satisfied:

1. A parallel reduction is performed to find $t_{\min}$. This step considers all potential $e_{\max,\text{global}}$ event positions in the global FEL and can hence be performed in $\mathcal{O}(\log(e_{\max,\text{global}}))$ operations.

2. Each thread iterates over one FEL segment to mark all events in the current lookahead window.
3. Each thread iterates over the global FEL to select marked events for one station each. On departure, the station status is set to "idle". On an "arrival" event, a token is added to the per-station queue. Since the previous step considers fewer events, the two steps require on the order of $\mathcal{O}(e_{\text{max,global}})$ operations.
4. Each thread sorts one station's new events. If the station is idle, the earliest of the new events represents the token currently occupying the station. Remaining events are inserted into the node's queue. We assume an efficient sorting algorithm such as quick sort is used and thus given $e_{\text{new,node}}$ new events, each thread requires $\mathcal{O}(e_{\text{new,node}} \times \log(e_{\text{new,node}}))$ operations for sorting. Subsequently, each event can be appended to the station's queue in constant time.
5. Each thread checks one event in the global FEL: if the event is currently marked, the thread unmarks the event and updates the event depending on whether the corresponding station is busy.

In simulations where each event creates exactly one new event, the new event is stored in place of the currently executed event. In case the number of events varies during the simulation, storage for each new event is selected by a linear search in the global FEL, i.e., using on the order of $\mathcal{O}(e_{\text{max,global}})$ operations.

The approach proposed by Tang et al. [WYF13, TY13] segments an unordered global FEL into a number of columns. Since each thread inserts new events into a unique column of the FEL, explicit mutual exclusion operations are not required. At maximum, each insertion of a new event must consider all of the n_{rows} rows of the FEL according to the configured segmentation of the FEL. Hence, inserting an event requires on the order of $\mathcal{O}(n_{\text{rows}})$ operations. The simulation proceeds as follows:

1. A parallel reduction of all $e_{\text{max,global}}$ positions in the global FEL is performed to find t_{min}. The reduction requires on the order of $\mathcal{O}(\log(e_{\text{max,global}}))$ operations.
2. Each thread determines whether one event resides in the lookahead window. If this is the case, the event is inserted into a linked list that holds the events of one simulated entity in timestamp order. The handling of parallel accesses to the linked list of a single entity by multiple threads is not specified. For instance, it is possible to enable parallel access to linked lists using atomic operations [Har01]. Assuming no parallel accesses to a linked list containing a maximum of $e_{\text{max,node}}$ events, inserting a new event requires on the order of $\mathcal{O}(e_{\text{max,node}})$ operations.
3. Each thread executes the earliest event pertaining to a single simulated entity.

In the approach proposed by Zhen et al. [ZGGB14], events assigned to an agent are stored in a local FEL that is ordered by timestamp. Hence, performing a parallel reduction to determine the minimum timestamp requires on the order of $\mathcal{O}(\log(n_{\text{nodes}}))$ operations. Disregarding the potential serialization of accesses, creating an event and appending it to an agent's list of incoming events requires constant time, i.e., on the order of $\mathcal{O}(1)$ operations. However, the authors do not describe in detail the data structure used to represent FELs or the mechanism used to maintain non-decreasing timestamp order in each agent's FEL. Hence, we assume that in the situation where only a single thread appends to an agent's FEL that can contain up to $e_{\text{max,node}}$ events, a new event can be inserted using on the order of $\mathcal{O}(e_{\text{max,node}})$ operations.

Table 10.1 summarizes the previous analysis of the existing approaches applicable to general discrete-event simulations, and compares the time complexity of the simulation steps with our proposed approach. The symbols used are listed in Table 10.2. Note that the listed time complexities for the individual steps are given on a purely algorithmic level. The runtime performance of GPU programs depends strongly on memory access patterns and on an efficient utilization of the memory hierarchy. Further, optimal values for parameters such as the number of blocks and the number of threads per block are hardware-dependent. Hence, our complexity comparison should be viewed as a rough indication of algorithmic efficiency and cannot directly estimate the relative runtime performance of the approaches.

Our proposed event management approach differs from most existing GPU-based simulators by not inserting new events into a global FEL in an unsorted fashion. Instead, events are immediately appended to small FELs that subsequently establish a per-node non-decreasing timestamp ordering. To the best of our knowledge, the only other approach that supports general discrete-event models and also applies this mechanism is the work by Zhen et al. [ZGGB14]. Where their description of the event management mechanisms lacks details required in the complexity comparison, we assume the lowest-complexity mechanisms that we are aware of. The comparison in Table 10.1 shows that if the maximum number of events in the simulation is larger than the number of simulated nodes, the time complexity of Zhen et al.'s approach compares favorably to the other previous approaches. However, in the time complexity analysis, some key performance-critical aspects of the different approaches are not visible:

- The $\mathcal{O}(1)$ time complexity of event creation listed for Zhen et al.'s and our own approach does not consider the costs of mutual exclusion between GPU threads: if many events are atomically appended to a node's FEL at the same time, parallel accesses by multiple threads are serialized. Tang et al.'s approach avoids the use of atomic operations for event creation. If many events are created targeting the same node at the exact same time, Tang et al.'s approach may potentially be more efficient. However, in their approach, a mutual exclusion mechanism seems to be required when inserting events into the sorted per-node FELs.

- The time complexity analysis focuses on the event management steps and does not consider the efficiency of the parallel execution of events itself. Obviously, if a large proportion of GPU threads is idle during execution, the computational resources of the GPU are not utilized efficiently. As discussed above, Tang et al. propose a mechanism that considers more events for execution than a strict YAWNS-based synchronization, achieving performance increases of up to 30%. In our proposed approach, nodes are aggregated into dynamically LPs in order to reduce the number of idle threads. On the one hand, our approach increases the time complexity of event insertion as well as the probability of parallel, and hence serialized, access to an individual FEL. On the other hand, aggregating nodes increases the probability for each FEL to contain safe events within the current lookahead window, which has a dominant effect on performance: our measurements in Section 10.4.2 show the substantial dependence of the optimal LP size on the scenario configuration.

	Parallel min-reduction	Create new event	Select per-node safe event	Sort new events ($e_n := e_{new,node}$)	Insert event
Park	$\mathcal{O}(\log(e_{max,global}))$	$\mathcal{O}(e_{max,global})$	$\mathcal{O}(e_{new,node})$	$\mathcal{O}(e_n \times \log(e_n))$	$\mathcal{O}(1)$
Tang	$\mathcal{O}(\log(e_{max,global}))$	$\mathcal{O}(e_{max,row})$	$\mathcal{O}(1)$	N/A	$\mathcal{O}(e_{max,node})$
Zhen	$\mathcal{O}(\log(n_{nodes}))$	$\mathcal{O}(1)$	$\mathcal{O}(1)$	N/A	$\mathcal{O}(e_{max,node})$
Andelfinger	$\mathcal{O}(\log(n_{LPs}))$	$\mathcal{O}(1)$	$\mathcal{O}(1)$	N/A	$\mathcal{O}(e_{max,LP})$

Table 10.1: Time complexity of the simulation tasks in the GPU-based simulation approaches, disregarding potential serialization of operations due to parallel access to data structures by multiple threads.

Symbol	Description
$e_{max,global}$	Maximum size of global FEL
$e_{max,row}$	Maximum size of each FEL row in [WYF13, TY13]
$e_{max,node}$	Maximum size of per-node FEL
$e_{max,LP}$	Maximum size of per-LP FEL
$e_{new,node}$	Number of newly created events for given node
n_{nodes}	Number of nodes
n_{LPs}	Current number of LPs

Table 10.2: Symbols used in the time complexity analysis.

Performance Measurements

We evaluate the performance of the implementation of the proposed simulator engine with respect to simulations of Kademlia-based networks by first comparing two variants of the fully GPU-based simulator: a GPU-based approach using the CUDA API for memory access synchronization and a fully GPU-based approach using software-based synchronization. Subsequently, we compare the performance of the GPU-based simulator with an optimized CPU implementation that supports both sequential simulations as well as conservatively synchronized parallel simulation. As processing time per event in the evaluation network model is quite low at about $1\mu s$ or less depending on the scenario, a large portion of simulation time is spent handling the FEL in the sequential variant. Hence, a meaningful comparison requires an efficient FEL implementation. In the CPU-based simulations, we used the *map* container class from the C++ standard library to implement the FEL, which is also the default in the well-known network simulator ns-3.

The CPU-based parallel simulations were executed on a 16-core Intel Intel Xeon E5-2670, using conservative synchronization according to the null message algorithm (cf. Section 2.1). Communication was performed via shared memory using the MPI [SOHL+98] implementation OpenMPI[2]. The GPU-based simulator was executed on a NVIDIA GTX 660Ti graphics card with 1344 cores in 7 SMs, allowing us to assign 7168 threads to the fully GPU-based simulator variant (cf. Section 10.1.2). The test system uses an AMD Phenom II X4 965 CPU. We used the same system to execute the sequential CPU-based simulation runs. In the API-based GPU-based simulator variant, we measured highest performance with 256 threads per block for any sufficiently large number of blocks. In our experiments, we used $\lceil n_{LPs,initial}/256 \rceil$ blocks, $n_{LPs,initial}$ being the initial number of LPs.

[2] http://www.open-mpi.org/

We demonstrate the efficiency of the LP size adaptation mechanism by comparing the runtimes of simulations using fixed LP sizes with simulations using the adaptation scheme. The performance plots show averages over three runs per configuration and include 95% confidence intervals.

Figure 10.7 shows the event rate, i.e., average number of events executed per second of wall-clock time for the two variants of the fully GPU-based simulator, varying the number of peers in the simulated network. We vary the computational load in the simulation by configuring different amounts of traffic: each peer executes lookups with a delay in milliseconds drawn from a uniform distribution on $\{0, 1, \ldots, d_{max}\}$ between lookups. With smaller d_{max}, the computational load of the simulation increases as more messages are generated per unit of simulated time. We can see that both of the GPU-based simulator variants benefit from the higher event density of larger network sizes. The maximum and minimum event rates of the API-based simulator were 6.76×10^6 events/s

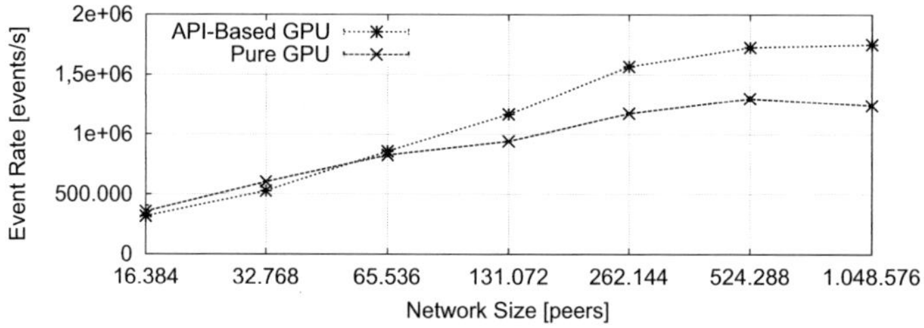

(a) Low amount of traffic (d_{max} = 10min).

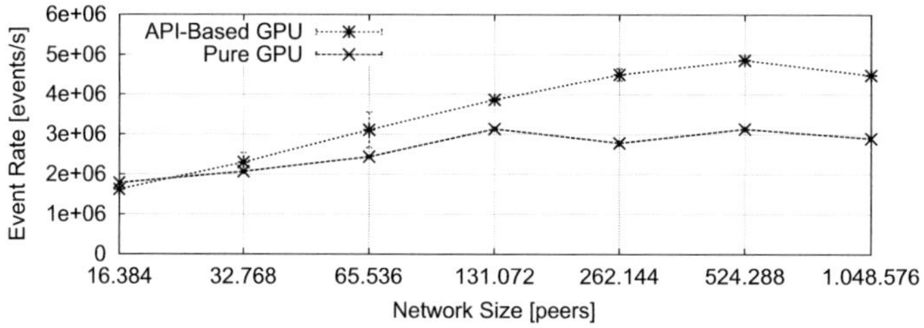

(b) Moderate amount of traffic (d_{max} = 1min).

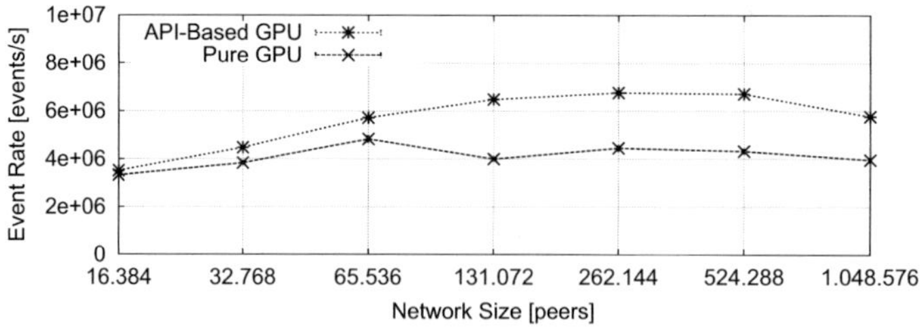

(c) Large amount of traffic (d_{max} = 10s).

Figure 10.7: Event rate for **Kademlia**$_C$ varying the memory access synchronization method of the GPU-based simulator variant, the amount of traffic in the simulated network, and the number of peers.

and 0.316×10^6 events/s, respectively. In almost all cases, the API-based memory synchronization achieved a significantly higher event rate than the simulator variant using the software-based barrier.

For networks of 1 048 576 peers, there is a decrease in the event rate incurred by the time required for initially populating the simulated peers' routing tables. Of course, the relative impact of the initialization phase diminishes for runs covering larger periods of simulated time.

To determine whether the software-based synchronization itself is more inefficient than API-based synchronization, or whether the limited number of blocks allowed in the fully GPU-based variant is insufficient to effectively hide memory access latencies, we configured the same number of threads for both GPU-based simulator variants and studied the resulting event rate for all network sizes with d_{max} = 10s. Even though the event rate of the API-based variant dropped by up to 12.7%, the API-based variant still achieved higher event rates than the pure variant in almost all

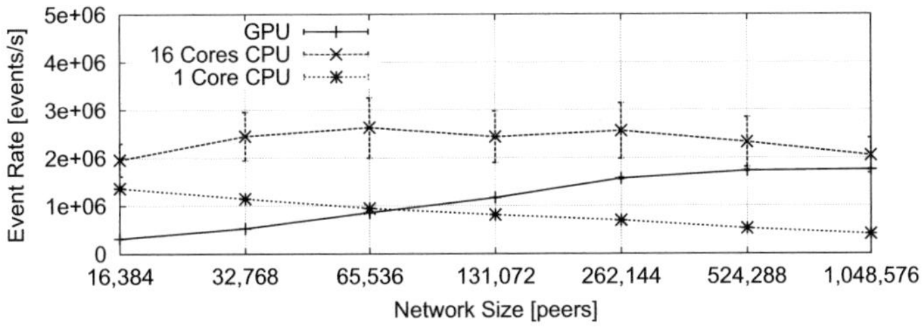

(a) Low amount of traffic (d_{max} = 10min).

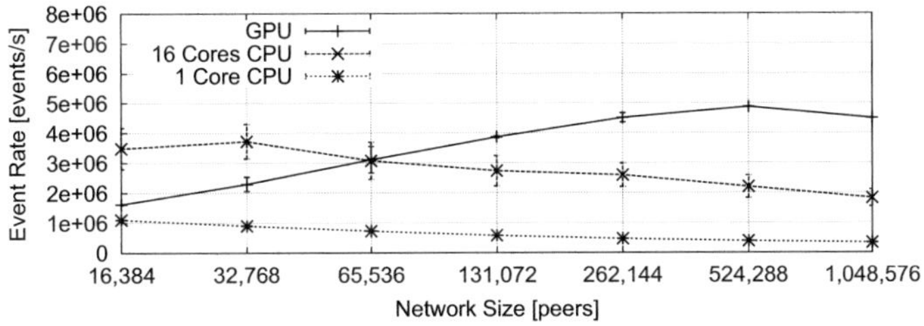

(b) Moderate amount of traffic (d_{max} = 1min).

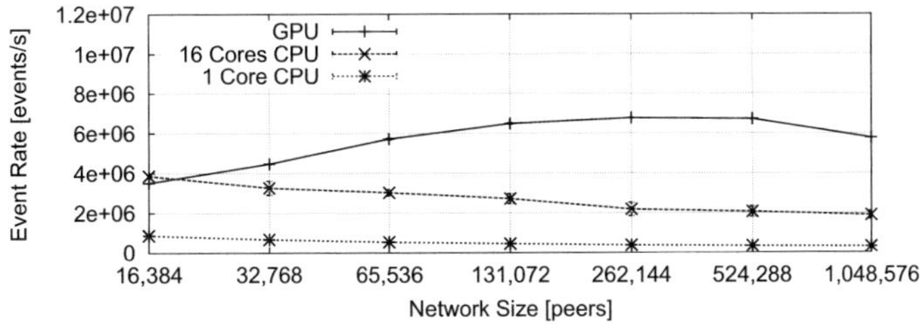

(c) Large amount of traffic (d_{max} = 10s).

Figure 10.8: Event rate for **Kademlia**$_{\mathbf{C}}$ varying the simulator variant, the amount of traffic in the simulated network, and the number of peers.

cases. Hence, we conclude that in our setup, software-based memory access synchronization on the GPU is less efficient than API-based synchronization.

Since in almost all cases, the API-based GPU variant was more efficient than the fully GPU-based variant, in the remainder of the performance evaluation we focus on the API-based approach.

Figure 10.8 compares the performance of three simulator variants: a sequential CPU-based simulation, a conservatively synchronized parallel simulation using 16 CPU cores, and the fully GPU-based simulator using API-based memory synchronization. The sequential simulation achieved a maximum event rate of 1.36×10^6 events/s with $d_{\text{max}} = 10\text{min}$ and a network size of 16 384 peers. Due to the larger costs of event management when increasing the number of events in the simulation, the event rate depends strongly on network size. The lowest event rate was 0.318×10^6 events/s with $d_{\text{max}} = 10\text{s}$ and a network size of 1 048 576. In the CPU-based parallel simulations, the maximum and minimum event rates were 3.86×10^6 events/s and 1.82×10^6 events/s, respectively. The largest measured speedup of a parallel CPU-based simulation compared to a sequential simulation was 6.00. Contrary to the CPU-based simulations, the GPU-based simulator achieves higher performance with larger network size, whereas the lower event density of smaller networks does not fully utilize the GPU's hardware resources. With $d_{\text{max}} = 10\text{min}$, the GPU-based simulation achieves lower event rates than the sequential simulation for network sizes below 131 072. With d_{max} at 1min and 10s, the GPU variant performed better than the sequential CPU variant in all scenarios. With $d_{\text{max}} = 1\text{min}$, the largest speedup was 13.47 with 1 048 576 peers. With $d_{\text{max}} = 10\text{s}$, the largest speedup was 19.50 with 524 288 peers, with a event rate of 6.71×10^6 events per second. The GPU-based simulation achieved higher event rates than the parallel CPU-based simulation in case of large event densities, with a maximum speedup of 3.25 with $d_{\text{max}} = 10\text{s}$ and a network size of 524 288.

To study the performance with respect to the **PHOLD** model, we varied the number λ of events per unit of simulated time and the proportion of remote traffic, i.e., the probability that an event e_2 created by an event e_1 is assigned to a different simulated node than e_1. The lookahead was set to 10 units of simulated time. We configured a network size of 131 072 nodes. The GPU-based simulation runs were performed 10 times for each parameter combination. Figures 10.9, 10.10 and 10.11 depict the performance measurements of the **PHOLD** model. The sequential CPU-based simulator achieved a maximum event rate of 4.08×10^6 events/s with 0% remote traffic, a population of 16 384 events and $\lambda = 100$. Due to the larger event management overhead with larger numbers of events, the performance decreases with larger **PHOLD** population settings. The lowest value of 0.69×10^6 events/s was measured with 100% remote traffic, a population of 1 048 576 events and $\lambda = 0.01$.

The parallel CPU-based simulator achieved event rates between 2.57×10^6 and 43.87×10^6. Accordingly, the maximum and minimum speedup of the parallel CPU-based simulator compared to the sequential CPU-based simulator was 18.35 and 1.73. The performance of the CPU-based parallel simulation depends strongly on the number of events in the simulation: up to a certain size of the **PHOLD** population, the event rate increases since more events can be executed by each LP before synchronization is required. However, at larger **PHOLD** populations, the event rate decreases significantly. A potential reason is the single-threaded nature of each LP in our implementation of the CPU-based parallel simulator: since the execution of events and the retrieval of messages cannot be performed at the same time, executing a large number of events before retrieving incoming messages can lead to a substantial waiting time for an LP that is sending a message. Still, considering

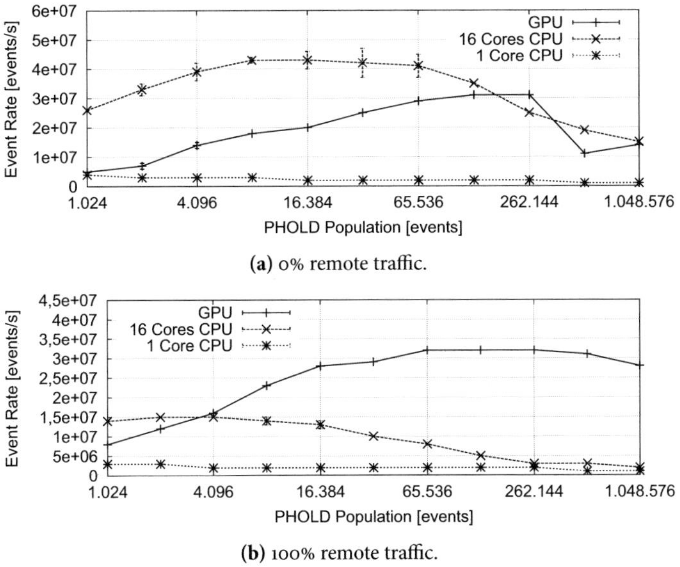

Figure 10.9: Event rate of GPU-based simulation of the **PHOLD** model with $\lambda = 100$.

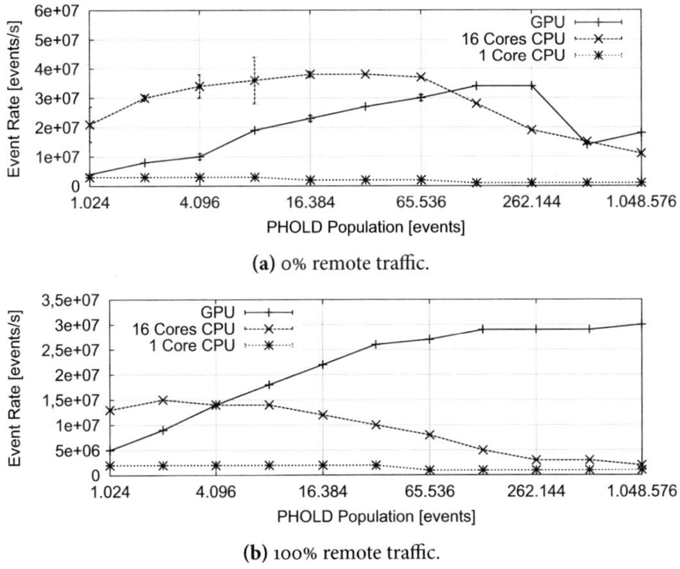

Figure 10.10: Event rate of GPU-based simulation of the **PHOLD** model with $\lambda = 1$.

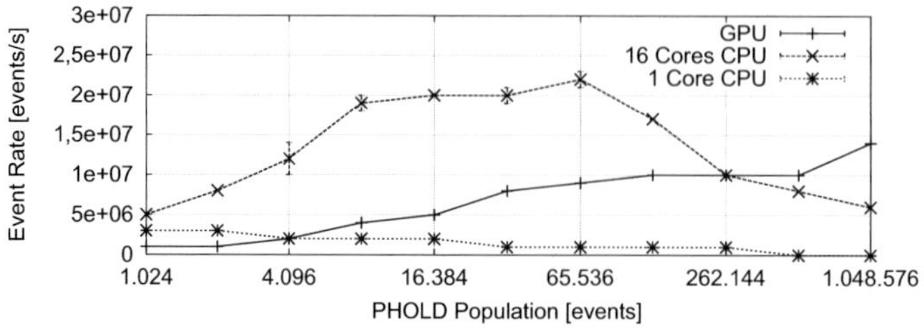

(a) 0% remote traffic.

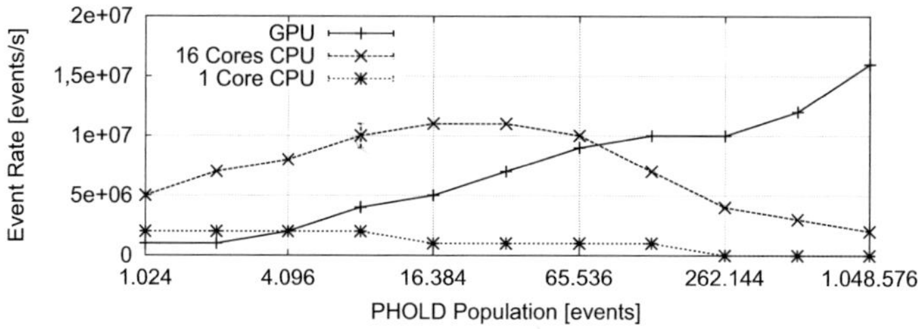

(b) 100% remote traffic.

Figure 10.11: Event rate of GPU-based simulation of the **PHOLD** model with $\lambda = 0.01$.

the measured event rates and the large speedup compared to the sequential CPU-based simulator, the CPU-based parallel simulator seems to provide a reasonable point of comparison.

The largest speedup of the GPU-based simulator compared to the CPU-based parallel simulator was 11.77 with a population of 1 048 576, 100% remote traffic and $\lambda = 1$. The largest speedup of the GPU-based simulator compared to the CPU-based sequential simulator was 23.55 with a population of 1 048 576, 100% remote traffic and $\lambda = 0.01$. The maximum event rate of the GPU-based simulator was 34.11×10^6 with a population of 262 144, 0% remote traffic and $\lambda = 1$.

In general, the GPU-based simulator achieves higher event rates with larger **PHOLD** populations. However, an exception can be observed in the results of Figures 10.9 and 10.10 with 0% remote traffic: the event rate declines sharply with a population of 524 288 and 1 048 576, although one would expect particularly large performance with these configurations. The reason lies in the configured number of 256 threads per GPU block. The choice of a suitable number of threads per block depends strongly on properties of the hardware as well as the performed computations and memory access patterns and is hence non-trivial [TGEL13]. Figure 10.12 shows a comparison of the event rate with 32 and 256 threads per block for two different configurations. We can see that with 0% remote traffic and $\lambda = 100$, using 32 threads per block results in higher event rates than using 256 threads per block for populations of 131 072 and above. Additionally, the constant event rate at larger populations seems to suggest that the GPU resources are utilized fully with these model parameter combinations. The largest event rate of 39.34×10^6 event/s is achieved with a population of 131 072. The largest speedup factor compared to the sequential CPU-based simulator was 27.52 with a population of 1 048 576. We provide an example of the results for the remaining PHOLD parameter combinations by a plot for 100% remote traffic and $\lambda = 0.01$: here, as in almost all other studied parameter combinations, 256 threads per block achieved larger event rates than 32 threads per block.

We now consider the percentage of simulation runtime spent on the individual steps of a simulation, focusing on the **Kademlia**$_C$ model. Table 10.3 lists measurement results for 16 384, 131 072 and 1 048 576 peers and $d_{max} = 10s$. For the CPU-based simulator, we distinguish two steps: event handling (Handle) and overheads (Other), including, and dominated by, FEL management. For the GPU-based simulator variants, there are four steps corresponding to the execution procedure described in Section 10.4.1: calculation of the smallest global timestamp (MinTs), event handling (Handle), insertion of events into FELs (Insert), and overheads (Other). While the CPU-based simulator spent 29.4% of its runtime executing events with 16 384 peers, with 1 048 576 peers, this value increased to 40%. As total runtime increased from 1 134s to 3 141s while the number of executed events remained constant, we can see that both the processing time per event as well as the FEL management overhead increased for larger networks. In the GPU-based simulator, in addition to the benefits of the large number of cores of the GPU, a larger portion of runtime was spent executing events than was the case for the CPU-based simulator. On the GPU, the results clearly show the superiority of the API-based variant: while in the fully GPU-based variant, the relative overhead for inserting events into FELs increases with larger network size, in the API-based variant, a larger portion of runtime was spent on event execution with larger network sizes. In all cases, finding the global minimum timestamp comprised only a small portion of the total runtime.

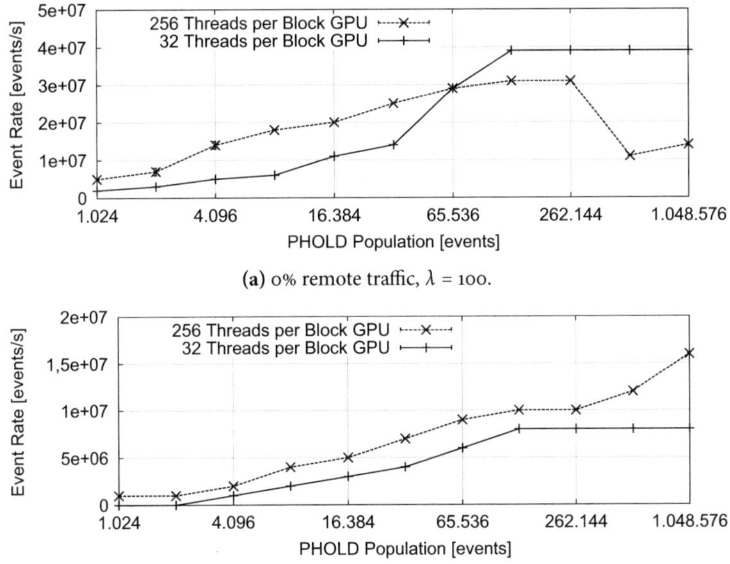

(a) 0% remote traffic, $\lambda = 100$.

(b) 100% remote traffic, $\lambda = 0.01$.

Figure 10.12: Event rate of GPU-based simulation of the **PHOLD** model when varying the number of GPU threads per block.

Network Size	*CPU* Handle	*CPU* Other	*API-Based GPU* MinTs	*API-Based GPU* Handle	*API-Based GPU* Insert	*API-Based GPU* Other	*Pure GPU* MinTs	*Pure GPU* Handle	*Pure GPU* Insert	*Pure GPU* Other
16 384 Peers	29.4%	70.6%	7.4%	52.7%	39.7%	4.7%	2.9%	46.5%	48.1%	0.0%
131 072 Peers	27.5%	72.5%	2.3%	60.1%	36.9%	0.7%	1.4%	45.1%	53.5%	0.0%
1 048 576 Peers	40.0%	60.0%	1.5%	71.4%	26.8%	0.3%	0.3%	36.3%	61.1%	0.2%

Table 10.3: Percentage of runtime spent on simulation steps for **Kademlia**$_C$ with d_{max} = 10s.

Optimal Logical Process Size

When assigning only a single peer to each LP, a sufficient portion of the concurrency of the Kademlia model is exploited to execute hundreds or thousands of events in each round. However, overheads due to idle GPU cores and for event selection increase with larger LP counts. To show that the proposed simulator successfully balances parallelism and overhead at runtime, Table 10.4 compares the event rate of simulation runs with fixed LP size to runs using adaptive LP size. In each run, the LP size was adapted a single time after initialization of the simulated network. The optimal fixed number of peers per LP varied between 2 and 16. In general, the lower the traffic in the simulated network and the fewer events there are per unit of simulated time, the more peers need to be aggregated in each LP to achieve best performance. In almost all cases, the adaptive simulator implementation was able to select an efficient LP size and hence closely approximated the largest event rate among the runs with fixed LP size. With 16 384 peers and d_{max} = 1min, the adaptive simulator even slightly outperformed the best fixed-LP run. With 1 048 576 peers and d_{max} = 10min, however, due to high variance of runtime performance, the chosen LP size achieved only 84.3% of the run with the largest event rate. When increasing the duration of each performance measurement from 10^5 to 10^6 events, 97.2% of the highest event rate was achieved.

We can observe that in nearly all of the parameter combinations considered in Table 10.4, the aggregation of simulated nodes increased the event rate of the simulation. The largest increase in event rates by a factor of 4.52 through the aggregation was achieved with 1 048 576 peers and d_{max} = 10min. In the simulation run with the largest speedup of 19.5 compared to a CPU-based sequential execution, about 15 600 events were processed per parallel execution.

Considering the **PHOLD** model, the largest benefit of the aggregation of simulated nodes is observed in case of low event density in simulated time. Table 10.5 lists the event rates achieved when considering a single simulated node per logical process, compared to the result achieved with

Network Size	16 384 Peers			131 072 Peers			1 048 576 Peers		
d_{max}	*10s*	*1min*	*10min*	*10s*	*1min*	*10min*	*10s*	*1min*	*10min*
1 Peer per LP	**3.87**	1.44	0.26	5.77	2.47	0.46	5.01	2.41	0.46
2 Peers per LP	3.82	1.58	0.30	**6.78**	3.31	0.74	**5.90**	3.27	0.77
4 Peers per LP	3.51	**1.61**	**0.32**	6.49	**3.98**	1.02	5.79	4.18	1.25
8 Peers per LP	2.22	1.29	**0.32**	4.39	3.87	1.18	4.49	**4.50**	1.78
16 Peers per LP	1.09	0.81	0.26	2.34	2.59	1.18	2.86	3.50	**2.08**
Adaptive LP Size	***3.51***	***1.62***	***0.32***	***6.48***	***3.86***	***1.17***	***5.77***	***4.49***	***1.75***
Percentage of Best	**90.6%**	**100.3%**	**99.4%**	**95.5%**	**96.9%**	**99.0%**	**97.7%**	**99.7%**	**84.3%**

Table 10.4: Event rates [10^6 events/s] using fixed-sized and adaptive LPs to execute **Kademlia**$_C$.

the aggregation. Depending on the configuration, the optimal degree of aggregation lies between between 1 and 16 nodes per logical process. The results show that in cases of low event density, the performance of the fully GPU-based simulator can be substantially improved by aggregating the simulated nodes. With larger event densities, the benefit of the aggregation diminishes, since in these cases, the GPU is utilized sufficiently when assigning a single simulated node to each logical process. With the listed parameter combinations, a speedup of up to 1.97 to can be achieved by the aggregation compared to a consideration of individual nodes.

Population	1024 Events			4096 Events			16384 Events			65536 Events		
λ	*0.01*	*1*	*100*	*0.01*	*1*	*100*	*0.01*	*1*	*100*	*0.01*	*1*	*100*
1 Node per LP	0.83	3.93	7.44	2.53	13.80	14.31	5.81	**25.00**	**24.57**	9.85	**31.70**	**31.54**
2 Nodes per LP	1.11	5.14	5.13	3.16	11.66	12.95	6.47	23.49	22.39	10.32	27.90	25.80
4 Nodes per LP	1.38	**6.39**	6.65	3.45	10.89	11.55	6.90	21.58	19.67	11.67	24.53	21.26
8 Nodes per LP	1.56	5.33	**7.45**	3.47	**14.78**	**15.28**	7.17	15.99	15.01	**13.46**	20.21	15.53
16 Nodes per LP	**1.64**	6.03	6.08	**3.64**	11.16	11.20	7.63	17.08	15.28	12.59	21.35	12.77
32 Nodes per LP	1.46	5.93	5.93	3.48	11.37	11.53	**8.63**	15.90	13.84	8.78	18.23	9.35
Max. Speedup	**1.97**	**1.62**	–	**1.43**	**1.07**	**1.06**	**1.48**	–	–	**1.36**	–	–

Table 10.5: Event rates [10^6 events/s] when varying the LP size and the maximum speedup achieved through the aggregation of nodes in simulations of the **PHOLD** with 0% remote traffic.

10.4.3 Discussion

The proposed simulator achieves a substantial simulation speedup compared to a sequential CPU-based implementation and in many configurations rivaled or significantly exceeded the performance of a parallel simulation on a 16-core CPU. Still, a number of aspects warrant further research in future work:

Per-LP FELs are represented as ring buffers, incurring linear time complexity when inserting an event into an FEL. The runtime adaptation of LP size implicitly determines the average number of events in each FEL so that insertion overhead remains acceptable. However, more sophisticated data structures may enable higher efficiency when inserting events into FELs. A systematic comparison of the efficiency of different data structures to represent priority queues on GPUs is a potential focus of future work.

We have shown that the use of a software-based barrier for memory access synchronization results in lower performance than using API-based memory access synchronization. A possibility for further performance increases is given by the "dynamic parallelism" feature of recent CUDA devices of compute capability 3.5 and larger, which allows for synchronization of memory accesses between all threads on the GPU.

Currently, all LPs are formed by aggregation of an identical number of nodes. Further, in our current implementation, nodes are selected for aggregation based on the positions of their FELs in GPU memory. Additional performance increases may be achievable when selectively aggregating particular nodes to LPs of varying sizes depending on the current distribution of events to the simulated nodes.

Furthermore, we have seen that the configured number of threads per block can have a substantial impact on the simulation performance. A consideration of additional parameters such as the overall number of threads may enable additional speedup. Since it is not clear whether there are significant interactions among these parameters, as well as between the parameters and the considered network model, it may be beneficial to consider applying generic autotuning approaches for GPU-based applications [TKDT13] in order to identify suitable parameter combinations.

The simulation performance depends on properties of the network model. Graphics memory is optimized for high bandwidth instead of low latency. Hence, if there are sequences of scattered memory accesses during event handling, large numbers of parallel events are required to allow for efficient hiding of memory access latencies, limiting the benefit of GPU-based simulation when considering small-scale networks. Additionally, since all threads of each warp operate in lockstep, heavy branching in the model code depending on the nodes' states must be expected to impede performance. Hence, GPU-based simulations of models with large variation in node behavior, such as state machine models of TCP connections, should be studied in future work.

10.5 Conclusions

In this chapter, we proposed and evaluated GPU-accelerated parallel simulation architectures. The proposed approaches utilize only a single GPU and are hence suitable for deployment on commodity hardware.

We first considered hybrid simulation where events are executed on a GPU, while the event management is performed on a CPU. The approach has the benefit of requiring only limited development efforts: it is possible to implement only computationally expensive event handlers on the GPU, whereas the remainder of the model is implemented targeting the familiar CPU environment. Similarly, an existing CPU-based simulator and model implementation can be extended for GPU-based execution of individual event types with relative ease. However, hybrid CPU-GPU-based simulation requires frequent and time consuming interaction and data transfer between the CPU and GPU context of the simulation. Starting from a data-parallel execution of individual events of a detailed model of wireless communications, we studied the impact of optimizations to the simulator architecture that aim to reduce the frequency of the CPU-GPU interactions.

The performance of the architectures was evaluated using a synthetic benchmark model that executes three computationally expensive algorithms required in detailed wireless network simulation. Whereas the GPU-based execution of individual events achieved only minor performance improvements compared to a purely CPU-based sequential simulation, significant speedup was achieved when aggregating multiple events to exploit the data parallelism in individual events as well as the parallelism across multiple events. Similarly to CPU-based parallel and distributed simulation, aggregated execution of events requires a consideration of the simulation correctness. For instance, conservative synchronization can exploit the speed-of-light propagation delay of radio waves to determine events that can safely be executed in parallel on the GPU. Further performance increases are achieved when avoiding data transfers between graphics and host memory in case the output data of event handlers will be used as input for future event handlers. Still, due to the remaining costs of CPU-GPU interactions, hybrid CPU-GPU-based simulation seems particularly suitable in case of models with computationally expensive and highly data-parallel events.

Subsequently, we studied the fully GPU-based network simulation. In fully GPU-based simulation, both the simulation events as well as the event management tasks are executed on a GPU. Since significant CPU-GPU interaction is required only during initialization and termination of a simulation run, the fully-GPU based approach can be applied to models where individual events require only small amounts of computation and are inherently sequential. We studied the performance achievable using fully GPU-based network simulation on the example of a model of an application-layer peer-to-peer network and the popular PHOLD benchmark model. Further, we compare two approaches for synchronizing the access of the GPU threads to graphics memory: an approach where the consecutive GPU-based simulation tasks are triggered from a CPU process, and an approach where a software-based barrier operation is used to completely avoid the use of the CPU. Since in case of the software-based barrier, the exploitation of the GPU resources must be restricted to eliminate the possibility for deadlocks, triggering the simulation tasks from a CPU process showed higher simulation performance in our experiments.

In the GPU-based network simulation approaches from the literature, each GPU thread considers the events of a single simulated node for processing in each execution step. Hence, if in each iteration of the simulation, only few nodes hold events that can be safely processed, many of the GPU threads will remain idle. To increase the utilization of the GPU's resources, similarly to CPU-based parallel and distributed simulations, our proposed event management scheme aggregates sets of multiple nodes of the simulated network into LPs. Since each thread considers the events assigned to an LP, the probability of idle threads is reduced. However, increasing the number of nodes per LP increases the costs of event management. Hence, the size of the LPs is adapted at simulation runtime based on performance measurements to select an LP size that achieves a large event execution rate with respect to wall-clock time. The dynamic selection of the LP size balances the utilization of the GPU's hardware resources during event execution with the costs of event management.

On a commodity GPU, the proposed simulation approach achieved event rates of up to 6.8×10^6 events per second for simulations of the peer-to-peer network model, and up to 39.3×10^6 events per second in case of the PHOLD model. We compared the results with a sequential CPU-based simulation and observed a speedup of up to 27.5. In comparison with a conservatively synchronized parallel simulation using 16 CPU cores, we achieved a speedup of up to 11.8.

In future work, it may be beneficial to focus on producing generalized insights into the performance of different GPU-based simulation approaches. In particular, a systematic performance evaluation of the various possible implementations of future event lists on a GPU based on a direct comparison using a fixed hardware platform and model implementation could clarify the advantages of the different approaches. Further, due to the execution of groups of GPU threads in a lockstep fashion and the large impact of memory access patterns on performance, interactions between multiple events that are executed in parallel may significantly affect the event rate. Identifying the impact of the characteristics of the event handlers on GPU-based simulation performance may enable simulationists to decide whether a model will benefit from GPU-based execution and may guide model optimizations.

11
Harnessing Concurrency – Conclusions

In this part of the thesis, we proposed CPU-based and GPU-based methods for accelerating models of peer-to-peer networks and wireless networks. We analyzed two partitioning strategies for a model of a large-scale peer-to-peer network, showing that a simple partitioning strategy that exploits the structure of the nodes' routing tables in a network based on the Kademlia protocol reduces the amount of inter-LP communication and the simulation runtime substantially, whereas a location-based partitioning strategy moderately increases the exploitable lookahead. We demonstrated that although the network model requires only fine-grained computations, a traditional CPU-based distributed simulation enables a speedups of up to 6.0 compared to a sequential execution, and near-linear reductions in the memory requirements per execution node. However, the increase in hardware requirements by distributing the simulation outpaces the runtime reduction by a wide margin. Hence, for distributed simulation of the considered network model to be useful, the benefit of an increased simulation scale or of the runtime reduction must outweigh the additional costs in hardware resources.

In order to accelerate the execution of a detailed wireless networks model that requires data-parallel and coarse-grained computations, we compared different architectures for a hybrid CPU-GPU coprocessing. To expose a sufficient amount of data parallelism and to achieve substantial performance gains, it is necessary to consider multiple events in a single processing step. Aggregating events introduces the need to apply mechanisms of parallel and distributed simulation in order to maintain simulation correctness. Although large speedup could be achieved for the considered computationally intensive network model, the coprocessing approach incurs substantial overhead through the interaction between the host system and the GPU and is hence suitable for models with large per-event computation times. In order to reduce the overhead of the CPU-GPU interaction, we proposed a fully GPU-based network simulator. The simulator enables high-performance simulations even for network models that require fine-grained computations and frequent interaction between simulated nodes. We applied an established synchronization algorithm used in CPU-based parallel simulation to the many-core realm and presented an event management mechanism suitable for GPUs. Contrary to existing approaches, sets of simulated nodes are aggregated to form logical processes, enabling a dynamic balancing of GPU utilization and event management overhead at runtime. While the supported simulation scale is limited by the available graphics memory, the reliance on a single GPU enables researchers to achieve high simulation performance using a single local workstation. Our approach achieved event rates of up to 39.3×10^6 events per second and a speedup of up to 27.5 compared to a sequential CPU-based execution.

In contrast to approaches that employ GPU clusters to increase the feasible simulation scale or approaches considering multiple replications of a simulation in parallel to increase the rate at which simulation results are obtained, our approaches can be considered to focus on reducing the latency between starting a simulation and obtaining the results. Hence, our approaches are particularly beneficial in exploratory phases of a simulation study, where short feedback loops are desirable.

12 Conclusions and Outlook

This dissertation considered methods for identifying and harnessing concurrency in discrete-event simulations of computer networks. Although computer networks are inherently parallel systems, network simulation models vary immensely in their potential for parallel execution. The performance gains should therefore be estimated prior to expending the development effort of a model implementation suitable for parallel and distributed simulation.

Identifying Concurrency – Conclusions

The concurrency of network models is frequently evaluated on an abstract level through the automated analysis of simulation event traces created in sequential model executions, e.g., using critical path analysis. However, such automated analysis methods provide only limited insights into the relationships between the properties of the original system, the simulation model and the observed degree of concurrency. This observation motivated our first research question: *How can the parallelization potential of discrete-event models of computer networks be estimated and explained?*

We proposed a concurrency estimation approach that reveals the relationships between model properties and the concurrency of a simulation based on a manual analysis of simulation models and basic network statistics gathered from sequential simulation runs. The approach estimates the number of cores that can be occupied by a parallel execution of a network model under common simplifying assumptions. The concurrency estimations can support decisions on parallelization of a network model and on suitable simulator architectures. Similarly to some of the works from the literature, the estimation approach is based on approximating the simulation progress of the well-known synchronization algorithm YAWNS. **A rigorous proof shows that under the given assumptions, the concurrency determined using YAWNS can deviate only to a limited degree from the results of critical path analysis.** Hence, these two methods can be used interchangeably in case a rough estimation of concurrency is sufficient. An empirical validation of the estimation approach was performed on the example of three network models implemented in popular network simulators. Our results support the following statement:

The concurrency of network simulations can be estimated at reasonable accuracy without relying on an automated analysis of event traces.

While the fundamental impact of the communication patterns in the modeled networks can be easily captured by a manual analysis, sequential simulation runs are still used to acquire network statistics such as the frequency of unsuccessful transmission attempts in a wireless network. The need for executing the model arises in case an accurate analytical estimation of the required statistic is elusive. As noted by Ewald [Ewa06], this observation points to a fundamental challenge in performance modeling of simulations: simulation is applied when a property of a system cannot be captured easily in an analytical form. If such a property significantly affects the performance of the simulation, a purely analytical performance estimation poses a similar challenge as the original modeling task.

The proposed analytical estimation approach determines the number of cores that can be occupied by a simulation under simplifying assumptions. We presented a refinement of our estimation approach that enables a consideration of the variable costs of the computational tasks defined by the network model. Still, if an accurate prediction of the runtime of a parallel model execution is desired, the estimation must consider the previously disregarded costs of synchronization and communication between processors and the impact of the partitioning strategy applied to the simulation model. **We proposed an estimation tool that considers all steps of a model execution by performing a second-order simulation, i.e., a sequential simulation of an envisioned parallel or distributed simulation.** Our results showed that when estimating the performance with respect to network models that require fine-grained computations and frequent inter-processor communication, variations in the communication costs must be considered to achieve reasonable estimation accuracy. Generally, by refining the estimation model with representations of components of the simulation platform such as processors and network interconnects at increasing levels of detail, the prediction accuracy can be expected to improve. However, the costs of development, parametrization and execution of highly detailed performance models must be weighed against the costs of the parallelization of the model itself.

Identifying Concurrency – Future Work

Future research could aim at a generalization of our performance modeling results: a categorization of classes of network models according to their parallelization potential would enable simulationists to avoid repeating performance estimations of network models that fall in a previously identified category. For instance, when considering a simulation's concurrency, a network model category might be characterized by the network topology and a simplified representation of communication patterns. A first step towards a categorization could be taken by repeating the performance analysis experiments presented in this dissertation on the example of network models with similar characteristics to the previously considered models. A strong match in the performance evaluation results with respect to network models of similar characteristics would justify assigning these models to a shared category.

Further, our proposed concurrency estimation approach approximates the assignment of events to the simulated nodes according to the network model analytically. The required analysis of the way the network model translates the simulated communication patterns to sequences of events is performed manually. Static code analysis tools might be able to partially perform this step in an automated fashion by tracing the discrete-event logic formulated in the network model code. Some ongoing work already applies static code analysis to identify sets of events that can be executed in parallel [SSGW15]. Similarly, static code analysis could also generate insights into the influencing factors to the model's concurrency as functions of the configured scenario parameters.

An additional goal that might be achievable by static code analysis is to reveal invariants or asymptotical results on network statistics such as packet rates or queue lengths. Such results may render some simple network simulations unnecessary by generating a direct analytical solution. Further, by translating parts of a simulation model of the original system into an analytical form, such an approach could provide insights into the original system, the simulation model and the causes for the observed results. Partial solutions to the described problem may be achievable using methods from the fields of model checking and automated theorem proving. Of course, the enormous state space of typical discrete-event models must be expected to severely limit the comprehensiveness of results achievable in reasonable time frames.

Harnessing Concurrency - Conclusions

In the subsequent part of the dissertation, we proposed methods to utilize the concurrency of network models in order to achieve reductions in simulation runtime. We considered two opposite cases: peer-to-peer overlay networks based on the Kademlia protocol comprised of millions of nodes represented by a model that abstracts from low-level network properties, and wireless networks of up to 100 nodes represented by a model that considers even low-level network properties in detail.

A distinctive property of many peer-to-peer overlay networks is the separation between the spatial and logical distance of nodes, which impacts the parallelization of models of such networks: a *spatial partitioning* of the simulated nodes to the processors used for simulation increases the average latency of simulated messages between nodes simulated on separate processors, potentially reducing the frequency of inter-processor synchronization. In contrast, a *partitioning based on the logical topology of the network* reduces the number of simulated messages that cross processor boundaries. **Our results showed that the benefit of a spatial partitioning of the considered peer-to-peer network is low, whereas a partitioning based on the logical network topology strongly improves the performance of distributed runs of the network model.** The distributed simulation achieved a speedup of up to 6.0 compared to sequential runs and reductions in memory requirements per execution node that scaled close to linearly with the number of execution nodes. Still, whether the runtime reductions through distributed simulation can be considered to justify the substantial amount of required hardware resources must be decided in light of the given time constraints. Our second research question was therefore: *How can computationally intensive network simulations be executed efficiently on commodity graphics cards?*

To enable high-performance network simulations without the need for traditional CPU-based high-performance computing resources, we studied parallel network simulations on many-core hardware in the form of graphics processing units (GPUs) readily available in recent commodity computers. GPU-based simulations can be performed directly on a simulationist's workstation, enabling a short feedback loop between modifications to the simulation model or scenario parameters, and the retrieval of simulation results. A short feedback loop is particularly desirable during model development and to identify suitable value ranges for scenario parameters, i.e., in exploratory phases of simulation studies.

We first considered **architectures for GPU-based coprocessing** in the context of traditional sequential CPU-based simulation. Due to their heritage in graphics rendering, GPUs are particularly suited for efficient executions of tasks characterized by enormous numbers of data elements to each of which an identical sequence of operations is applied. In the case of a detailed model of a wireless network, highly data-parallel signal processing tasks can be executed efficiently on a GPU. However, our performance measurements showed that significant runtime reductions require an aggregated consideration of the processing tasks associated with multiple simulated messages, while maintaining the correctness of the simulation results. **Thus, even in the base case of GPU-based coprocessing, synchronization methods from parallel and distributed simulation are required to achieve significant performance gains.** The coprocessing approach is beneficial in cases where parts of the simulator cannot be efficiently executed on a GPU or where the costs of fully porting a model to the GPU are to be avoided, but where highly data-parallel tasks dominate the simulation runtime. Since a frequent crossing of the CPU-GPU boundary is associated with substantial overhead, a GPU-based coprocessing is inefficient in the case of network models comprised of events that require only fine-grained computations. Hence, we proposed a **fully GPU-based simulation approach that executes all tasks of a network simulation on a commodity GPU.** The fully GPU-based simulation does not require the considered network model to contain any explicit data parallelism. By exploiting the concurrency given by independent events in network models, our implementation of the approach achieved a speedup of up to 27.5 compared to a sequential CPU-based execution, and a speedup of up to 11.8 compared to a parallel CPU-based execution on 16 processor cores, using a single inexpensive commodity graphics card. We observed event execution rates of up to 39.3×10^6 events per second. Contrary to existing works, our approach aggregates the simulated nodes to form logical processes, in analogy to CPU-based parallel and distributed simulation. Through the aggregation, the simulation performance can be increased by considering a tradeoff arising in the assignment of simulation tasks to the GPU's processing elements: aggregating *smaller* sets of simulated nodes increases the frequency of periods of inactivity of the nodes assigned to a GPU core, resulting in low utilization of the GPU's computational resources; however, aggregating *larger* sets of simulated nodes increases the overheads of event management. Further, since the events assigned to a single logical process' nodes are executed sequentially, aggregating larger sets of simulated nodes can conceal some of the concurrency of the network model. The optimal logical process size depends on the GPU hardware and on the runtime behavior of the network model, which in general cannot assumed to be easily predictable prior to a simulation run. **Hence, in order to balance the utilization of GPU cores and the event management overhead, the proposed approach dynamically adapts the logical process size based on performance measurements conducted during simulation runtime.** Our results support the following statement:

A dynamically adaptable aggregation of simulated nodes substantially reduces the runtime of fully GPU-based network simulations.

The presented performance measurements showed the strong dependence of the optimal logical process size on the simulation scenario.

Harnessing Concurrency – Future Work

The issue of choosing a suitable partitioning strategy to minimize the need for physical communication between logical processes is central in the case of distributed simulations. This consideration seems less crucial in the case of GPU-based simulations since a communication across logical process boundaries is not inherently associated with additional costs, although low-latency regions of graphics memory could potentially be utilized to optimize simulated communications within each logical process. Still, depending on the considered network model, workload imbalances between logical processes may significantly limit the simulation performance. A possible focus of future work could be a selection of variable sizes for separate logical processes. As in CPU-based parallel and distributed simulation, static or dynamic partitioning strategies could be applied. Hence, the introduction of logical processes augments the dimensions that can be considered in the performance optimization of fully GPU-based simulations.

Outlook

In general, the proposed performance evaluation approaches and our measurement results show that fundamentally different simulator architectures and hardware platforms are required for efficient execution of different model types. Some works from the literature have already considered a dynamic assignment of simulation tasks to different components of heterogeneous hardware platforms [BR13] and an automated selection of simulation algorithms [Ewa11].

Finding an efficient assignment requires knowledge about the characteristics of the tasks and the properties of the execution environment, i.e., a performance model of the given network simulation model and the available hardware. Already, a partial performance model of network models is created and utilized in many parallel and distributed simulation approaches: for instance, the lookahead of a model or runtime statistics such as the frequency of communication between simulated nodes can be considered as parts of a performance model that is used to guide the assignment of the simulation to the hardware as well as the selection and parametrization of synchronization algorithms.

We consider a more systematic and comprehensive formulation of the optimization problem underlying the hardware assignment of network simulations a key direction for future research in parallel and distributed simulation. Although the degrees of freedom in the formulation of discrete-event models and in the hardware assignment of simulations are immense and make a fully comprehensive performance model seem unlikely, even a partial formulation of the optimization problem may suggest appropriate simulator realizations and decrease the need for the development of specialized simulators. The methods for evaluation of network models and their efficient execution presented in this dissertation are contributions towards this goal of a more comprehensive performance modeling of network simulation models and suitable execution environments.

Bibliography

[ABN92] B. C. Arnold, N. Balakrishnan, and H. N. Nagaraja. *A First Course in Order Statistics*, volume 54. Siam, 1992.

[ADM94] P. J. Ashenden, H. Detmold, and W. S. McKeen. Execution of VHDL Models Using Parallel Discrete Event Simulation Algorithms. *VLSI Design*, 2(1):1–16, 1994.

[AH13] P. Andelfinger and H. Hartenstein. Towards Performance Evaluation of Conservative Distributed Discrete-Event Network Simulations Using Second-Order Simulation. In *Proceedings of the Conference on Principles of Advanced Discrete Simulation*, pages 221–230. ACM, 2013.

[AH14] P. Andelfinger and H. Hartenstein. Exploiting the Parallelism of Large-Scale Application-Layer Networks by Adaptive GPU-Based Simulation. In *Proceedings of the Winter Simulation Conference*, pages 3471–3482. IEEE, 2014.

[AH15] P. Andelfinger and H. Hartenstein. Model-Based Concurrency Analysis of Network Simulations. In *Proceedings of the Conference on Principles of Advanced Discrete Simulation*, pages 223–234. ACM, 2015.

[AH16] P. Andelfinger and H. Hartenstein. Validity and Application of Model-Based Concurrency Estimation for Network Simulations. *Submitted to ACM Transactions on Modeling and Computer Simulation*, 2016.

[AJH14] P. Andelfinger, K. Jünemann, and H. Hartenstein. Parallelism Potentials in Distributed Simulations of Kademlia-based Peer-to-Peer Networks. In *Proceedings of the Conference on Simulation Tools and Techniques*, pages 41–50. ICST, 2014.

[AKK10] M. J. Arif, S. Karunasekera, and S. Kulkarni. GeoWeight: Internet Host Geolocation Based on a Probability Model for Latency Measurements. In *Proceedings of the Australasian Conference on Computer Science*, pages 89–98. Australian Computer Society, Inc., 2010.

[Amd67] G. M. Amdahl. Validity of the Single Processor Approach to Achieving Large Scale Computing Capabilities. In *Proceedings of the Spring Joint Computer Conference*, pages 483–485. ACM, 1967.

[AMH11] P. Andelfinger, J. Mittag, and H. Hartenstein. GPU-Based Architectures and Their Benefit for Accurate and Efficient Wireless Network Simulations. In *Proceedings of the International Symposium on Modeling, Analysis and Simulation of Computer and Telecommunication Systems*, pages 421–424. IEEE, 2011.

[And11] P. Andelfinger. Analysis and Evaluation of the Potential of GPGPUs on Network Simulator Runtime Optimization. Diploma Thesis, Karlsruhe Institute of Technology, 2011.

[APS10] B. G. Aaby, K. S. Perumalla, and S. K. Seal. Efficient Simulation of Agent-Based Models on Multi-GPU and Multi-Core Clusters. In *Proceedings of the International Conference on Simulation Tools and Techniques*, pages 29:1–29:10. ICST, 2010.

[BB93] G. Bottoni and R. Barzaghi. Fast Collocation. *Bulletin Géodésique*, 67(2):119–126, 1993.

[BCB+13] V. Bertacco, D. Chatterjee, N. Bombieri, F. Fummi, S. Vinco, A. M. Kaushik, and H. D. Patel. On The Use of GP-GPUs for Accelerating Compute-Intensive EDA Applications. In *Proceedings of the Conference on Design, Automation and Test in Europe*, pages 1357–1366. EDA Consortium, 2013.

[BF00] A. Boukerche and A. Fabbri. Partitioning Parallel Simulation of Wireless Networks. In *Proceedings of the Winter Simulation Conference*, pages 1449–1457. IEEE Computer Society, 2000.

[BGL98] J.-P. Briot, R. Guerraoui, and K.-P. Lohr. Concurrency and Distribution in Object-Oriented Programming. *ACM Computing Surveys*, 30(3):291–329, 1998.

[BJ85] O. Berry and D. Jefferson. Critical Path Analysis of Distributed Simulation. In *Proceedings of the SCS Multiconference on Distributed Simulation*, 1985.

[BKR07] S. Becker, H. Koziolek, and R. Reussner. Model-Based Performance Prediction with the Palladio Component Model. In *Proceedings of the International Workshop on Software and Performance*, pages 54–65. ACM, 2007.

[BM02] R. Buyya and M. Murshed. Gridsim: A Toolkit for the Modeling and Simulation of Distributed Resource Management and Scheduling for Grid Computing. *Concurrency and Computation: Practice and Experience*, 14(13-15):1175–1220, 2002.

[BN08] S. Bai and D. M. Nicol. GPU Coprocessing for Wireless Network Simulation. Technical report, University of Illinois at Urbana-Champaign, 2008.

[Bou01] A. Boukerche. An Adaptive Partitioning Algorithm for Conservative Parallel Simulation. In *Proceedings of the International Parallel & Distributed Processing Symposium*, page 133, 2001.

[BR13] B. Ben Romdhanne. *Large-Scale Network Simulation over Heterogeneous Computing Architecture*. Dissertation, EURECOM, 2013.

[BRA95] L. Barriga, R. Ronngren, and R. Ayani. Benchmarking Parallel Simulation Algorithms. In *Proceedings of the IEEE International Conference on Algorithms and Architectures for Parallel Processing*, pages 611–620, 1995.

[BRM12] R. Birke, G. Rodriguez, and C. Minkenberg. Towards Massively Parallel Simulations of Massively Parallel High-Performance Computing Systems. In *Proceedings of the International ICST Conference on Simulation Tools and Techniques*, pages 291–298, 2012.

[Bry77] R. E. Bryant. Simulation of Packet Communication Architecture Computer Systems. Technical report, Massachusetts Institute of Technology, 1977.

[BS88] W. L. Bain and D. S. Scott. An Algorithm for Time Synchronization in Distributed Discrete Event Simulation. In *Proceedings of the SCS Multiconference on Distributed Simulation*, pages 30–33, 1988.

[BT00] R. Bagrodia and M. Takai. Performance Evaluation of Conservative Algorithms in Parallel Simulation Languages. *IEEE Transactions on Parallel and Distributed Systems*, pages 395–411, 2000.

[CK06] M.-K. Chung and C.-M. Kyung. Improving Lookahead in Parallel Multiprocessor Simulation Using Dynamic Execution Path Prediction. In *Proceedings of the Workshop on Principles of Advanced and Distributed Simulation*, pages 11–18. IEEE Computer Society, 2006.

[CM79] K. Chandy and J. Misra. Distributed Simulation: A Case Study in Design and Verification of Distributed Programs. *IEEE Transactions on Software Engineering*, SE-5(5):440–452, 1979.

[CPF99] C. Carothers, K. Perumalla, and R. Fujimoto. Efficient Optimistic Parallel Simulations Using Reverse Computation. *ACM Transactions on Modeling and Computer Simulation*, pages 224–253, 1999.

[CS89] B. Cota and R. Sargent. Automatic Lookahead Computation for Conservative Distributed Simulation. *Technical Report*, 1989.

[DLTM08] T. T. A. Dinh, M. Lees, G. Theodoropoulos, and R. Minson. Large Scale Distributed Simulation of P2P Networks. In *Euromicro Conference on Parallel, Distributed and Network-Based Processing*, pages 499–507, 2008.

[DMVB13] S. De Munck, K. Vanmechelen, and J. Broeckhove. Revisiting Conservative Time Synchronization Protocols in Parallel and Distributed Simulation. *Concurrency and Computation: Practice and Experience*, 26(2):468–490, 2013.

[DTM08] T. T. A. Dinh, G. Theodoropoulos, and R. Minson. Evaluating Large Scale Distributed Simulation of P2P Networks. In *International Symposium on Distributed Simulation and Real-Time Applications*, pages 51–58. IEEE/ACM, 2008.

[DYB10] Z. Du, Z. Yin, and D. Bader. A Tile-Based Parallel Viterbi Algorithm for Biological Sequence Alignment on GPU with CUDA. In *International Symposium on Parallel Distributed Processing, Workshops and Phd Forum*, pages 1–8, 2010.

[EHU+06] R. Ewald, J. Himmelspach, A. Uhrmacher, D. Chen, and G. Theodoropoulos. A Simulation Approach to Facilitate Parallel and Distributed Discrete-Event Simulator Development. In *International Symposium on Distributed Simulation and Real-Time Applications*, pages 209–218. IEEE, 2006.

[EMP97] G. Ewing, D. McNickle, and K. Pawlikowski. Multiple Replications in Parallel: Distributed Generation of Data for Speeding Up Quantitative Stochastic Simulation. In *Proceedings of the Congress of International Association for Mathematics and Computers in Simulation*, pages 397–402, 1997.

[Ewa06] R. Ewald. Simulation of Load Balancing Algorithms for Discrete Event Simulations. Diploma Thesis, University of Rostock, 2006.

[Ewa11] R. Ewald. *Automatic Algorithm Selection for Complex Simulation Problems*. Dissertation, University of Rostock, 2011.

[FGF00] N. Fröhlich, V. Glöckel, and J. Fleischmann. A New Partitioning Method for Parallel Simulation of VLSI Circuits on Transistor Level. In *Proceedings of the Conference on Design, Automation and Test in Europe*, pages 679–685. ACM, 2000.

[Fuj87] R. M. Fujimoto. Performance Measurements of Distributed Simulation Strategies. Technical report, DTIC Document, 1987.

[Fuj88] R. M. Fujimoto. Lookahead in Parallel Discrete Event Simulation. *Proceedings of the 1988 International Conference on Parallel Processing, Vol. 3*, pages 34–41, 1988.

[Fuj00] R. M. Fujimoto. *Parallel and Distributed Simulation Systems*. Wiley New York, 2000.

[Fuj01] R. M. Fujimoto. Parallel Simulation: Parallel and Distributed Simulation Systems. In *Proceedings of the 33nd Winter Simulation Conference*, pages 147–157. IEEE Computer Society, 2001.

[GID10] D. Gianni, G. Iazeolla, and A. D'Ambrogio. A Methodology to Predict the Performance of Distributed Simulations. In *Proceedings of the Workshop on Principles of Advanced and Distributed Simulation*, pages 31–39. IEEE, 2010.

[HAP12] X. He, D. Agarwal, and S. K. Prasad. Design and Implementation of a Parallel Priority Queue on Many-Core Architectures. In *International Conference on High Performance Computing*, pages 1–10. IEEE, 2012.

[Har01] T. L. Harris. A Pragmatic Implementation of Non-Blocking Linked-Lists. In *Proceedings of the International Conference on Distributed Computing*, pages 300–314. Springer, 2001.

[HHSS08] C. Harris, K. Haines, and L. Staveley-Smith. GPU Accelerated Radio Astronomy Signal Convolution. *Experimental Astronomy*, 22(1-2):129–141, 2008.

[HLJ+13] D. M. Hughes, I. S. Lim, M. W. Jones, A. Knoll, and B. Spencer. InK-Compact: In-Kernel Stream Compaction and Its Application to Multi-Kernel Data Visualization on General-Purpose GPUs. *Computer Graphics Forum*, 32(6):178–188, 2013.

[HMS+09] S. D. Hammond, G. R. Mudalige, J. A. Smith, S. A. Jarvis, J. A. Herdman, and A. Vadgama. WARPP: a Toolkit for Simulating High-Performance Parallel Scientific Codes. In *Proceedings of the International Conference on Simulation Tools and Techniques*, pages 19:1–19:10, 2009.

[JAH11] K. Jünemann, P. Andelfinger, and H. Hartenstein. Towards a Basic DHT Service: Analyzing Network Characteristics of a Widely Deployed DHT. In *Proceedings of the International Conference on Computer Communications and Networks*, pages 1–7, 2011.

[JB96] V. Jha and R. Bagrodia. A Performance Evaluation Methodology for Parallel Simulation Protocols. *ACM SIGSIM Simulation Digest*, 26(1):180–185, 1996.

[Jef85] D. R. Jefferson. Virtual Time. *ACM Transactions on Programming Languages and Systems*, 7(3):404–425, 1985.

[JLL+10] X. Jia, Y. Lou, R. Li, W. Y. Song, and S. B. Jiang. GPU-Based Fast Cone Beam CT Reconstruction from Undersampled and Noisy Projection Data via Total Variation. *Medical Physics*, 37(4):1757–1760, 2010.

[JTKG01] Z. Juhasz, S. Turner, K. Kuntner, and M. Gerzson. A Performance Analyser and Prediction Tool for Parallel Discrete Event Simulation. In *UKSIM: Conference on Computer Simulation*, pages 148–155, 2001.

[JTL+13] J. Jin, S. J. Turner, B.-S. Lee, J. Zhong, and B. He. Simulation of Information Propagation Over Complex Networks: Performance Studies on Multi-GPU. In *International Symposium on Distributed Simulation and Real Time Applications*, pages 179–188. IEEE, 2013.

[Jün15] K. Jünemann. *Confidential Data-Outsourcing and Self-Optimizing P2P-Networks: Coping with the Challenges of Multi-Party Systems.* Dissertation, Karlsruhe Institute of Technology, 2015.

[KHW95] K. L. Kapp, T. C. Hartrum, and T. S. Wailes. An Improved Cost Function for Static Partitioning of Parallel Circuit Simulations Using a Conservative Synchronization Protocol. *ACM SIGSIM Simulation Digest*, 25(1):78–85, 1995.

[KSGW12] G. Kunz, D. Schemmel, J. Gross, and K. Wehrle. Multi-Level Parallelism for Time- and Cost-Efficient Parallel Discrete Event Simulation on GPUs. In *Proceedings of the Workshop on Principles of Advanced and Distributed Simulation*, pages 23–32. IEEE Computer Society, 2012.

[KY91] P. Konas and P.-C. Yew. Parallel Discrete Event Simulation on Shared-Memory Multiprocessors. In *Proceedings of the Simulation Symposium*, pages 134–148, 1991.

[KY95] P. Konas and P.-C. Yew. Partitioning for Synchronous Parallel Simulation. *ACM SIGSIM Simulation Digest*, 25(1):181–184, 1995.

[Law14] A. M. Law. *Simulation Modeling and Analysis*. McGraw-Hill, fifth edition, 2014.

[LB10] J.-Y. Le Boudec. *Performance Evaluation of Computer and Communication Systems*. EPFL Press, 2010.

[LCSH07] R. LaFortune, C. D. Carothers, W. D. Smith, and M. Hartman. An Abstract Internet Topology Model for Simulating Peer-to-Peer Content Distribution. In *Proceedings of the International Workshop on Principles of Advanced and Distributed Simulation*, pages 152–162. IEEE Computer Society, 2007.

[LCT13] X. Li, W. Cai, and S. J. Turner. GPU Accelerated Three-Stage Execution Model for Event-Parallel Simulation. In *Proceedings of the Conference on Principles of Advanced Discrete Simulation*, pages 57–66. ACM, 2013.

[Leo06] P. Leopardi. A Partition of the Unit Sphere into Regions of Equal Area and Small Diameter. *Electronic Transactions on Numerical Analysis*, 25(12):309–327, 2006.

[LF00] M. L. Loper and R. M. Fujimoto. Pre-Sampling as an Approach for Exploiting Temporal Uncertainty. In *Proceedings of the Workshop on Parallel and Distributed Simulation*, pages 157–164. IEEE Computer Society, 2000.

[LH07] D. Luebke and G. Humphreys. How GPUs Work. *IEEE Computer*, 40(2):96–100, 2007.

[Liv85] M. Livny. A Study of Parallelism in Distributed Simulation. In *Proceedings of the SCS Multiconference on Distributed Simulation*, pages 94–98, 1985.

[LL90] Y.-B. Lin and E. Lazowska. Exploiting Lookahead in Parallel Simulation. *IEEE Transactions on Parallel and Distributed Systems*, 1(4):457–469, 1990.

[LLH09] J. Liu, Y. Li, and Y. He. A Large-Scale Real-Time Network Simulation Study Using PRIME. In *Proceedings of the Winter Simulation Conference*, pages 797–806. IEEE Press, 2009.

[LN02] J. Liu and D. M. Nicol. Lookahead Revisited in Wireless Network Simulations. In *Proceedings of the Workshop on Parallel and Distributed Simulation*, pages 79–88. IEEE Computer Society, 2002.

[LN08] A. Loewenstern and A. Norberg. BitTorrent Enhancement Proposal 5: DHT Protocol. `http://www.bittorrent.org/beps/bep_0005.html`, 2008.

[LNPP99] J. Liu, D. Nicol, B. Premore, and A. Poplawski. Performance Prediction of a Parallel Simulator. In *Proceedings of the Workshop on Parallel and Distributed Simulation*, pages 156–164. IEEE, 1999.

[LPGZ05] S. Lin, A. Pan, R. Guo, and Z. Zhang. Simulating Large-Scale P2P Systems with the WiDS Toolkit. In *International Symposium on Modeling, Analysis, and Simulation of Computer and Telecommunication Systems, 2005.*, pages 415–424. IEEE, 2005.

[Mar72] G. Marsaglia. Choosing a Point from the Surface of a Sphere. *The Annals of Mathematical Statistics*, 43(2):645–646, 1972.

[MB98] R. Meyer and R. Bagrodia. Improving Lookahead in Parallel Wireless Network Simulation. In *Proceedings of the International Symposium on Modeling, Analysis and Simulation of Computer and Telecommunication Systems*, pages 262–267, 1998.

[MB99] R. A. Meyer and R. L. Bagrodia. Path Lookahead: a Data Flow View of PDES Models. In *Proceedings of the Workshop on Parallel and Distributed Simulation*, pages 12–19. IEEE, 1999.

[Mit12] J. Mittag. *Characterization, Avoidance and Repair of Packet Collisions in Inter-Vehicle Communication Networks.* Dissertation, Karlsruhe Institute of Technology, 2012.

[MM02] P. Maymounkov and D. Mazieres. Kademlia: A Peer-to-Peer Information System Based on the XOR Metric. *Peer-to-Peer Systems*, pages 53–65, 2002.

[MPHS11] J. Mittag, S. Papanastasiou, H. Hartenstein, and E. G. Strom. Enabling Accurate Cross-Layer PHY/MAC/NET Simulation Studies of Vehicular Communication Networks. *Proceedings of the IEEE*, 99(7):1311–1326, 2011.

[MS81] W. M. McCormack and R. G. Sargent. Analysis of Future Event Set Algorithms for Discrete Event Simulation. *Communications of the ACM*, 24(12):801–812, 1981.

[Nic93] D. M. Nicol. The Cost of Conservative Synchronization in Parallel Discrete Event Simulations. *Journal of the ACM*, 40(2):304–333, 1993.

[Nic96] D. M. Nicol. Principles of Conservative Parallel Simulation. In *Proceedings of the Winter Simulation Conference*, pages 128–135. IEEE Computer Society, 1996.

[NKPS12] M. Nanjundappa, A. Kaushik, H. D. Patel, and S. K. Shukla. Accelerating SystemC Simulations Using GPUs. In *International High Level Design Validation and Test Workshop*, pages 132–139. IEEE, 2012.

[NL93] B. Nandy and W. M. Loucks. On a Parallel Partitioning Technique for Use with Conservative Parallel Simulation. In *Proceedings of the Workshop on Parallel and Distributed Simulation*, pages 43–51. ACM, 1993.

[NMI89] D. Nicol, C. Micheal, and P. Inouye. Efficient Aggregation Of Multiple LPs In Distributed Memory Parallel Simulations. In *Proceedings of the Winter Simulation Conference*, pages 680–685. IEEE Computer Society, 1989.

[NS88] D. Nicol and J. Saltz. Dynamic Remapping of Parallel Computations with Varying Resource Demands. *IEEE Transactions on Computers*, 37(9):1073–1087, 1988.

[PA08] K. S. Perumalla and B. G. Aaby. Data Parallel Execution Challenges and Runtime Performance of Agent Simulations on GPUs. In *Proceedings of the Spring Simulation Multiconference*, pages 116–123. Society for Computer Simulation International, 2008.

[Pao10] G. Paoloni. How to Benchmark Code Execution Times on Intel® IA-32 and IA-64 Instruction Set Architectures. Technical report, Intel Corporation, 2010.

[PAYS09] K. S. Perumalla, B. G. Aaby, S. B. Yoginath, and S. K. Seal. GPU-Based Real-Time Execution of Vehicular Mobility Models in Large-Scale Road Network Scenarios. In *Proceedings of the Workshop on Principles of Advanced and Distributed Simulation*, pages 95–103. IEEE Computer Society, 2009.

[Per06] K. S. Perumalla. Discrete-Event Execution Alternatives on General Purpose Graphical Processing Units (GPGPUs). In *Proceedings of the Workshop on Principles of Advanced and Distributed Simulation*, pages 74–81. IEEE Computer Society, 2006.

[Per08] K. S. Perumalla. Efficient Execution on GPUs of Field-Based Vehicular Mobility Models. In *Proceedings of the Workshop on Principles of Advanced and Distributed Simulation*, pages 154–154. IEEE, 2008.

[Per13] K. S. Perumalla. *Introduction to Reversible Computing*. CRC Press, 2013.

[PF08] H. Park and P. A. Fishwick. A Fast Hybrid Time-Synchronous/Event Approach to Parallel Discrete Event Simulation of Queuing Networks. In *Proceedings of the Winter Simulation Conference*, pages 795–803. IEEE Computer Society, 2008.

[PF10] H. Park and P. A. Fishwick. A GPU-Based Application Framework Supporting Fast Discrete-Event Simulation. *Simulation*, 86(10):613–628, 2010.

[PF11] H. Park and P. A. Fishwick. An Analysis of Queuing Network Simulation Using GPU-Based Hardware Acceleration. *ACM Transactions on Modeling and Computer Simulation*, 21(3):18, 2011.

[PF13] R. S. Pienta and R. M. Fujimoto. On the Parallel Simulation of Scale-Free Networks. In *Proceedings of the Conference on Principles of Advanced Discrete Simulation*, pages 179–188. ACM, 2013.

[PFP04] A. Park, R. M. Fujimoto, and K. S. Perumalla. Conservative Synchronization of Large-Scale Network Simulations. In *Proceedings of the Workshop on Parallel and Distributed Simulation*, pages 153–161. IEEE, 2004.

[PFT+05] K. Perumalla, R. Fujimoto, P. Thakare, S. Pande, H. Karimabadi, Y. Omelchenko, and J. Driscoll. Performance Prediction of Large-Scale Parallel Discrete Event Models of Physical Systems. In *Proceedings of the Winter Simulation Conference*, pages 356–364. IEEE, 2005.

[PL90] B. R. Preiss and W. M. Loucks. The Impact of Lookahead on the Performance of Conservative Distributed Simulation. In *Proceedings of the European Multiconference-Simulation Methodologies, Languages and Architectures*, pages 204–209. Citeseer, 1990.

[PR11] J. Pelkey and G. Riley. Distributed Simulation with MPI in ns-3. In *Proceedings of the Conference on Simulation Tools and Techniques*, pages 410–414. ICST, 2011.

[Pro01] J. G. Proakis. *Digital Communications*. McGraw Hill, New York, 2001.

[PVM09] P. Peschlow, A. Voss, and P. Martini. Good News for Parallel Wireless Network Simulations. In *Proceedings of the International Conference on Modeling, Analysis and Simulation of Wireless and Mobile Systems*, pages 134–142. ACM, 2009.

[QD11] H. Qian and Y. Deng. Accelerating RTL Simulation with GPUs. In *Proceedings of the International Conference on Computer-Aided Design*, pages 687–693. IEEE Press, 2011.

[QRT12] M. Quinson, C. Rosa, and C. Thiery. Parallel Simulation of Peer-to-Peer Systems. In *CCGrid 2012 – The IEEE/ACM International Symposium on Cluster, Cloud and Grid Computing*, pages 668–675, 2012.

[RA97] R. Rönngren and R. Ayani. A Comparative Study of Parallel and Sequential Priority Queue Algorithms. *ACM Transactions on Modeling and Computer Simulation*, 7(2):157–209, 1997.

[RHB+11] A. F. Rodrigues, K. S. Hemmert, B. W. Barrett, C. Kersey, R. Oldfield, M. Weston, R. Risen, J. Cook, P. Rosenfeld, E. Cooper-Balls, and B. Jacob. The Structural Simulation Toolkit. *SIGMETRICS Performance Evaluation Review*, 38(4):37–42, 2011.

[RJD89] P. F. Reynolds, Jr., and P. M. Dickens. SPECTRUM: A Parallel Simulation Testbed. In *Proceedings of the Hypercube Conference*, 1989.

[RRM+15] S. Raghav, M. Ruggiero, A. Marongiu, C. Pinto, D. Atienza, and L. Benini. GPU Acceleration for Simulating Massively Parallel Many-Core Platforms. *IEEE Transactions on Parallel and Distributed Systems*, 26(5):1336–1349, 2015.

[RSPM98] R. Reussner, P. Sanders, L. Prechelt, and M. Müller. SKaMPI: A Detailed, Accurate MPI Benchmark. In *Proceedings of the European PVM/MPI Users' Group Meeting on Recent Advances in Parallel Virtual Machine and Message Passing Interface*, pages 52–59, 1998.

[SF87] S. M. Swope and R. M. Fujimoto. Optimal Performance of Distributed Simulation Programs. In *Proceedings of the Winter Simulation Conference*. IEEE Press, 1987.

[SG08] R. Szerwinski and T. Güneysu. Exploiting the Power of GPUs for Asymmetric Cryptography. In *Cryptographic Hardware and Embedded Systems*, pages 79–99. Springer, 2008.

[SIR14] B. P. Swenson, J. S. Ivey, and G. F. Riley. Performance of Conservative Synchronization Methods for Complex Interconnected Campus Networks in ns-3. In *Proceedings of the Winter Simulation Conference*, pages 3096–3106. IEEE Press, 2014.

[SK12] M. G. Seok and T. G. Kim. Parallel Discrete Event Simulation for DEVS Cellular Models Using a GPU. In *Proceedings of the Symposium on High Performance Computing*, pages 11:1–11:7. Society for Computer Simulation International, 2012.

[SLRK13] J. Sang, C.-R. Lee, V. Rego, and C.-T. King. A Fast Implementation of Parallel Discrete-Event Simulation on GPGPU. In *Proceedings of the International Conference on Parallel and Distributed Processing Techniques and Applications*, page 501. The Steering Committee of The World Congress in Computer Science, Computer Engineering and Applied Computing, 2013.

[SOHL+98] M. Snir, S. Otto, S. Huss-Lederman, D. Walker, and J. Dongarra. *MPI-The Complete Reference, Volume 1: The MPI Core.* MIT Press, Cambridge, MA, USA, 2nd. (revised) edition, 1998.

[SSGW15] M. Stoffers, T. Sehy, J. Gross, and K. Wehrle. Analyzing Data Dependencies for Increased Parallelism in Discrete Event Simulation. In *Proceedings of the Conference on Principles of Advanced Discrete Simulation*, pages 73–74. ACM, 2015.

[SVS11] L. Savioja, V. Välimäki, and J. O. Smith. Audio Signal Processing Using Graphics Processing Units. *Journal of the Audio Engineering Society*, 59(1/2):3–19, 2011.

[Swe15] B. P. Swenson. *Techniques to Improve the Performance of Large-Scale Discrete-Event Simulation.* Dissertation, Georgia Institute of Technology, 2015.

[TGEL13] Y. Torres, A. Gonzalez-Escribano, and D. R. Llanos. uBench: Exposing the Impact of CUDA Block Geometry in Terms of Performance. *Journal of Supercomputing*, 65(3):1150–1163, 2013.

[TKDT13] M. Tillmann, T. Karcher, C. Dachsbacher, and W. F. Tichy. Application-Independent Autotuning for GPUs. In *International Conference on Parallel Computing*, pages 626–635, 2013.

[TY13] W. Tang and Y. Yao. A GPU-Based Discrete Event Simulation Kernel. *Simulation*, 89(11):1335–1354, 2013.

[VCBF12] S. Vinco, D. Chatterjee, V. Bertacco, and F. Fummi. SAGA: SystemC Acceleration on GPU Architectures. In *Proceedings of the Design Automation Conference*, pages 115–120. ACM, 2012.

[VD75] J. G. Vaucher and P. Duval. A Comparison of Simulation Event List Algorithms. *Communications of the ACM*, 18(4):223–230, 1975.

[Vit67] A. Viterbi. Error Bounds for Convolutional Codes and an Asymptotically Optimum Decoding Algorithm. *IEEE Transactions on Information Theory*, 13(2):260–269, 1967.

[WDYR13] J. Wang, Z. Dong, S. Yalamanchili, and G. Riley. Optimizing Parallel Simulation of Multicore Systems Using Domain-Specific Knowledge. In *Proceedings of the Conference on Principles of Advanced Discrete Simulation*, pages 127–136. ACM, 2013.

[WHL95] Y.-C. Wong, S.-Y. Hwang, and J. Y.-B. Lin. A Parallelism Analyzer for Conservative Parallel Simulation. *Transactions on Parallel and Distributed Systems*, 6(6):628–638, 1995.

[WYF13] T. Wenjie, Y. Yiping, and Z. Feng. An Expansion-Aided Synchronous Conservative Time Management Algorithm on GPU. In *Proceedings of the Conference on Principles of Advanced Discrete Simulation*, pages 367–372. ACM, 2013.

[XB07] Z. Xu and R. Bagrodia. GPU-Accelerated Evaluation Platform for High Fidelity Network Modeling. In *Proceedings of the International Workshop on Principles of Advanced and Distributed Simulation*, pages 131–140. IEEE Computer Society, 2007.

[XF10] S. Xiao and W.-c. Feng. Inter-Block GPU Communication via Fast Barrier Synchronization. In *International Symposium on Parallel and Distributed Processing*, pages 1–12. IEEE, 2010.

[YM89] C.-Q. Yang and B. P. Miller. Performance Measurement for Parallel and Distributed Programs: a Structured and Automatic Approach. *IEEE Transactions on Software Engineering*, 15(12):1615–1629, 1989.

[ZGGB14] L. Zhen, Q. Gang, G. Gang, and C. Bin. A GPU-Based Simulation Kernel within Heterogeneous Collaborative Computation on Large-Scale Artificial Society. *International Journal of Modeling and Optimization*, 4(3):205, 2014.

[ZKK04] G. Zheng, G. Kakulapati, and L. Kale. BigSim: a Parallel Simulator for Performance Prediction of Extremely Large Parallel Machines. In *Proceedings of the International Parallel and Distributed Processing Symposium*, pages 78–87, 2004.

[ZKP00] B. P. Zeigler, T. G. Kim, and H. Praehofer. *Theory of Modeling and Simulation*. Academic Press, Inc., 2nd edition, 2000.

[ZLC+13] P. Zou, Y.-s. Lü, L.-l. Chen, Y.-p. Yao, et al. Epidemic Simulation of Large-Scale Social Contact Network on GPU Clusters. *Simulation*, 2013.

[ZP01] B. Zarei and M. Pidd. Performance Analysis of Automatic Lookahead Generation by Control Flow Graph: Some Experiments. *Simulation Practice and Theory*, 8(8):511–527, 2001.

[ZWD11] Y. Zhu, B. Wang, and Y. Deng. Massively Parallel Logic Simulation with GPUs. *ACM Transactions on Design Automation of Electronic Systems*, 16(3):29, 2011.